☟ P9-BVG-722

DATE

Black Pearls

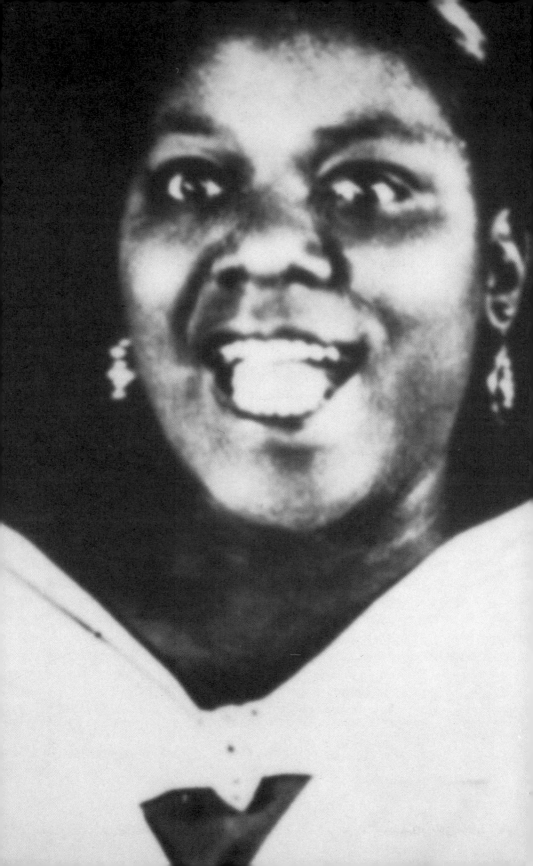

BLUES

QUEENS

OF THE

1920S

Black Pearls

Daphne Duval Harrison

RUTGERS UNIVERSITY PRESS New Brunswick   and London

LIBRARY OF CONGRESS CATALOGING-IN-PUBLICATION DATA

Harrison, Daphne Duval, 1932–

    Black pearls.

    Bibliography: p.

    Includes index.

    1. Blues (Songs, etc.)—United States—History
and criticism. 2. Blues musicians—United States—
Biography. 3. Afro-American women musicians—
Biography. I. Title.
ML3521.H38   1988   784.5'3'0922   87-14084
ISBN 0-8135-1279-4

British Cataloging-in-Publication
information available

"Graveyard Dream Blues," by Ida Cox, © 1923 Northern Music Company, renewed, rights administered MCA Music Publishing, a division of MCA Inc. All rights reserved. Used by permission of MCA Music Publishing.

"He May Be Your Man, But He Comes to See Me Sometimes," by Edith Wilson, used by permission of the Jerry Vogel Music Company, Inc.

"I Hate a Man Like You," by Ferd "Jelly Roll" Morton, © 1930, 1931 Southern Music Publishing Co., Inc., renewed 1958, 1959 Edwin H. Morris & Company, a division of MPL Communications, Inc. International copyright secured. Used by permission of Edwin H. Morris & Company.

"I'm a Mighty Tight Woman," by Sippie Wallace, © 1946 Cherio Corp., renewed 1974. International copyright secured. Used by permission of the Cherio Corp.

"Poor Man Blues," by Bessie Smith, © 1930, 1974 Frank Music Corp., renewed 1958. International copyright secured. Used by permission of the Frank Music Corp.

"Trouble in Mind," by Richard M. Jones, © 1926, 1937 MCA Music Publishing, a division of MCA Inc., renewed. All rights reserved. Used by permission of MCA Music Publishing.

IN
MEMORY
OF
SIPPIE
WALLACE
AND
EDITH
WILSON

SARAH
MARTIN

Exclusive
Okeh Artist

Contents

● ●

1   SARA MARTIN PUBLICITY PHOTOGRAPH FROM
    OKEH RECORDS

List of Illustrations

Acknowledgments

This book has become a reality because of the help and encouragement of many people along the pathway from its conception to its completion. They have stood with me as I have tossed away what I thought were precious pieces of the whole and have given me the insight that led me to a broader vision of the contemplated finished product. Their belief in the value of this study and in my ability to weave it into the fabric of black history and culture has been the beacon that has guided me through the entanglements of obfuscation and unclarity. Foremost among them were my family: my mother, Daphne Sr.; my son and daughter, Michael and Stephanie; and my loving, patient husband, Daniel Comegys. I am indebted to them for their unflagging faith and support as I have struggled to bring the book to fruition. Sometimes this meant haphazard schedules, missed vacations, or total abandonment as I cloistered myself away from home to work on the manuscript.

To my mother, I offer this book as an expression of my appreciation for the loving care with which she wisely taught me the value of knowledge, the courage freely to express my thoughts, and the ability to laugh and not take myself too seriously. Maybe that accounts for my affinity with the blues women, because I could see and feel some of me in the way that they dealt with a wretched situation by making fun of it. Both my mother and husband were sympathetic yet critical sounding boards, as well as mainstays when I was ready to abandon ship.

Support for the initial portion of the research was provided in part by a grant from the R. R. Moton Center for Independent Studies in 1976–1977. That time would have been less productive were it not for the unstinting assistance and interest given by Louise Coursey, the special collections librarian assigned to the Moton Center. She ferreted out valuable information and introduced me to persons who provided me with print, oral, and memorabilia materials. She continued to assist me, long after we had finished our stay at the Center, by computer searches and by accompanying me on trips to archives in New York, Philadelphia, and Washington. Dan Morgenstern and Ed Berger guided my search for recordings at the Institute for Jazz Studies, Rutgers University, as well as connecting me with informants who were valuable to my work. Debra Willis-Thomas, curator of prints and photographs, Schomburg Center for Research on Black Culture, helped me to locate visuals related to the subject. Len Kunstadt gave freely of his time as informant for the oral data on Victoria Spivey, who died shortly after she had consented to an interview session with me. He also gave me materials from the Record Research archives regarding Spivey and other singers.

The spirit of Sterling Brown pervades this book, because it was he who early on stated that it was important and necessary to write about the blues women. As we talked about and listened to the blues in his living room I began to understand more deeply what he meant when he wrote about the blues. He and Stephen Henderson gave the critical commentary that I needed to begin the tedious task of reordering and refining the manuscript.

Without Leslie Mitchner and Craig Werner's sincere commitment to the value of this work the manuscript would still be in search of a home. Leslie's untiring support in all phases of review and Craig's meticulous, knowledgeable editorial work have made my efforts worthwhile. Eleanor Levieux also provided expert editing at a crucial point during revision. To my colleagues in the Department of African American Studies, I am appreciative for their encouragement and suggestions from inception to the final stages; especially Robert Hall and Acklyn Lynch, who gave their precious time to read the manuscript and discuss each section with me. Julia Banks has tirelessly and patiently typed thousands of pages as the manuscript went from revisions to final copy. I am indebted to her for her willingness and cheerfulness throughout the process.

My thanks to all who I may have not named but who have in many ways contributed to the success of this work.

Columbia, Maryland
June 1987

NEST CLUB
JOHN CAREY and MAC FRAZIER
169 West 133d St., New York
Two Doors East of Seventh Avenue
DINING. DANCING. ENTERTAINING
TEL. MORNINGSIDE 9478

2   INTERIOR OF THE NEST CLUB IN HARLEM

Black Pearls

Pace & Handy Music Co.
390 BEALE AVENUE
MEMPHIS, TENNESSEE

Please send for the 15 cents inclosed "The Yellow Dog Rag" which I learn is an answer to "I Wonder Where My Easy Rider's Gone," Mr. Shelton Brooks' song hit.

I hear your music on all phonographs, electric and player-pianos, minstrel and circus bands and no vaudeville bill seems complete without one of Handy's Blues.

Send it to "Where the Southern Crosses the Dog."

Yours truly,

E. Z. Rider

Introduction

Train's at the station, I heard the whistle blow,
Train's at the station, I heard the whistle blow,
I done bought my ticket but I don't know where I'll go.
                    —Ma Rainey, "Traveling Blues"

Rainey's lyrics are one woman's interpretation of the dilemma—to
stay or to go, to find a new life and love or to endure the humiliation
of remaining faithful to an unfaithful man. Frustration, despair,
alienation—how could one escape the feelings that wrenched the
soul and spirit? Would a different town or city offer a brighter future
with love, money, a home, friends, and family; or would it be better
to go on down home to face more poverty, and possibly shame and
desolation? Maybe the home folks would welcome her back, maybe
not. Maybe her man would take her back, maybe not; and maybe
she doesn't care if he doesn't. The many uncertainties that race
through the mind of the woman in Rainey's blues illustrate the dilemma of many black women in the 1920s who lived on the fringe

• •

3   ADVERTISEMENT ON THE BACK COVER OF SHEET
     MUSIC PUBLISHED BY PACE & HANDY MUSIC
     COMPANY

of the community, outside of its norms and controls. Her desire to return to the warmth and companionship of family and friends is complicated by the circumstances surrounding her departure. The initial apprehension, however, would often give way to her longing to be among other women; women who could identify with her sorrow and pain and who would accept her without passing judgment.[1] The moment of truth comes as the train whistle blows and a ticket is bought—a ticket to nowhere in particular, just anywhere but here. But a new place cannot fill the void left by a failed love affair, or heal a spirit wounded by economic, racial, and sexual oppression. So the frustration remains, along with the hurt and the gnawing anger that threaten to destroy the will to go on. That is why the blues women sang—Ma, Bessie, Mamie, Sippie, Clara, Chippie, Sara, and a host of others. They knew the blues was always lurking in the shadows, coming out to grab you, messing with you just when you thought things were going right. So the women sang—in tents, theaters, dance halls, cabarets, and on records; they exorcised the blue feelings in a communal ritual with other black folk.[2]

> Fare-thee-well, Mama's gone, good-bye. No need to cry, no need
>   to sigh.
> For years you dogged me around, but now it's my time to wake up
>   and tell you what's on my mind.
> I'm going away, don't beg me to stay,
> Fare-thee-well, I been excused, now there's brand new rules and I
>   ain't no fool.
> I'm going to get me a Daddy, one who treats me right,
> Comes home and sleeps every night.
> Fare-thee-well, Mama's gone, good-bye.[3]

A woman stood on stage in glittering sequins and satins, sang the blues, and captivated her audience, convincing them that she undoubtedly was *the* queen of the blues—at least for that night's performance. She may have been statuesque with a deep bronze complexion and a handsome face; perhaps honey-colored with big saucer eyes and a petite figure; buxom, fair-skinned, and pretty; or even short, fat, and not so handsome. It did not matter when the lights were dimmed and the curtain was drawn to reveal the idol of their eyes, "the fabulous ——, uncrowned queen of the blues." On any night of any week during the 1920s, the circuit shows included blues singers on their bills. The latest record release of the blues singer often appeared in advertisements for the show. By the mid-twenties every tent show and theater billed a blues sensation.

In Chicago, Baltimore, Pittsburgh, Houston, Dallas, Chattanooga, Atlanta, and Birmingham blue singers always brought out huge crowds for a show. Enterprising musicians, record scouts, and managers promoted the latest queen of the blues as fast as she could be found. Some of those overnight sensations made one or two recordings and faded into obscurity. Others found admirers who bought their records and stampeded the theaters whenever they were in town. Theirs were the voices that sparked the fires of creativity in the fledgling jazz instrumentalists. Their phrasing and timing provided the opportunity for new improvisational interplay. They had grandeur and bravado to transform humble settings into palaces and to add fire and ice to the velvet-draped stages of the grand theaters, cabarets, and clubs. These uncrowned queens were the impetus for recorded black music in the twenties. They forged into a densely populated field during a marvelously exciting decade. In many eyes, these aspirants were no match for Bessie Smith, but each was admired for the unique qualities that distinguished her. In the show business world, blues women perceived themselves as queens and convinced their fans that they were deserving of the title.

Just what is the blues and how did it have such enormous cultural and social impact on the black community? A definition of the blues is crucial to understanding its lasting appeal in the community that created and performed the music; and its added significance when women dominated the stage and recorded performances of the blues. I have drawn upon two sources—blues artists and black writers—in the search for a satisfactory answer. The most cogent statements come from the blues men and women who have re-created the state of the mind, feelings and realities of the black experience through music.

The blues artist speaks directly of and to the folk who have suffered pain and assures them that they are not alone; someone understands. Willie Dixon, composer, band leader, and producer of blues acts put it bluntly, yet very succinctly. "The blues ain't nothing but the facts of life."[4] For Sippie Wallace, singer and songwriter, the blues was a part of her total being and a source of solace. "I sing the blues to comfort me on. . . . Most all my [blues] is about myself."[5] Victoria Spivey once said that the blues is life and since blues was her business she sang about life.

The essence of blues poetry, whether sung by women or men, is life itself—its aches, pains, grievances, pleasures, and brief moments of glory. Life for working-class black women in the United States has been especially difficult because of their bottom-rung status due to racism and sexism. The grief of a broken love affair is always poignant; it is more so when cast within a racist system. Black women's quest for independence is constrained by racial and sexual barriers and sometimes leads to types of behavior that appear to be arrogant, promiscuous, or violent, but are in fact manifestations of a large repertoire of defense mechanisms employed to gain or defend respect in a hostile environment. Dependency upon a capricious welfare system often spawned dishonesty in personal dealings, or sent some to the street seeking a better way to obtain the finer things in life. Others, like Spivey, Wallace, and Cox, turned to the church for solace and strength; to the other sisters in the community for companionship; or to the local lounge for warmth and good times.

The black writer addresses a broader, sometimes entirely different, audience. Nevertheless, the writer validates and reinterprets the experiences of the folk and acknowledges the blues as the embodiment of the black experience. In some cases, blues music is the implement of prediction, power, or change. Ralph Ellison uses the blues in *The Invisible Man* to resolve a horrible inner conflict for a character.

> I leaves tryin' to pray, but I cain't. I thinks and thinks, until I thinks my brain go'n bust, 'bout how I'm guilty and how I ain't guilty. I don't eat nothin' and I don't drink nothin' and cain't sleep at night. Finally, . . . I starts singin'. I don't mean to, I didn't think 'bout it, just start singin'. I don't know what it was, some kinda church song, I guess. All I know is I ends up singin' the blues . . . and while I'm singin' them blues I makes up my mind that I ain't nobody but myself and ain't nothin' I can do but let whatever is gonna happen, happen. I made up my mind that I was goin' back home and face Kate; yeah, and face Matty Lou too.[6]

In this scene, Ellison reveals the extraordinary power of the blues. Later, in a critical essay on the blues, he attributed the same potency to the blues queens.

> Bessie Smith might have been a "blues Queen" to the society at large, but within the tighter Negro community where the blues were a total way of life, and major expression of an attitude toward life, she was a priestess, a celebrant who affirmed the values of the group and man's ability to deal with chaos.[7]

All of the statements illustrate that the blues is about life; it has the power to reaffirm the values and worth of the people; and it is a wellspring of solace and hope. This power that enables one to cope with grief and disappointment, whether figuratively, vicariously, or literally, is central to my discourse on the blues women. I view the blues as the driving force with which the women could act on personal and artistic agendas simultaneously. In short, the blues is life which is art.

The women singers came to the forefront when the recording industry discovered their high profit potential in the race market in 1920, for their records were to be sold exclusively in the black community. Their careers were influenced greatly by the record industry, and in most cases, the industry also contributed to the demise of their careers as the shift was made to the recording of male blues singers and the increasingly popular dance bands in the last years of the 1920s and early 1930s.

In his sociocultural treatise on the evolution of black American music, LeRoi Jones states that phonograph records by women blues singers actually created whole styles of blues singing. "It is easy to see how this must have affected the existing folk tradition and created another kind of tradition that was unlike any other in the past," states Jones.[8] Linda Dahl asserts that the blues women "held and molded the power of the word in black music," implying that while they were faithful to the nature and spirit of the blues they also added innovations.[9] These included increased improvisation on melodic lines, unusual phrasing which altered the emphasis and impact of the lyrics, and vocal dramatics using shouts, groans, moans, and wails. The blues women thus effected changes in other types of popular singing that had spin-offs in jazz, Broadway musicals, torch songs of the 1930s and 1940s, gospel, rhythm and blues, and eventually rock and roll. The following statement by historian Lawrence Levine is consonant with the observations of Jones and Dahl. "Whatever the style is called it was closer to traditional blues than anything else on records, it fit in with the eclecticism so characteristic of black music, and it obviously had great appeal to Negroes, North and South."[10] The tradition begun by the women singers—

especially those who had vaudeville experience—brought a new emphasis and importance to musicianship, showmanship, varied repertoire, and a sense of artistry. Their live performances influenced local, lesser-known artists, and their recordings set the standard for the performance and interpretation of traditional material and introduced new material.[11]

David Evans states, and I agree, that the two major problems in the study of the blues are "the relationship of a singer's blues to those of his sources—the other singers that he learned from" and "the variation or stability from one performance . . . to another by the same performer."[12] The subjects of this study learned from show business peers, piano rolls, local musicians, Sunday School and church, and sometimes, as in the cases of Sippie Wallace and Victoria Spivey, from members of their families. They were apt to be more flexible and eclectic in their choice of texts and music than their rural counterparts because they had more sources to draw upon. Further, they were not mere mimics who imitated white music-hall singers, but were active participants in the evolution of the blues as it moved from the countryside to the cities and back. They transformed their personal feelings into artistic expression, which bonded them to other black women, by skillfully mixing the ingredients of heartbreak and joy to create the songs that caused thousands of black people to flock to their shows and to buy their recordings. Through the blues, these women became the principal spokespersons for black women in the North and the South.

Previously, writers such as Paul Oliver, Sam Charters, Giles Oakley, and Paul Garon have provided valuable information on the general themes and lyrics of the blues sung by men and women, but the main focus has generally been on men. More recently, Dahl and Sally Placksin have devoted some attention to the blues women in their works on American jazz women. Of particular importance, however, are the biographies of Bessie Smith and Ma Rainey by Chris Albertson and Sandra Lieb, respectively, for they were the first in-depth examinations of the blues woman as a distinct personality and creative artist. The autobiographies of Billie Holiday and Ethel Waters have also informed my study of the 1920s blues women from a personal and sociocultural standpoint.[13]

My main objective is to show the contributions of these women in the creation, development, and performance of the blues; to enlarge the reader's understanding of the music by examining it through the lives of the women who were instrumental in popularizing the blues via recorded and stage performances during the 1920s; to identify some of the most outstanding women of that era in terms of their particular styles, popularity, and influence; and, in the cultural context of the black experience in the 1920s, to discuss the blues that these women sang.

This study provides a comprehensive profile of the blues women of the 1920s and their important contributions to American music history. It also provides the reader with an opportunity to see these women as pivotal figures in the assertion of black women's ideas and ideals from the standpoint of the working class and the poor. It reveals their dynamic role as spokespersons and interpreters of the dreams, harsh realities, and tragicomedies of the black experience in the first three decades of this century; their role in the continuation and development of black music in America; their contributions to blues poetry and performance. Further, it expands the base of knowledge about the role of black women in the creation and development of American popular culture; illustrates their modes and means for coping successfully with gender-related discrimination and exploitation; and demonstrates an emerging model for the working woman—one who is sexually independent, self-sufficient, creative, assertive, and trend-setting.

Women's blues worked its way through the interpreter's personal experience; therefore, there was a divergence in style and depth of feeling from one singer to the next. The country sound of Ma Rainey, for instance, was imbued with the horror and despair of floods, blight, or crop failure, as well as mistreatment by lovers. Her focus on topics familiar to southern rural folk was enhanced by her boisterous wit, which she displayed in live performances. Wallace and Spivey employed a modified country style but their subject matter had a definite urban perspective. Nevertheless, both of them retained the style of singing and playing that they had developed back home in Texas. Ida Cox, Bessie Smith, and Clara Smith moved away from the country style and developed sophisticated, flexible blues styles that could handle the tough or slick sounds that city listeners were accustomed to. Yet, they employed the husky, throaty pathos, moans and groans which appealed to urban and rural blues listeners alike. This style—the city blues—grasped the issues of urban violence and neglect and rendered them in shouting, wailing, aggressive tempos and shadings.

Fancy-dressed smart-stepping vaudeville blues singers added pep, comedy, and showmanship to their performances in order to attract and entertain a more diverse audience than that of the country tent-show singers. They took familiar nonblues numbers and, with the assistance of pianists or jazz bands, jazzed them up or bluesed them down, thus expanding the blues repertoire and the blues listening audience. Some of these women built their careers in vaudeville and retained a decidedly vaudeville flavor in their recordings also. Mamie Smith is the most remembered because of her historic first recording, but Sara Martin had a lengthy career as a vaudeville blues queen—flashy, polished, glamorous, and cosmopolitan. On the other end of the spectrum was the minstrel-type vaudeville performer such as Trixie Smith, who was guileless, somewhat provincial, and less refined.

Alberta Hunter and Edith Wilson proved that the blues could appeal to a totally different constituency than the black masses in the South or the rowdy males in the dives, dance halls, and whiskey joints run by the underworld in the North. Their rise to prominence as entertainers in the more glamorous settings of the cabarets frequented by frolicking, adventure-seeking, wealthy whites created a new type of blues and blues singer—more cosmopolitan, less emotional. The Chicago and New York cabarets where they worked employed bands such as King Oliver's and Fletcher Henderson's to provide dance music for the so-called sophisticated gamblers and businessmen and their women. Their styles utilize wider vocal ranges, a greater variety of music, and often an upbeat rhythmic rendition more akin to vaudeville singing. They, and other cabaret blues singers such as Lucille Hegamin and Lizzie Miles, deserve credit for popularizing and standardizing blues performance so that it became a staple in American song repertoire.

Ma Rainey and Bessie Smith are the pivotal figures in an examination of blues singers, especially women blues singers, because of their enormous talent and popular appeal. Both of them have already received excellent coverage in previous works.[14] They will serve mainly as reference points in my discussion of the four singers whose lives I have probed more deeply—Hunter, Spivey, Wallace, and Wilson. Other singers, although obscure today, were highly ranked as blues queens in the 1920s, and will also be discussed here. These recording and stage performers transformed and enlarged the scope of blues performance beyond the vaudeville circuit and phonograph. Some went on to the radio or into the movies, others to musical comedy and theater, and others to Europe's stages.

Wallace, Spivey, Hunter, and Wilson are featured in this study for several reasons: they were all still active in the blues world as this book evolved; they could provide personal accounts of their experiences, as well as comments about other aspects of the era; each had recorded in recent years—between 1960 and 1983; and their vocal and performing styles were distinct. Spivey and Wallace came closer to the traditional standard blues style; while Hunter and Wilson had a more swinging cabaret or supper-club style. They, along with Eva Taylor, were the only known survivors of the classic blues era who were still living at the time this study began.

Chapter 1 examines the impact of the migration of blacks at the turn of the century on the nature and development of black communities in cities and the resultant effects on black women's lives. The changes brought about by increased mobility, expanded economic and employment opportunities, and shifts in personal and familial relationships are reflected in the social and religious activities of these migrants. Among them are increased leisure and recreational outlets and the institutions to support them. Theaters replaced tents as more black entertainers joined the ranks of vaudeville and other organized shows. The Theatre Owner's Booking Association (TOBA), was instrumental in the career development of many black artists. Its importance to the women's careers, the treatment of artists and the conditions under which they performed will also be discussed in that chapter.

The role of the phonograph industry—producers, scouts, studio managers, and publicity agents—are examined in Chapter 2. Mamie Smith and Bessie Smith will be discussed in the context of their significance in the development of the recording industry.

Since the most neglected aspect about women blues singers is the analysis of the principles and perspective that guided their choice of lyrics and interpretation, Chapter 3 examines the singers' lyrics and styles and illustrates an emerging feminist perspective. It also asserts that interpretation and analysis are a critical key to understanding the general nature of black cultural expression and the movement of black women toward self-determination and independence. Although the blues women sang about the same topics that men did, they provided new slants. They dealt openly with the issues that were of particular concern to black women in the urban setting—freedom from social and religious constraints, sexual and economic independence, alcoholism and drugs. Issues of sexuality and sex were addressed directly and indirectly in their lifestyles and their blues. The desire to find and express affection, love, and sensuality in various ways and under less scrutiny was a central issue for them. Lesbianism was practiced and sung about by such diverse singers as Bessie Smith, Ma Rainey, and Gladys Bentley—the last was known as a tough-talking, singing piano player who some believed to be a male transvestite and others, a lesbian. The blues themes in this chapter include the sexual and social concerns of the women.

Chapters 4–7 are profiles of Wallace, Hunter, Wilson, and Spivey. Their accounts of their careers during and after the "race" records era give us an inside glimpse of how these talented artists coped with the problems arising from the fluctuations in the entertainment industry.

I will also briefly discuss how the lives of some of the women, such as Hunter and Wilson, were affected by the rapid changes during the Harlem Renaissance. Their contributions to the cultural milieu of Harlem and other cities were noted by writers as diverse as Langston Hughes and Carl Van Vechten. Some were blasphemed and stereotyped, while others were photographed and idolized in the black and white press. Their social activities were followed here and abroad by black reporters and their performances were sought after and imitated by curious whites who trekked to Harlem in fine cars and furs in search of thrills.[15]

Those and other women, such as Sara Martin, Clara Smith, and Ida Cox, dominated the music scene for thousands of fans in the span of one decade, traveling from city to city, in successful and failing shows, developing the body of music now labeled the classic blues. They raised the status of black women entertainers to a new height and were adored at home and abroad for a brief moment in history; then after this swift burst of notoriety, they passed from the American cultural scene into obscurity. Many of the women were overlooked because they recorded for small record companies that went bankrupt by the mid-1920s; others, because they did not receive the kind of publicity that big companies like Columbia and Okeh gave to Bessie and Mamie; others, because the original wax masters of their recordings disappeared when the companies folded; and others, because their talents could not adjust to the vagaries of public taste.

I have attempted to demonstrate through the blending of oral and written data the strong relationship between the lifestyles of these women and their creative mode of expression—the blues. I have listened to and transcribed the 1920s versions of blues sung by approximately twenty singers in order to provide a sense of their performance styles, vocal abilities, and textual emphases. Finally, I have, wherever possible, used contemporary newspapers, journals, and magazines to capture the essence of the 1920s with regard to the struggle by blacks to assimilate or to gain equality; the moral questions raised about women on the stage, singing and dancing jazz and the blues; and the popularity and critical reception of the blues women.

Black readers in general will find that this book will add to the body of social history; clarify the role of black women in American history; illustrate the dynamics of work, personal relationships, and religion in black culture; demonstrate the economic impact of the blues women on a major American industry. For those readers who can recall the era that this book deals with, I hope I have conjured memories of a special time and place.

Other scholars will quickly recognize that I raised questions about the blues women and the evolution of the entertainment industry and its relationship to the development and promotion of the arts and artists. I encourage further investigation of these questions not only because there is a need, but also because the surge in scholarship on women and on American music has made information more accessible, and because the American music industry plays such a major role in the recognition and promotion of creative talent.

Riding "Joby" to the Big Time

> You didn't ask me but I'm gonna tell you anyway
> You might'ner . . . never heard old "Ma" sing them blues
> If it wasn't for the T.O.B.A.

We might never have heard the recordings of Ma Rainey, Bessie Smith, and many other great blues singers if the Theatre Owners' Booking Association circuit had not showcased so many black entertainers during the early years of the twentieth century. The TOBA organized and scheduled appearances of black vaudeville and tent acts in sixty-seven theaters across the South and Midwest. The throngs of blacks who paid twenty-five cents to a dollar for a variety show were rewarded with two to four hours of nonstop entertainment: dancing girls, comedians, blues singers, light classics singers, snake or magic acts, and a jazz band. And eventually audiences demanded recordings of those singers they had heard on the TOBA circuit.

• •

4   LIZZIE MILES PUBLICITY PHOTOGRAPH

The demand for entertainment in the hammocks of the country mill towns and the avenues of southern and northern cities came from a black population that was on the move geographically and economically at the turn of the century. The emigration of thousands of blacks from the rural areas to towns and cities created a major shift in the institutions and activities all along the eastern seaboard and in the midwestern regions of the country. Blacks were fleeing the violence and oppression of the post-Reconstruction South— lynchings, a new form of peonage called sharecropping, labor farms and chain gangs, and poll taxes. They sought improvement through better jobs, education, and housing in the booming urban and industrial areas. They rode the rails, riverboats, and steamers to the North and, ostensibly, freedom.

The black exodus was fraught with real and imagined dangers as inexperienced youths and adults maneuvered through Jim Crow laws, tricky employment schemes, and city temptations. The mass migrations sent thousands of rural men and women into the strangeness of the city with its crowded housing, glittering nightlife, faster pace, and impersonal atmosphere. Those who traveled North were prey to the harsh climatic changes, exploitation of their labor, and, in the instance of some young women, slavelike conditions of servitude as domestics for the wealthy.[1] Allan Spear notes that in Chicago at the turn of the century nearly 80 percent of its black population was born in states other than Illinois.[2] In New York City the black population had increased by 79 percent by 1900, the South Atlantic states accounting for the major portion of that increase. As black males moved north they shifted from domestic or agricultural occupations to industrial work prior to World War I. During the war, black females entered industry in large numbers for the first time and continued in these occupations after the war at an increase of nearly 70 percent.[3]

The rapid push northward presented problems for blacks already in the city. This warning appeared in a 1907 *New York Age:* "South-

ern Negroes should 'think carefully' before coming to New York. . . .
Native New Yorkers were severely limited in their choice of responsible positions . . . and the steady stream of newcomers only complicated the situation."[4] Similar articles appeared in the *New York
Age,* pleading with southern race members to consider the problems
they caused by their migration. Some southern whites attempted to
discourage the migration by claiming that the big cities were "lur-
ing" poor Negroes northward "by false promises of good positions,
reasonable hours and big money."[5]

One unusual aspect of this black migration was that not just men
but women and children often left their homes and kin to seek a
better life. More of these women were single than married, many
traveling to jobs promised in service to families—jobs that often did
not materialize. Turn-of-the-century census data includes children
as young as ten years in its population of gainfully employed.[6]
E. Franklin Frazier reported,

> Some of the women had their first experience with city life when they
> went to a near-by town to work for a few dollars a month in domestic
> service. . . . these towns offered comparative freedom from the reli-
> gious restraints imposed by the rural churches. In the dance halls,
> [they] . . . could give rein to their repressed impulses without incur-
> ring the censure of the elders for "their sinful conduct." . . . Once
> having caught a glimpse of the world beyond . . . these men and
> women were lured to a world beyond the small towns where they
> might enjoy even greater freedom and more exciting adventures.[7]

Agents who sought cheap labor for the rapidly expanding industrial North often resorted to devious means to attract young black
women. Many of the women arrived in cities expecting to work for
families who resided in suburban areas and found no means of
transportation to and from their jobs. Some were forced to live in
unsavory environments because they lacked the money to obtain

decent housing. Others who were inexperienced were let go by disappointed employers. Still others lost their jobs in garment factories because white female workers refused to work with them.[8] Francis Kellor wrote as early as 1905 that young girls responding to dubious job offers were often left at the mercy of agents who kept their clothes and money until they earned enough to pay their transportation costs. For some young women, this meant working in the red-light districts or being forced to live with undesirable persons. The problem was so acute that Kellor pleaded for the establishment of missions for the protection of young women as they arrived in cities such as Baltimore, Philadelphia, and New York.[9]

All was not totally bleak for blacks as they migrated to the cities. Many of the jobs, though physically demanding, provided far better salaries than those earned by the southern and rural blacks. Black women were moving into some of the light industry slots in factories; black men were finding more factory jobs, and although blacks were grossly underrepresented in manufacturing and mechanical occupations, the increased demand for personal and domestic service did provide additional employment.[10] The black female was more likely to benefit from these employment opportunities than the black male. In the burgeoning working class, people began to exercise their newly gained freedom from the church and tightly knit communities they had left and sought entertainment in the small bars and cafés that sprang up in the cities. The blues that they had heard in Memphis and Birmingham was transported by the New Orleans jazz men and women to Chicago; the minstrel troupes and tent shows followed the hordes of blacks northward carrying the sounds of the blues which told of their "disappointments . . . disillusionments . . . nostalgic yearnings for the . . . folk left behind."[11]

Segregated, overpriced housing forced blacks into enclaves, which developed into separate communities apart from whites. Blacks created institutions to accommodate their religious, social, and cultural needs. Among these were churches, burial societies, fraternal orders, theaters, dance halls, and clubs. The fraternal and social orders were organized by more affluent blacks, initially as benevolent and burial societies such as those found in the South. They eventually branched out to become more social by presenting balls and other affairs. For the working-class blacks, masonic orders and clubs competed with public recreational facilities. In both cases, theatrical performances and churches were of special interest. Black audiences flourished as black-owned theaters "burst forth lining Harlem streets. Such theaters as the famous Lafayette displayed the finest of black talent and music which was becoming unique and refined as a black nationalism was forming."[12]

This trend was evolving in other cities as well during the decade between 1915 and 1925. The Grand, Pekin, and Monogram theaters in Chicago, the Turpin in St. Louis, the Cass and Koppin theaters in Detroit, the Regent in Baltimore, and the Standard and Gibson theaters in Philadelphia flourished as black communities began to nurture their own talent. So, ironically, that scourge of black life, discrimination, was a catalyst in the establishment of a loosely organized network of entertainment centers for city blacks. In these settings a host of comedians struggled for recognition, fame, and fortune as they lightened the burdens of their brothers and sisters.

Young black women with talent began to emerge from the churches, schools, and clubs where they had sung, recited, danced, or played, and ventured into the more lucrative aspects of the entertainment world, in response to the growing demand for talent in the theaters and traveling shows. The financial rewards often outweighed community censure, for by 1910–1911 they could usually earn upwards of fifty dollars a week, while their domestic counterparts earned only eight to ten dollars. Many aspiring young women went to the cities as domestics in hope of ultimately getting on stage. While the domestics' social contacts were severely limited, mainly to the white employers and to their own families, the stage performer had an admiring audience in addition to family and friends.[13]

Young black women were often so dazzled by the opportunity for freedom, fortunes, and fame offered by the stage that they were willing to accept questionable living and working conditions to achieve them. Neither the rugged conditions on the road nor their families' disapproval could dissuade them. The black community's expressed concern about the young women performing in what were sometimes raunchy whisky joints was understandable in light of the history of unsavory employment situations for black women. Their limited job opportunities, on one hand, and the attractive pay and perquisites of the jobs attached to cheap dance halls, cabarets, and brothels, on the other, made them especially susceptible to phony deals with unscrupulous employers. As early as 1910, black newspapers directed attention to these threats to the moral fiber of their citizens, especially females. An example of the hue and cry appeared in the article entitled, "Mothers Taking Innocent Daughters to Houses of Ill Fame to Play Piano"; the subtitle asked, "Still Our Christians' Cry of White Slave Is Heard in the Community—What about Black Ones?" The article claimed that girls ranging from fourteen to nineteen could be found playing the piano in the red-light district of Chicago's State and Archer Streets. Black girls were purportedly sought because the wealthy white male clientele disapproved of the cozy relationships that developed between white prostitutes and black male piano players. This article pleaded with black organizations to speak out for these "unknown" black slaves.[14] In other expressions of concern, "streetwalkers" on Wabash Avenue in Chicago were considered a menace and disgrace; meetings were held to set up aid for women and girls who would be unemployed as a result of the closing down of the red-light district of Norfolk, Virginia, in spring 1916; the 1922 Chicago Commission on Race Relations reported objections raised by the black community against the Pekin Café because it offered jazz, vulgar dances, and mixed couples, all considered immoral enticements for the young black women who performed there.[15]

Women blues singers were likely to be among the performers in vaudeville routines on theater circuits as early as 1914. Their performances were not written about but the demand for blues on music rolls coupled with the presence of their names on broadsides was indicative of their popularity. White female singers such as Sophie Tucker and Blossom Seeley capitalized on the popular appeal of the blues by copying the songs and performance styles of black women.[16] Between 1910 and 1920, many black patrons in the South were becoming acquainted with the form through the renditions of Gertrude "Ma" Rainey and Lillian Glinn, as they traveled on the theater circuits with shows such as the Rabbit Foot Minstrels. Blacks who had moved away from family and friends could reminisce with Ma as she groaned those "Traveling Blues" with a jugband accompaniment. The whistle-stops on the circuit often provided the only link between the itinerant or migratory black and her life back home. And unlike comedy, acrobatic, or dance routines, the blues singers brought a reality to the stage that struck a responsive chord in the hearts of their listeners.

The market for black stage talent was lucrative enough to attract exploiters; living and performing conditions often bordered on the hazardous; black talent and audiences remained under the financial control of white theater owners and booking agencies; and the quality of some acts and shows was sometimes amateurish.

TOBA had a reputation that ranged from laudable for its regularizing of engagements and management to despicable depending on who was telling it. It was called "Tough on Black Asses" by those who were booked under its auspices. Acts and theater owners bickered constantly about salaries, conditions of theaters and housing, and scheduling of engagements.

Let us take a closer look at TOBA and its real value to the black entertainment world. The TOBA was organized in 1909 by Anselmo Barrasso in Memphis after he had noted the success that his brother had had running a number of southern theaters that catered to blacks.[17] Barrass noted the potential market for black acts, and created a booking association to supply the demand. The TOBA scheduled acts for the theaters that belonged to its network, much as a movie distribution company might rent films to a favored chain. This became the busy circuit for many black vaudeville shows and acts, reaching from Chicago to Florida, and from Oklahoma to New Orleans, with Memphis, Toledo, Chattanooga, Atlanta, Pittsburgh, and other towns in between. A long string of outstanding headliners appeared on the circuit and indeed a few received good salaries, often working year round. The most notable included Bessie Smith, Rainey, Sara Martin, Butterbeans and Susie, Kid and Coot, S. H. Dudley, the Whitman Sisters, Sweet Mama Stringbean (a.k.a. Ethel Waters), and Hamtree Harrington. Some of the theaters that prospered on the Toby circuit, as it was sometimes called, were the Regent in Baltimore, the Howard in Washington, the 81 in Atlanta, the Booker T. in St. Louis, and the Monogram in Chicago. For nearly thirty years the circuit provided many black entertainment professionals with the opportunity to appear on a regular basis along its route, if they were good.[18]

Although the TOBA favored its headliners with good salaries and provided the stock companies with an opportunity for regular bookings, it treated everyone below top billing poorly, subjecting performers to low salaries, inadequate or no housing accommodations, cramped and makeshift dressing areas, poor lighting and staging, cheating managers, racist managers, haphazard schedules, abandonment and so on. Artists often worked on stages that were so small there were no wings, no backstage, no dressing rooms. Some even had to dress underneath the stages and then slip on stage by climbing up through the orchestra pit when the house lights went down. Performers who were not headliners did not receive traveling expenses or guarantees of continuous runs. Hence, there were complaints about long "jumps," that is, a few nights in one town then the ride hundreds of miles away for another engagement.

With low salaries they could ill-afford the additional expenses for food and housing while traveling between shows. This problem was often exacerbated by squalid, unsavory housing. An item in *The Afro-American* warned, "Colored acts playing Carbondale, Pa., had better take a camping outfit along with them." An act on the Keith circuit, a consortium of white theaters which also hired blacks, claimed they "could not find accommodations in town."[19] A jazz band had had to sleep in the depot when they performed there the previous season. A possible explanation given was that since no black people lived in Carbondale, no housing was available, because blacks were prohibited from staying in white establishments. In small towns where there were no rooming houses for "colored," or no black families to house them, performers slept under hazardous circumstances; sometimes in empty buildings, in train stations, or in warehouses.

This was a period in American history when lynchings were still a common occurrence throughout the South.[20] Traveling from one Jim Crow town to another, the performers were haunted with fears of being dragged from a train or theater at the whim of some racist white person who wanted to have some fun or demonstrate his superiority. One headline read, "Orchestra Lured from Fashionable Hotel to Distant Forest and First Robbed, Then Clubbed and Stoned—Another Instance of Barbarism of South."[21] Another described the harassment of blacks in New Orleans by the Ku Klux Klan. There is little wonder there were complaints about long jumps with unsure wages. These and other problems gave a bittersweet taste to what little successes the showpersons had.

Disgruntled showpeople often turned to the black press as a medium for expressing concern or registering complaints. Consequently, the TOBA was the subject of many letters and articles in papers such as the *Pittsburgh Courier, The Afro-American,* and the *Chicago Defender* for most of the 1920s. As early as 1921 letters of protest deploring the behavior of certain theater managers appeared in the major black newspapers. These served to warn acts and companies about certain engagements so they could avoid working them. In one such letter, Garnett Warrington reported on his TOBA time in the summer of 1921: "I have just returned from a very successful 16 week's engagement over the T.O.B.A. time and with only two exceptions the entire engagement was a very pleasing one."[22] A Mr. Cummings, however, one of the theater managers whom Warrington and his company encountered on the circuit, was described as deceitful and unscrupulous.

> . . . I was fool enough to think that Mr. Cummings was a real man and a friend to the performers and meant my people well. . . . and although he claims to be a New Yorker he is a typical Southerner and hates a Negro like poison.
>
> The salaries of nearly all the acts . . . were cast under all kinds of pretenses. . . .
>
> [He] is an enemy not only to the performers but also to the T.O.B.A.

Warrington continued with a diatribe against an Atlanta manager, Charles Bailey, who he called "Marse." Bailey required performers to sleep and eat where he assigned them and charged them for meal tickets whether they used them or not. Those who refused were cancelled. Warrington's letter ended with a plea to his fellow performers and the TOBA officers not to book with such managers: "We can live without Cummings and Bailey and unless they change their tactics, no self-respecting performer has any business playing for them."[22]

The complaints made by Warrington illustrate the continuing stranglehold whites had on blacks even when blacks owned the companies. Whites were stockholders in the TOBA; they owned and managed many of the member theaters; and they often controlled the concessions and living arrangements which the companies had to use. As could be expected, there would be some abuse of black performers as they battled for power over their own domain. To put it mildly, the Toby was "grueling and humiliating," especially for minor performers, who were often harassed by the white theater bosses like Marse Bailey of the 81 Theatre. Bailey was described in the press as a "vindictive and arrogant 'czar' in his own theatre" as well as outside. He issued passes to the black performers who worked for him so that they could break Atlanta's curfew, which required blacks to be off the streets after certain hours.[23] Even carrying his passes, however, they were exposed to harassment and arrest.

On the positive side, the TOBA provided opportunities for a variety of acts, single and group, to develop expertise, to refine their talents. Although it booked white acts also, it was referred to in the black show business community as the "Colored Circuit" because of the predominance of black acts and audiences. The regular press coverage of the grievances brought against Toby led to improvements.

Ironically, Cummings, who was one of the subjects of Warrington's 1921 letter, was to become the manager for the southern territory of the TOBA within a year. He, along with two others, S. H. Dudley, a black businessman, and Martin Klein, a Jewish businessman, were responsible for booking acts and increasing the number of theaters on the circuit. J. A. Jackson, entertainment reporter for the black press, reported that the association had improved the living conditions and schedules for performers by providing a route of "comparatively easy jumps and with several cities where they may remain for more than the usual week . . . several weeks in one city permits a bit of homelike living, a chance for social activities, . . . and to do essential shopping."[24] This comment implies that there may have been a desire by some showpersons to have closer contact with the townspeople who offered them rented rooms in private homes or rooming houses.

Dudley made strong appeals to those in vaudeville, both actors and theater managers, regularly through his news column in the

Chicago Defender. In 1923, he urged the TOBA to select a person to serve as a commissioner. He felt that a man who was familiar with the problems of both sides—the box office and backstage—and who commanded their respect, would be able to resolve pay squabbles, contractual difficulties, and problems over low-quality acts. He also felt that performers would fare better with members of a circuit who would be able to offer fixed salaries rather than shaky percentages. Another concern was to provide acts with consecutive working dates so that their "railroad jumps" would be short and their salaries stable.[25] The prevailing practice at the time was "pay-as-you-go," so performers were never sure of receiving their wages until after the receipts for the day were counted and totaled enough to cover expenses. If the sales were poor, the performers were often left with nothing except promises to pay later. The organization of theaters into circuits thus benefited managers because they could plan and book shows well in advance and maximize the opportunity for good gate receipts. Circuit owners could then control and manipulate the flow of talent to their profit advantage. As an incentive for becoming a member of the association, the TOBA franchise allowed member theaters a 6 percent rake-off of the salaries for each engagement received, practically guaranteeing good profits.

Milton Starr, president of the TOBA in 1924, made great strides in improving the organization and quality of the shows it booked. The bookings were expanded to include the renowned Lafayette Theatre Players and Broadway revues such as *Liza.* These, of course, attracted a wider audience. Schedules for all acts and shows appeared weekly on the entertainment pages of black newspapers such as *The Afro-American, Chicago Defender,* and *Norfolk Journal and Guide,* providing added publicity.[26]

Many factors affected the development of the TOBA, as well as other circuits that included blacks on their roster of talent. The northward migration caused a reduction of the patronage in some southern theaters as the wage-earning population declined. Some theaters closed, making it necessary for acts to take longer stretches to travel from one place to another. However, benefits were correspondingly gained up North as migrants expanded black audiences and provided a larger outlet for black talent. One journalist suggested that the smaller cities, such as New Haven, Connecticut; Allentown, Pennsylvania; and Youngstown, Ohio, were logical places for new acts and shows to shakedown before going to the big houses in Baltimore, Philadelphia, and Atlanta.[27]

The expansion of circuits was inevitable as whites capitalized on the lucrative market created by the ballooning black population in the North. The Keith, Pantage, and Columbia circuits captured the cities in the North and Midwest, while the Orpheum captured those in the West—in the week of 31 October 1925, TOBA acts were booked in Chattanooga, Nashville, Dallas, Houston, New Orleans, St. Louis, Columbus, Macon (Georgia), and Chicago; while Montreal, Boston, Syracuse, Newark, Erie (Pennsylvania), New Britain (Connecticut), and Woonsocket (Rhode Island) received the Keith bookings.[28] One obvious difference in these routings was the audiences—blacks on the TOBA and whites on Keith. Black acts were even booked for Europe and Africa as their popularity registered high in the gate receipts.[29] However, the politics of racism inevitably pervaded the entertainment world. One circuit, the Mutual Burlesque, ordered its houses not to book any mixed or colored shows, demonstrating that for some people profit was less compelling than maintaining racial discrimination.[30]

The problem of white control and exploitation of black stage life was aired in columns by black newswriters. Not only did the numerous white circuits book more black acts than TOBA, but they also determined what those acts would do. This practice became so brazen that there was an outburst from several noted black showpersons. For example, when Carl Van Vechten devoted two of his *Vanity Fair* columns to his criticism of black blues singers and Negro entertainment, this enraged S. T. Whitney, an entertainment columnist, to the point of responding via *The Afro-American*. Whitney stated that white capitalists would not consent to departure from the mammy songs, cork face, and rude comedy, but insisted on perpetuating the stereotypes. He wisely acknowledged that "the real musical show and drama of race life will have to be promoted by our men before the desired result is obtained."[31] The struggle by blacks to wrest control of the content and management of black theaters and music continued. Meanwhile, the blues singers who came into greater demand on the circuits between 1915 and the early 1920s were subject to that exploitation and control.

Eventually, there was public reaction in the black community to the effect of show business on morals. Some people felt that the acts used lewd language and too much nudity. Others felt that they were receiving shows of poor quality. The small towns in the South were particularly vulnerable to the wiles of the exploitative theater owners who paid the least in order to book acts, often taking performers with little or no experience or talent. The heads of the TOBA were clearly the ones responsible for bilking the public since their percentage policy did not have any restrictions or quality guidelines.[32]

In a series of articles, "Gang" Tines, an entertainment reporter for the *Chicago Defender,* denounced contemporary vaudeville shows as "purveyors of putrid puns" and "filth furnishers." Another article blamed degenerates for catering to the degraded tastes of white theater-goers by offering nudity on stage. Tines also chided black showmen for jeopardizing the opportunities of other blacks on the white circuits when they got too involved with women while on the road. Vivienne, another *Defender* reporter, chastised, "Stage folks have a wonderful opportunity to help elevate the race—help to lift the stamp of inferiority. . . . Vulgarity is a yoke or burden. See it for what it is—a hindrance to our standard of respectability and success."[33] To press the point further, the *Defender* featured a reprint of a review in the *Detroit News* which lambasted Ethel Waters's rendition of an "unspeakably rotten blues" in her "Miss Calico" revue. William Gibson, another reporter, took the position that the public cared little about the morals of showfolk, believing them to be a bad lot anyway. He felt that they were more interested in the acts and their quality of entertainment, leaving morality for another arena.

On more than one occasion, churches were criticized for trying to monitor stage shows, to prevent young people from attending, and in some instances, to prohibit showpeople from taking communion.[34] No consensus on the morals issue was achieved during that period—nor has it been since.

Despite the numerous snares and pitfalls of stage life, young black women continued their quest for stardom via the Toby time or small traveling tent shows, or other means. Ads in papers encouraged them to apply for movie roles, chorus lines, and singing parts which would allegedly bring them fame and fortune.

> Wanted—A Girl for Vaudeville. One that can sing. Experience unnecessary. Must be reliable. $20. a week. Apply between 7 and 8 p.m. to MEL-VERN, 1106 McCullough Street, City [Baltimore]

> GET IN THE MOVIES
> Great field for advancement. Fame, wealth and a happy life already earned by many motion picture stars. St. Louis fast becoming the Colored Hollywood. The Colored public is now demanding Good Colored pictures. Complexion or age should prove no bar. Write, send photo, or call.

> MECCA STUDIOS
> Suite 302-4 Midway Building
> Olive and Jefferson   St. Louis, Mo.[35]

Such notices elicited responses from all over the country as black women sent pleas for jobs to the entertainment editors of black papers, since it was common practice for persons connected with show business to leave their addresses with newspapers. Their mail or messages would be printed in the papers because most of them were on the road so much. An enterprising Kansas girl, "Miss L.M.," followed that procedure by writing this letter to the manager of Detroit's Koppin Theatre, E. B. Dudley:

> Dear Sir: I am 20 years of age, height five feet three, one-half inches, weight 118 pounds. Am light complexioned, have black curly, bobbed hair. I am Colored. I am a poor girl and would like for some respectable man, who is interested in theatre work to help give me a start. I want a one-act man. I want to take Spanish dancing lessons, Japanese dancing lessons, and Hawaiian dancing lessons and learn a good character reading that would take. I want to go on the stage but I don't want anything trashy. I am sure that in two or three months I would be ready, and I'm not hard to learn and . . .
>
> Yours truly,
Miss L.M.[36]

Her letter reveals much about herself and the prevailing tastes—the preference for light-skinned women, with curly hair; the naive belief that a few dance lessons would prepare her for a stage career; her hope to find a mentor, as well as a mate; and the popularity of the exotic act. The color vogue was reinforced by ads for complexion and hair products endorsed by some of the stars of the day, such as Esther Bigou, a creole actress from New Orleans billed as the "Girl with the Million Dollar Smile."[37] A reader of *The Afro-American* was so disappointed by the unattractiveness of girls in previous shows that he was moved to write to that paper's theatrical editor to complain about the "crooked lower limbs, often spindly. With the girls ranging in color from ebony hue to that desired by every conventional comedian, 'high yaller.'"[38] Complexion and hair that approximated white standards of beauty continued for decades to be plus factors for women who sought stage careers as singers, chorus girls, or actresses, contrary to the so-called trend noted in an *Afro-American* article.

BROWN SKIN NOW BROADWAY'S FAVORITE

Light girls in Broadway shows and night club revues seem to have had their day.

. . . In the new Ziegfeld show, "Show Boat," there will be a number of girls, all "dark brown."

Heretofore the fair-typed were preferred, . . . as a novelty and a "draw" and . . . "essential" to musicals using a colored female ensemble.[39]

Neither these nor other barriers dampened the spirits of the women who pursued the glamour and glitter which they perceived that the TOBA offered. They wanted to be seen at the elaborate dinners and parties sponsored by well-to-do blacks and whites for the big-time singers such as Bessie Smith, Mamie Smith, and Sara Martin. High style and high living were the goals of the showfolk and their patrons. The Toby helped to spread the Harlem lifestyle from Dallas to Kansas City, Chattanooga, Birmingham, and up the rails.

Big, gorgeous Bessie was the center of attraction not only at affairs given by the Van Vechtens and Frank Walker of Columbia Records in New York but also the Detroit dinner parties of Viola Chesapeake, a former showgirl turned socialite. Bylines in the black newspapers mentioned the parties in Norfolk, Philly, Chicago, and Kansas City. The monotony of the clickety-clacking train wheels, the cramped sleeping quarters, lousy food, haggles over wages, loneliness, and other hardships were temporarily forgotten as the whiskey flowed and the music played—sometimes all night. These occasions sometimes provided the opportunity for the showwomen to offset the negative attitudes about them; however, they also had the reverse effect in some instances. Ma Rainey's escapades with some of her chorus girls got out of hand at a party after a show in Cincinnati and the police raided the place. Bessie Smith was said to have raised the roof at a swank party given by the Van Vechtens when she had had too much of her favored whiskey.[40]

In spite of its many liabilities, the TOBA must be credited with facilitating the growth of black entertainment during a critical period in American show business history. That growth also benefited the black community, which reaped economical and cultural benefits when the train uncoupled the show railcar at the local siding. The traditional parade that followed not only brought folks to the show, it brought business to the little shops, cafés, and "joints" as people crowded in to mingle with the showpeople. And high spirits remained for weeks after the train was gone.

Many women and men who rode the Toby time have passed unnoticed out of stage hisory, but the blues queens left a special mark. Some were heard by scouts for the record companies who seized the opportunity to promote and exploit their talents while leaving us a permanent trace. Few left as powerful a mark as Ma Rainey and Bessie Smith, who were undisputedly the greatest blues stars in the 1920s. Rainey's experiences on the TOBA circuit are illustrative of the tensions caused by a developing career, high visibility, publicity, and fame, accompanied by unscrupulous management, callous treatment, and grueling conditions.

Gertrude Pridgett was born 26 April, 1886 in Columbus, Georgia. The second oldest of five children, Gertrude appeared in a local talent show, *Bunch of Blackberries,* at the Springer Opera House when she was about fourteen years old. Will Rainey, a comedy singer, was traveling with one of the minstrel shows passing through Columbus when he met and fell in love with the young Gertrude. He married her on 2 February 1904. The couple did a song-and-dance act for many years billed as "Ma" and "Pa" Rainey, "Assassinators of the Blues," with the Rabbit Foot Minstrels, but her blues singing soon became the drawing card of the performances.[41]

She is said to be the first singer to use blues as a part of her reper-

toire in minstrel acts. Her voice was described as an earthy, powerful, and deep contralto with an "authentic manner of singing the
blues."[42] Her ability to capture the mood and essence of black rural
southern life quickly endeared her to throngs of followers throughout the South. Ma's straightforward singing style was especially
suited to the content of her blues, which described the drudgery,
pain, and joys of her folk.

> You see me ravin', you hear me crying,
> Oh Lawd, this lonely heart of mine,
> Sometimes, I'm grieving from my hat down to my shoes.
> I'm a good-hearted women that's a slave to the blues.[43]

Rainey was almost unheard of outside the South until she was
picked up by Paramount Records in 1923. Until then, although she
had toured with several minstrel shows including the Rabbit Foot
Minstrels, Tolliver's Circus and Musical Extravaganza, the C. W.
Parker, Al Gaines, and Silas Greene shows, she had rarely gone any
farther north than Virginia.[44] When Paramount Records announced,
"Discovered at Last"—"Mother of the Blues," she had been performing for nearly twenty-five years. The half-page ad for the first issue
of the recording "Moonshine Blues" featured a picture of Rainey, resplendent in the gold necklace and gold-plated grin.[45] Paramount
had a winner because she had developed the most faithful followers
of any of her contemporaries. With the establishment of her recording career new audiences joined her band of followers in the South.
Chicago, Detroit, and Pittsburgh were added to the southern cities
on the TOBA route Rainey followed. Newspapers heralded her coming and praised her shows lavishly. Rainey's career received a decided boost when she moved to Toby time around 1924, according
to her biographer. She earned added prestige with the more polished, professional performances found on the circuit than in the
rural, small-town traveling tent shows, and her audience was greatly

expanded because she was booked into theaters in major cities of the North and Midwest.[46]

Rainey was highly respected by jazz musicians as well as other musicians. Thomas Dorsey, her former pianist, said she was a "natural-born" artist who knew more about music than he did although she did not have his formal training. He said she just opened up and "issued" out the blues just as they were supposed to sound.[47] The highlight of their shows was the moment Madame Rainey, as she was billed, emerged from "a big Paramount talking machine. Oh Boy! What a flash Ma does make in her gorgeous gowns backed up by her Georgia Jazz Band."[48] But it was her compassion, her tenderness, and her willingness to share her money, time, or experience with others that made her just plain "Ma" to her fellow troupers and audiences on the TOBA. Her audiences reacted to her with affection because she maintained a bond with them; she understood their lives and had the ability to interpret them through the blues she sang. Sterling Brown, the poet who studied and wrote much on the blues, captured the feelings Ma aroused throughout the South in his eloquent elegy, "When Ma Rainey Comes to Town."

> . . . O Ma Rainey, Li'l and low
> Sing us 'bout de hard luck Round our do',
> Sing us 'bout de lonesome road We must go
> I talked to a fellow an' the fellow say
> "She jes' catch hold us some kind way . . ."[49]

Thomas Fulbright, a member of a drama stock company, met Rainey when her company toured with TOBA and played in the same East Texas towns as his company around 1930. His accounts of her singing reports that she made her people "weep with her and laugh with her."[50]

A professional who was reputed to be always willing to help others, Ma took time to provide coaching for the newcomers to the shows. Years earlier she had supposedly coached the young Bessie Smith when she joined the Rabbit Foot Minstrel Show around 1914. In fact, her bandleader, Thomas Dorsey, claimed that he spent more time practicing with newcomers than he did with Ma.[51] Butterbeans and Susie, a comic duo, got their start with her; so did many others. Little Daniel Rainey, one of seven children for whom she served as foster mother, performed his song-and-dance act with their troupe. Rainey was confident enough to use top-rate acts in her company, which numbered around twenty-five, including her jazz band. Other singers, as well as dancers, comedians, and choristers, performed in her company. Rainey was a good businesswoman; Dorsey cited the stability of pay as one of the reasons he stuck with her as a band leader for several years.[52] She knew that well-paid help meant fewer worries.

Ma Rainey was a flashy dresser who loved jewelry, the more glittery, the better. Announcements for shows often included pictures of her in a lamé headband, necklace and earrings fashioned from gold eagle dollars, and a heavily beaded dress draped over her stocky torso. Her penchant for helping those less fortunate than herself, coupled with her weakness for jewels, got her into a scrape with the law in 1924 after she had purportedly paid $25,000 for jewelry offered by a man posing as a down-and-out actor in Tennessee. Those jewels adorned a dress Dorsey described as "nothing but flashing lights," which she wore in an engagement in Cleveland, Ohio, one Sunday night in the autumn of 1924. Two detectives traced the jewels to Rainey and arrived at the theater to arrest her. She was allowed to finish the show but then they hustled her on to Nashville and a waiting jail cell. While she was trying to extricate herself, the rest of the show went on to Washington, Pennsylvania, for a performance scheduled the following Tuesday. To keep their contract alive and avoid losing money Dorsey and some others dreamed up what they thought was a pretty good scheme to cover up her absence. They selected one of the plumper chorus girls, dressed her in Rainey's finery, and proceeded to drill her in Rainey's songs. Dorsey said that they practiced all night getting the routine down pat. Before a screaming audience anxious to see Rainey, the lights lowered, a spotlight zoomed in on a Victrola at stage center as the band began "Moonshine Blues," and a nervous young lady stepped out singing. Suddenly from the far reaches of the balcony, a voice yelled, "Hey, hell, that ain't Ma Rainey. That ain't Ma Rainey." The curtain went down and the show closed, leaving the company stranded for four days. Rainey reappeared at the Lincoln, a TOBA theater in Pittsburgh, Pennsylvania, after the delay caused by her being detained by police in Nashville for questioning about the stolen goods. Nevertheless, the *Pittsburgh Courier* hailed her first visit to the Steel City with the headline, "Ma Rainey, Record Artist, at Lincoln Next Week."[53] After some shaky moments with little money, the company went on in Pittsburgh with Rainey back in the spotlight. Dorsey, however, decided to return to Chicago. He did not consider the incident as bothersome for Rainey because her reputation was so solid that she could borrow a thousand dollars at any time with no difficulty.[54]

Rainey played on the TOBA until the final years of her career with Paramount. During those years she packed in audiences wherever she appeared, and continued to receive rave reviews in the waning years of the vaudeville revues, 1928 and 1929. She still wowed them in Arkansas, Kansas, Alabama, Texas, and Kentucky as she had in the early years. Although the blues recordings and TOBA were suffering a severe decline, Rainey kept going by returning to the tent show routines with which she had begun.

Rainey made ninety-two records during the five-year period that she worked for the Paramount label. She had some of the finest musicians accompanying her—Lovie Austin, Fletcher Henderson, Don Redmon, Buster Bailey, Tom Dorsey, Tommy Ladnier, and the incomparable Louis Armstrong.[55] But today, our evaluation of her output suffers from the poor quality of the Paramount sides.

What of the music of Ma Rainey? She was a versatile singer who sang variety songs and blues in a voice with a gravelly timbre and a range of approximately one octave. Dorsey says she was a "natural-born artist" who "didn't need no school didn't go to no school; didn't take no music, didn't need no music."[56] He said Bessie Smith had more of the groaning and moaning in her than did Ma. On the other hand, "Ma had the real thing she just issued out there. It had everything in it it needed, just like somebody issue a plate of food out say everything's on the plate. And that's the way Ma handed it to 'em—take it or leave it."[57] Her singing retained those characteristics most admired by Africans and Afro-Americans—buzzing sound, huskiness, satirical inflections, ability to translate everyday experiences into living sound. Her dynamism fueled with empathy drew her listeners into the mood of a blues.

Rainey's naturalness coupled with her flair for comedy showed in the topics she sang about. They are typical of those of many blues singers—mistreatment, desertion, infidelity, revenge, sex, alienation. The same ambivalence about whether to go or stay, or to call him back or "crown" him, to brag about other men, or moan about the lost one, to defy sexual norms, appeared in her blues and were dealt with equally as well. Rainey sometimes took everyday situations and created an outrageously funny picture. A fine example is "Those Dogs of Mine," a mournful, draggy blues about the aching corns on her feet. Every line is so funny that one can just see this fat woman tiptoeing ever so carefully to avoid another twinge of pain. In each of her blues, regardless of whether she presented the dilemma with wry humor, sardonic irony, or mocking sadism, the message is clear—"I am pained," "My sense of worth is threatened," "I'm lonely, I need love."

The record industry did not develop Rainey as an artist; she was already an artist when they "discovered" her; the industry merely preserved on wax a voice that would serve as a striking example of the diversity of the black experience. And though some said that

Rainey's singing was too country to keep recording after the 1920s, she continued to pack them in on the circuits in the South and Southwest.

The good-humored, rollicking Rainey loved life, loved love, and most of all, loved her people. Her voice bursts forth with a hearty declaration of courage and determination—a reaffirmation of black life. The life of those riding Toby time is reflected in the lines from one of her blues:

> I went to the depot, looked up and down the board,
> I went to the depot, looked up and down the board,
> I asked the ticket agent, "It's my time on this road?" [58]

And so it would be for other blues women such as Ida Cox and her Raisin' Cain company, Mamie Smith and her Jazz Hounds, Sara Martin, and later, Spivey, the Black Snake Moaner, and dozens of others, who rode the rails to fame, glamour, and, in some cases, fortune, as they belted out, moaned, and groaned the blues to the screaming delight of their audiences. A new industry emerged and earned a fortune from their vocal talents when Okeh records gambled on Mamie Smith and won. As with most of the gains made by blacks in America, their stage success was attained despite extraordinarily difficult odds, and, as with most of the gains, the industry that produced the success lay outside of the black community, and subject to forces beyond their control. TOBA was instrumental in the development and expansion of the black entertainment industry from 1907 until its destruction by the economic forces of the Depression. It could not compete with the competition from "talkie" movies, radio programs, and dance music as opposed to vaudeville and minstrel acts. Member theaters were crushed if they could not muster the funds to renovate to accommodate sound movies. Local musicians and stage crews went without jobs as the economy slowed to a halt.[59] Fortunately for some of the blues women, there were opportunities in brief roles in the movies; for others the radio weekly shows kept them singing for a while; and those who could adjust their style and repertoire were able to continue as cabaret or revue performers. Mamie and Bessie Smith, Hunter, Wilson, and Spivey all appeared in at least one film during their careers. Hunter, Wilson, Spivey, and Trixie Smith also performed in plays and musicals on Broadway during the 1930s. But none of these activities brought them the fame and fortune that were theirs in the heyday of the 1920s. Like the TOBA, the blues women lost in a market that disappeared.

CRAZY BLUES

By PERRY BRADFORD

MAMIE SMITH AND HER JAZZ HOUNDS

Get this number for your phonograph on Okeh Record No. 4169

PUBLISHED BY
PERRY BRADFORD
MUSIC PUB. CO.
1547 BROADWAY, N. Y. C.

"Crazy Blues" Starts a New Craze

One of the phonograph companies made over four million dollars on the Blues. Now every phonograph company has a colored girl recording. Blues are here to stay.

—*The Metronome*, January 1922

Rainey's experiences traveling with the Rabbit Foot Minstrels and other roadshows were typical of other blues singers who rose to fame in the second decade of this century. Ida Cox, Bessie Smith, Eva Taylor, Sippie Wallace, and Bertha "Chippie" Hill are only a few of the singers who were first noticed on the stage of a road company. From this fertile source enterprising songwriters and recording scouts plucked much of the talent of the classic blues era. After World War I, when the hot jazz bands began to flourish on the night scene in Harlem and Chicago, practically every cabaret fea-

• •

5   SHEET MUSIC COVER FOR "CRAZY BLUES,"
FEATURING MAMIE SMITH AND HER JAZZ HOUNDS

tured one or two singers who strolled among the patrons between solos to encourage them to spend more. The black theaters and fancy clubs put on musical revues that showcased a singer of vaudeville and fox-trot melodies, as well as the blues. One of these women, Mamie Smith, was destined to change the course of show business history when she made the first blues recording by a black singer.

Blacks were heard on records as early as 1895, when George W. Johnson recorded "Laughing Song" on an Edison phono-cylinder. There were also a 1901 Victor recording by the brilliant young comedian, Bert Williams; a 1902 recording by the Dinwiddie Colored Quartet; recordings by Carroll Clark, a vocalist who sang so-called plantation melodies; the Fisk Jubilee Singers singing their "sorrow songs"; and coon songs by a few black minstrel men (some of whom would express their regret a few years later).

These early recordings featured comic monologues and black college choral versions of religious music, but no blues, except for one blues title among forty-nine music rolls issued in a 1906 series, *Music for the Aeolian Grand.*[1] Perhaps this was an anomaly, but it was the precursor of blues rolls issued ten years later. With typical irony, it was the active search for and use of blues songs by major white entertainers that thrust the blues into the center of the entertainment industry. According to Ronald Foreman, a scholar on the history of jazz and race records, it was Sophie Tucker's interest in the blues and their subsequent adoption by Blossom Seeley, Al Bernard, Nora Bayes, and other white headliners that "invested the word [blues] with musical meaning for many vaudeville and theatre patrons."[2] For persons who could not attend live performances, there were occasional issues of blues on music rolls prior to World War I; and between March 1917 and April 1918, G.R.S., Connorized, Standard Music, Universal Music, and Vocalstyle released lists of new blues titles.[3]

The profitable sales of jazz and blues piano rolls was the impetus for the phonograph companies' search for black or white talent to feature on jazz and blues recordings. The rise in race consciousness among blacks after the war facilitated the search. In 1919, James Reese Europe and his Army band were instrumental in pointing out the value and beauty of black music to blacks. This raised consciousness led black musicians and entertainers to seek involvement in the entertainment industry beyond stage performances. The phonograph companies initially made only modest attempts to respond to blacks' aspirations for acceptance as both buyers and producers of recordings.[4] The popularity of black artists was not attributed to their talent by white promoters but rather to the type of music they played. Many hours were spent by Perry Bradford and W. C. Handy trying to convince the record companies that black women blues singers had a ready market of black consumers who wanted to buy their recordings. They repeatedly approached the companies from 1919 on and were rebuffed by managers who claimed that the black women's voices were unsuitable, or that their diction was different from that of white women, or that they could not fill the requirements.[5]

But Bradford was a hustler. His persistence may have been considered a nuisance by some but that did not deter him. As he pounded the New York pavements, he hit upon what he thought was a sure-fire plan—convince a recording company to sign up a singer for his songs and win a big audience. He had been writing, playing, publishing, and hawking his compositions for quite a few seasons when he decided that Mamie Smith, the star of *Maid of Harlem,* a musical revue, would be an attractive offering on the recording market. To his credit, Bradford had produced some tuneful, danceable melodies which were already on piano rolls and sheet music, and this helped him get an appointment with RCA Victor Records on 10 January 1920 for a trial session featuring Mamie Smith singing "That Thing Called Love," a vaudeville-type ballad. Although Victor did not release it, Bradford and Smith did not give in to one failure. They continued up and down Tin Pan Alley, knocking on the doors of recording studio managers, seeking a fair shake in the expanding record market. Bradford hit pay dirt on 14 February at General Phonograph's Okeh studios, with Smith singing "That Thing Called Love" coupled with "You Can't Keep a Good Man Down." A stellar group of musicians led by Johnny Dunn, trumpet, and including Willie "The Lion" Smith, piano, backed the vocals.[6] The recording lay dormant until summer when General Phonograph released it in its regular series of popular titles without any special attention or fanfare.[7]

In March 1920, the black press hailed the upcoming release as an event:

> Now we have the pleasure of being able to say that they [the record company] have recognized the fact that we are here for their service; the Okeh Phonograph Company has initiated the idea by engaging the handsome, popular and capable vocalist, Mamie Gardener Smith of 40 W. 135th Street, N.Y.C., and she has made her first record, . . . apparently destined to be one of that great company's big hits.[8]

Although General Phonograh did no special promotion, the recording was an overwhelming success. Blacks purchased every copy that could be found. Some estimates were in the 100,000 range, stupendous for the times, especially because these were sold exclusively to blacks.[9]

Okeh rushed to capitalize on its new find by recording "Crazy Blues" on 10 August of the same year. At that session the studio orchestra was dubbed Mamie Smith's Jazz Hounds and was expanded to include Johnny Dunn on cornet, Dope Andrews on trombone, and Leroy Parker on violin. The cover for the sheet music of "Crazy Blues" featured a photograph of Smith and the band and the Okeh record catalog number. This time, much advertising fanfare accompanied its release.

"Crazy Blues" set off a recording boom that was previously unheard of. The target of the publicity campaigns soon became known as the "race market," a term supposedly coined by Ralph Peer, the Okeh recording manager.[10] In less than a year, the race market was jumping with "discovery after discovery" of blues singers touted as the "best yet" by their record companies. Meanwhile, Mamie Smith was propelled into the limelight by the rave reviews appearing in the black press. She was pointed to with pride as the first artist of the race to record popular songs. Her entry in the market was a boon to music publishing companies as well as to music stores in every town and city. The *Chicago Defender* ran an ad by the Pace and Handy Music Company for their latest sheet music release, which included Bradford's "You Can't Keep a Good Man Down." The interesting feature of this ad was its exploitation of Smith's name: "Sung by Mamie Smith on Okeh record. The first Colored girl to make a record of a popular song, and it's great."[11] W. C. Handy acknowledged in an article appearing a few weeks later that the increase in profits for publishers and writers, and in the number of contracts for other singers, was "following up the good works of Mamie Smith with the Okeh record people."[12] Between September and December 1920, Smith had cut six more sides for Okeh; they included a mixture of blues and vaudeville type songs.

The General Phonograph company began promoting the Smith recordings by linking them to her stage appearances. Her record releases boosted her stage career dramatically and vice versa: in 1921 her output rose to twenty-nine sides as she made promotional tours that took her to the South, the Midwest, and the Southwest. In April Smith appeared at the Dallas Coliseum, where her revue was acclaimed "one of the best accelerated musical treats of the year. [She] is a master of the art of Negro blues' songs."[13] The "phenomenal success of her Southern Tour" was crowned with her being feted while in Dallas by Portia Washington Pittman, the concert artist and acclaimed pianist, daughter of the highly respected educator, Booker T. Washington.[14] Recognition by Pittman was quite an honor, and forecast the emergence of a rise in status of the blues singers. Mamie Smith was rapidly building a reputation for herself. Because she understood that her record success was related to that of her stage appearances, and that her public had certain expectations with regard to their newly-made star, she set a standard for the blues queens who followed her with her lavish costumes and scenery. She made the following remarks in the *Norfolk Journal and Guide* on the occasion of one of several appearances at Billy Sunday's Tabernacle in 1921.

> . . . thousands of people who come to hear me . . . expect much, and I do not intend that they shall be disappointed. They have heard my phonograph records and they want to hear me sing these songs the same as I do in my own studio in New York. . . . Another thing, I believe my audiences want to see me becomingly gowned, and I have spared no expense or pains, . . . for I feel that the best is none to good for the public that pays to hear a singer.[15]

By 1922, her star status prompted Okeh to feature the "Mamie Smith Blues," an early version of a recorded commercial.

> I've got the Mamie Smith Blues . . .
> And when I hear that Okeh . . . record play "I Want My Daddy
> Blues."
> "Saxophone blues" thrill me with bliss . . . so Mamie
> Don't you feel blue
> 'Cause lots of girls wish they were Mamie Smith too . . .[16]

The recording industry was beginning to have a dynamic effect on the development of performers' careers and on the transmission of black popular music.

Okeh's unprecedented success with Mamie Smith sent many other record companies in search of women blues singers for promotion in the lucrative race market. The year 1921 burst forth with newly discovered blues on a variety of labels. Columbia touted Mary Stafford as the "First Colored Girl to Sing for Columbia" in their promotion of her January release of "Crazy Blues."[17] Edith Wilson was signed by Columbia in early 1921 mainly because she was already established as a stage star in New York. By the next year her name was only one among many showing up in music store ads in the black community. Cardinal Records introduced "Sweet Mama Stringbean," the twenty-year-old Ethel Waters, who recorded one single. Lillyn Brown was described in the Emerson Phonograph catalogue as "not only a favorite with her own people, but with white audiences as well."[18] In its attempt to overtake Okeh, Arto Records, a subsidiary of the Standard Music Roll Company, recorded Lucille Hegamin, a well-known New York cabaret singer, in March 1921. Though other women recorded for Arto, it did not survive.

Among the labels that began to proliferate in 1921 was the Black Swan label of the black-owned Pace Phonograph Company, which opened in May. Its first blues release was by Ethel Waters. Although Waters had reportedly been earning only thirty-five dollars a week at the time, she convinced Harry Pace to pay her one hundred dollars to record "Down Home Blues." He acquiesced to her demand and was rewarded by good sales, which pulled Black Swan out of debt for a short while.[19] Katie Crippen and Lula Whidby also recorded blues for Black Swan but the company could not compete in the market and was eventually taken over by Paramount in 1923.

By the end of 1922, names like Leona Williams, Kitty Crippen, Lula Whidby, Daisy Martin, Esther Bigeou, Lavinia Turner, Laura Smith, Trixie Smith, Monette Moore, and Gladys Bryant had joined the ranks of blues recording artists. Black newspapers were bombarded with ads for individual artists and titles.

The Columbia Gramophone Company has more colored artists than any other record manufacturer.

Try WEAVER'S for
Victor, Brunswick, Okeh, and Arto Records
$.75 Each $.75 Each

One enterprising proprietor borrowed from the Heinz Foods slogan to illustrate the breadth of his blues inventory.

If It's Blues You Like

We Have 57 Varieties, And Then Some

Sung by	Played by
Trixie Smith	Johnny Dunn's Jazz Hounds
Mamie Smith	Ted Lewis
Lucille Hegamin	Black Swan Orchestra
Ethel Waters	Connorized Jazz Hounds[20]
Mary Stafford	

As the competition got hotter, the Pace, Arto, and Pathé companies folded. The big labels such as Okeh, Columbia, and Paramount shifted the nature of their ads from dignified, attractive photos of the featured singer to caricatures with pickaninnies, big-mouthed "Sapphires," men with bulging eyes and oversized lips, and heavy dialect. Record sales continued to soar. Singers moved from studio to studio. Although the big three recording companies, Columbia, Paramount, and General Phonograph (Okeh), had relied on the proven talent of professionals in New York and later Chicago in the first three or four years of the blues decade, later they began to set up temporary recording laboratories in other major cities, such as Atlanta and New Orleans, in order to expand their roster of artists and catalogue of offerings to meet the demand of the race market. Soon the companies sent scouts ahead or announcements to music stores, community leaders, and newspapers to inform them of upcoming field recording sessions. They relied on artists to scout out possible talent, as well.

Records were sold through many outlets—furniture stores, music stores, variety and five-and-dime stores, as well as direct mail order. Sales in the hamlets and rural areas were often based upon word-of-mouth rather than paid advertising. Company scouts also used public reaction as the means for selecting the song to be recorded by field units.[21] As field recordings increased, a greater variety of black musicians were recorded who were not professionals but who represented the broader spectrum of black music— preachers, jubilee quartets, college choirs, country blues men, jazz groups, and comedians.[22]

The meteoric rise of the recording industry depended heavily upon the talents of many women, including several Smiths, the most renowned blues singer among them being Bessie, "The Empress." Bessie's emergence on the Columbia label produced a dramatic change in the race market. Hers was a genuine talent that had developed under the tutelage of the likes of Ma Rainey, when she began as a singer-dancer on the tent-show circuit. When "discovered" by Clarence Williams on one of his talent-seeking forays in the South, Smith was a seasoned performer with a drive for stardom nurtured by her childhood of poverty and deprivation. Her naturally magnificent voice, coupled with her dramatic flair, brought to the stage and recordings a new vibrancy which drove her audiences wild while enriching Columbia Records.

This big-boned handsome woman from Tennessee, who sang on street corners as a youngster, was born in 1898 and was said to be stage-struck by the time she became a teenager. Although her gift was untutored and unrefined, she won a school talent show. She hit the circuit quite early, at about fourteen, as a dancer who had aspirations to become a singing star. Bessie Smith spent the next decade traveling with various tent shows; among them the Rabbit Foot Minstrels with Rainey and Pete Worleys' Florida Cotton Blossoms. Five of those years were on the TOBA circuit, where she eventually headed her own show at the 81 Theatre in Atlanta. She performed in clubs in and around New York and New Jersey for a while during 1920 but did not succeed in attracting a recording offer.

Returning South in 1922 to resume her stage career, Bessie was pursued by Frank Walker, a Columbia scout who had heard her several years earlier in an Alabama mining town.[23] When Columbia Records signed her, she was a seasoned performer, though still a bit rough around the edges. Whereas Rainey drew on her country roots for her blues style and content, Smith derived hers mainly from the city. She moved quickly into a city-oriented life style as she became an immediate recording success. The best instrumentalists—Louis Armstrong, Fletcher Henderson, Sidney Bechet—played on her recordings, and they influenced her as she did them.

The record industry got a tremendous boost from the astounding sales of her records. By the time her career ended during the Depression, her records had sold an estimated six to ten million copies.[24] Jazz musicians, gospel singers, and popular song vocalists all acknowledge Bessie as a major influence because of her keen sense of timing, her expressiveness, and her flawless phrasing. Some noted disciples were Mahalia Jackson, Bix Beiderbecke, Mezz Mezzrow, Charlie Parker, and Coleman Hawkins. She drained each phrase of its substance and bathed each tone with warmth, anger, or pathos. But above all, her naturally fine voice and her uncanny ability to transform any material into a great performance earned her a superb reputation.[25] None of her recordings is of poor quality thanks to Columbia's superior equipment. Although both Rainey and Smith generally confined the melodic range of their songs within intervals of a fifth or a sixth, Smith employed more improvisation—rhythmic and melodic—which endowed the lyrics with added power and meaning. Her association with jazz musicians had a mutually beneficial effect and she developed vocal techniques as sophisticated as the techniques used by a horn player.[26]

Through Bessie Smith, the blues were raised to an artform that was to be the hallmark for every woman blues singer who recorded during the 1920s. Smith's blues songs covered many of the same themes as did Rainey's; she could sing about violence or the threat of prison without any hint of tears or remorse, or loneliness and abandonment with a wrenching mournfulness. Her blues emanated from the violence and complexities of the urban experience and its effects on black women. Langston Hughes said that Smith's blues were the essence of "sadness . . . not softened with tears, but hardened with laugher, the absurd, incongruous laughter of a sadness without even a god to appeal to." [27]

> You can send me up the river or send me to that mean ole jail,
> You can send me up the river or send me to that mean ole jail,
> I killed my man and I don't need no bail. [28]

Like so many of her lyrics, these lines reveal her identification with the anxieties, alienation, and disaffection of the urban black woman. Her rowdy behavior stemmed from the need to be independent, yet recognized a defenselessness in the face of rigid realities. Bessie's almost manic-depressive paranoia was symptomatic of the existence of many black females; hers just happened to have a public forum. [29] She was a multi-talented performer who was constantly tripping herself in public and private arenas. Her known bisexuality was not a problem for her but it led to incidents which gave her a notoriety beyond her singing achievements. Affairs with women were sometimes as intense as those with men and ended in hostility and excruciating bouts of depression. The on-again, off-again relationship with her husband, Jack Gee, was characterized by fights that were not only loud but physically brutal. Yet, she was also adored and admired by members of her family and friends who had been the recipients of her generosity. Contrary to the myths surrounding her acquaintance with Rainey as being that of a protégée and mentor, theirs was a very close relationship which, according to Lieb, may have been sexual. Smith would deny that relationship with Rainey in later years after she was a star in her own right. [30]

In defense of Bessie Smith and her peers, Eva Taylor, blues singer

and wife of Clarence Williams, noted that the women were quite aware of their responsibility to uphold a professional image.

> . . . they were a rough class, let's face it. But when they went in these hotels . . . they lived their life; when they came on stage they were artists. And it made it hard, but like they speak of Bessie Smith in the book, a lot of things in the book [Albertson, *Bessie*] . . . were untrue, because they . . . didn't make a research on what the niece told them. She was an enemy of the niece, anyhow . . . because the niece was going with her husband. And anything terrible the niece could say about her, she said.
>
> Bessie Smith was rough, but she was a soulful woman; she was a good woman inside. And the roughness that they tried to portray her as a person—she drank, she swore—but she wouldn't go in a hotel and belittle herself by being noticed with ill habits, ill doings. She knew how to act when she went out in a hotel or show business or an office. Now she could get up in Harlem and show her colors, but she had sense enough to know that she couldn't come down on Broadway and do that. So she wasn't half the woman, the bad woman that they portrayed her.[31]

Taylor's comments confirm that the blues women were subject to the same expectations as other artists and responded accordingly. The tension between private and public behavior was ever-present to temper and constrain the outbursts of volatile personalities such as Bessie Smith. Yet, it was that tension that also gave her and Rainey that soulful expressiveness that makes their music immortal and memorable.

Ironically, Rainey did not receive a recording contract until after Smith, although she had been an established performer before the

• •

6   BESSIE SMITH

younger woman. Nevertheless, she captured a place in the race market that was inimitably hers and undeniably unique because of her particular style and appeal. Her life was dissimilar to Smith's in some ways and therefore may account for the manner in which her career developed, especially during the 1920s.

Before the decade was over, dozens of blues singers had passed through the portals of Columbia, Okeh, Pace, Ajax, Pathé, Paramount, Arto, Brunswick, and finally, RCA Victor studios. The voices ranged from light soprano to rich contralto. Although their renditions were often quickly forgotten, like much of today's popular music, the black community was glorying in its own cultural power and paid happily for the sound of black music sung by black voices. Singers who did not sing the blues did not last long on wax or on the show circuit.

The immense sales of Mamie Smith's second issue, "Crazy Blues," convinced record companies that there was a market in the black community. Eventually the largest record companies were selling up to five million copies of blues records per year, most of them to blacks, from 1920 through the 1930s. The recording industry may indeed have commercialized a folk art by standardizing format, cleaning up lyrics, and featuring women singers. Though W. C. Handy started the process ten years earlier when he put blues lyrics down on paper and published them, Perry Bradford and Mamie Smith thrust the blues into high gear. It is idle to argue whether they were closer to vaudeville blues or jazz singing than to authentic blues; what counts is that the audience for the recordings accepted and endorsed them as blues. "The Negro market not only existed, it was able to impose its own tastes upon the businessmen who ran the record companies and who understood the music they were recording imperfectly enough so they extended a great deal of freedom to the singers they were recording. Though blues became part of the commercial world of the entertainer and the recording industry, they remained communal property and were vehicles for individual and group expression."[32]

Jeff Todd Titon found that among southern blacks in the 1920s, the phonograph was played at parties and picnics, much as present-day tapeplayers are, as well as at home for private listening. Persons who did not own phonographs still purchased records (for seventy-five cents) by their favorite artists.[33] They would then gather on Saturday nights at a home where there was a phonograph to share an evening of listening and dancing to their latest records. Although the appearance of the phonograph surely influenced tastes in blues, even in rural black areas where the authentic blues were born, blacks were not passive receptacles. They flooded the record producers with requests for certain singers and thus imposed their tastes on the industry.[34]

The blues singers' products were validated by their audiences, no mean feat given the role and behavior of black audiences. The performer was aware that her audience knew the music as well as she and would actively participate with singing, clapping, dancing, and shouts of approval. That instant feedback—a common practice in the black community, which linked the performer to her audience spiritually—was the catalyst for topnotch performances. Oakley perceived the relationship as a "shared communal feeling half as entertainment and half as public ritual and celebration."[35] Those women, as they became the first major stage and recording stars, represented black pride, strength, and power.[36]

As with all popular culture, the advancements in technology paired with the shifts in public tastes eventually brought about significant changes in the demands on the recording industry. The radio began to take the place of the phonograph as the medium of choice for music, news, and variety programs. In their search for a new gimmick to maintain their sales, the record scouts sought the

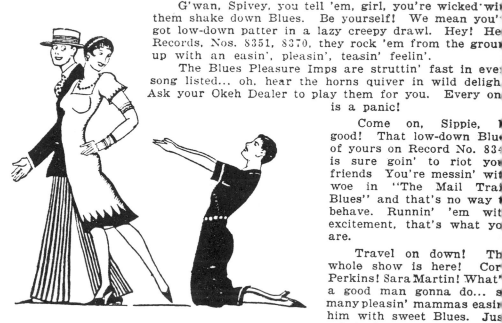

G'wan, Spivey, you tell 'em, girl, you're wicked wit them shake down Blues. Be yourself! We mean you' got low-down patter in a lazy creepy drawl. Hey! He Records, Nos. 8351, 8370, they rock 'em from the grou up with an easin', pleasin', teasin' feelin'.

The Blues Pleasure Imps are struttin' fast in ever song listed... oh, hear the horns quiver in wild deligh Ask your Okeh Dealer to play them for you. Every on is a panic!

Come on, Sippie, good! That low-down Blu of yours on Record No. 834 is sure goin' to riot yo friends You're messin' wit woe in "The Mail Trai Blues" and that's no way behave. Runnin' 'em wit excitement, that's what yo are.

Travel on down! Th whole show is here! Cor Perkins! Sara Martin! What' a good man gonna do... s many pleasin' mammas easir him with sweet Blues. Jus ask to hear them all.

Dirty Woman's Blues

8351
10 in. .75
> DIRTY WOMAN'S BLUES—Contralto and Piano.
> LONG GONE BLUES—Contralto, with Piano Accomp. b
> De Lloyd Barnes and Cornet by Pierce Gist.
> Both sung by **Victoria Spivey.**

8345
10 in. .75
> THE MAIL TRAIN BLUES—Contralto.
> I FEEL GOOD—Contralto.
> Both sung by **Sippie Wallace,** with Piano by Hersa
> Thomas and Cornet by Louis Armstrong.

8346
10 in. .75
> LISTEN TO MA—Contralto.
> G'WAN I TOLD YOU (She Just Won't Have)—Contralto
> Both sung by **Hociel Thomas,** with Piano by Hersa
> Thomas and Trumpet by Louis Armstrong.

8348
10 in. .75
> WHEN I RISE BLUES—Contralto, Accomp. by Piano an
> Violin.
> TODAY BLUES—Contralto, Accomp. by Violin, Mandoli
> and Piano.
> Both sung by **Cora Perkins.**

8354
10 in. .75
> YOU DON'T WANT ME, HONEY—Contralto.
> DON'T NEVER FIGURE—Contralto.
> Both sung by **Sara Martin,** with Piano by Eddi
> Heywood.

The Original Race Records

Butterbeans and Susie

Shout, brother, shout! The Bluest shoutin' team is starrin' in Jimmie Cooper's Black and White Revue. None other. BUTTERBEANS AND SUSIE! Stoppin' the show in every big City... Sure, we knew it... they're the demons! Get 'em quick, the world's best Blues entertainers. There will be a waiting list for this record... and you'll be on it; if you don't get No. 8355 today! Butter and Sue are your sugar.

This page is groanin' with the weight of Blues wonder. It's the berries for messin' with happy feelin's. You just can't behave with Lonnie waitin' on Record No. 8358 to sing you mad with temptation! It's a way with wimmin he has! More power to you, Lonnie, wow, wow!

8355
0 in. .75
- **I CAN'T DO THAT**—Vocal Duet, with Piano by Lovey Austin.
- **HE LIKES IT SLOW**—Vocal Duet, Accomp. by Louis Armstrong and His Hot Five.
  - Both sung by **Butterbeans and Susie.**

8356
0 in. .75
- **LONESOME AND SORRY**—Contralto.
- **BABY O' MINE**—Contralto.
  - Both sung by **Lillie Delk Christian,** with Banjo Accomp. by John St. Cyr and Clarinet by Jimmie Noone.

8358
0 in. .75
- **WOMAN CHANGED MY LIFE.**
- **GOOD OLD WAGON.**
  - Both sung and fiddled by **Lonnie Johnson,** with Piano by James Johnson.

8359
in. 1.25
- **IF THAT DON'T GET IT—THIS SHO' WILL**—Tenor.
- **HANNAH FELL IN LOVE WITH MY PIANO**—Tenor.
  - Both sung by **Frankie Jackson,** with Piano by De Lloyd Barnes.

363
in. .75
- **DID SHE FALL OR WAS SHE PUSHED.**
- **INDIVIDUAL BLUES**—Contralto.
  - Both sung by **Katherine Adkins,** with Piano by W. M. Gill.

8364
in. .75
- **HEART BREAKING BLUES**—Contralto.
- **BLACKVILLE AFTER DARK**—Contralto.
  - Both sung by **Hazel Meyers,** Accomp. by Starks Hot Five.

male folk blues singers and the singing preachers in the South to beef up their roster of race artists. These included Blind Lemon Jefferson, Robert Johnson, Reverend J. M. Gates, and Reverend Sutton Griggs.[37]

By 1932, record sales had dropped to 6 million compared with approximately 104 million in 1927. Phonograph machine sales declined steadily as radio sales and inventories rose; ads in the papers dropped and eventually the last one appeared in the *Chicago Defender* in 1931.[38] The reduction in the size and number of ads was symptomatic of the decrease in the number of records that the companies recorded. Ironically, the Victor Talking Machine Company was entering the blues and race market when the other companies were beginning to suffer the effects of the plummet. Its sales were healthy when it recorded nearly forty artists during the last half of the 1920s—Spivey and Wallace included. Subsequently, shifts to radio, talking movies, and the reorganization or dissolution of failing record companies brought the decline in the number and quality of recordings in the race market in general, and especially of the blues women.[39]

The cabaret crowd was now being entertained by the hot dance rhythms of the bands of Ellington, Henderson, Benny Moten, and others. White dance bands smoothed out the jagged rhythms for the supper club crowd and offered the ballads of the torch singer rather than the blues. These and a combination of economic factors brought the recorded classic blues to an end and with it the careers of most of those who had been recorded.

• •

8   PARAMOUNT AND BLACK SWAN NEWSPAPER AD

"Wild Women Don't Have the Blues": Blues from the Black Woman's Perspective

Now, when you've got a man don't ever be on the square,
If you do, he'll have a woman everywhere.
I never was known to treat one man right,
I keep 'em working hard both day and night,
Because wild women don't worry,
Wild women don't have the blues.
                    —Ida Cox, "Wild Women Don't Have the Blues"

These lines do not come from the southern black rural experience; rather, they depict the "new" city woman who had fled from medieval to modern America, in the words of E. Franklin Frazier, seeking the glamour of Harlem and other urban centers and the prospect of better jobs in factories. She had escaped the religious sanctions that had been imposed in her church down home and was eager to ex-

• •

9   IDA COX PUBLICITY PHOTOGRAPH, c. 1926

plore the outlets for leisure-time activities that were not approved by her elders. The dance hall, gay house, whiskey joint, and brothel offered unbridled pleasure and entertainment previously unavailable to the men and women who migrated North after World War I. The typical black woman emigrant left home at age fifteen or sixteen, around 1915–1920, seeking the better life that itinerant laborers and songsters described in their stories and songs about the cities. In those black odysseys, as Frazier called them, a life of good times, good living, and good money was to be had by anybody who dared to venture.[1] Hard times or abandonment required women to fend for themselves, armed with cynicism and an extraordinary drive to achieve economic and personal independence.

The blues women of Ida Cox's era brought to their lyrics and performances new meaning as they interpreted and reformulated the black experience from their unique perspective in American society as black females. They saw a world that did not protect the sanctity of black womanhood, as espoused in the bourgeois ideology; only white middle- or upper class women were protected by it. They saw and experienced injustice as jobs they held were snatched away when white women refused to work with them or white men returned from war to reclaim them. They pointed out the pain of sexual and physical abuse and abandonment. They sought escape from the oppressive controls of the black church but they did not seek to sever their ties from home, family, and loved ones. They reorganized reality through surrealistic fantasies and cynical parodies such as "Red Lantern Blues," "Black Snake Moan," and "Stavin' Chain."

James Baldwin claims that while the blues express the pain of black experience they also bring relief, even joy.

> Now, I am claiming a great deal for the blues; I'm using them as a metaphor. . . . I want to talk about the blues, not only because they speak of this particular experience of life and this state of being, but

because they contain the toughness that manages to make this experience articulate. . . . And I want to suggest that the acceptance of this anguish one finds in the blues, and the expression of it, creates also, however odd this may sound, a kind of joy.[2]

Baldwin does not see the contradictions as problematical because his life experiences as a black person in America often consisted of a joy born from pain.

The "bluesman, grappling with the fundamental issues of his existence, takes action against his fate by articulating his woes and thus, in effect, creating himself anew," according to Kimberly Benston.[3] In other words, the blues transcend conditions created by social injustice; and their attraction is that they express simultaneously the agony of life and the possibility of conquering it through the sheer toughness of spirit.[4] That is, the blues are not intended as a means of escape, but embody what Richard Wright calls "a lusty, lyrical realism, charged with taut sensibility."[5]

The blues, therefore, are a means of articulating experience and demonstrating a toughness of spirit by creating and re-creating that experience. Two qualities highly valued in the black community, articulateness and toughness, are thus brought together in this artform. Fluency in language is considered a powerful tool for establishing and maintaining status in the black community. Thus a man or woman who has mastered the art of signifying, rapping, or orating can subdue any challenger without striking a blow and is held in high esteem. (The present-day phenomenon of the grand masters of rap music demonstrate the continuation of this value among blacks in cities.) The resilience developed by black folks in the face of slavery and post-Reconstruction violence armed them with a will to survive against seemingly insurmountable odds. Those who did were the heroes and heroines of the black world—Frederick Douglass, Sojourner Truth, Harriet Tubman, Mary McLeod Bethune, John Henry, Marcus Garvey, and so on. To summarize, the blues are paradoxical in that they contain the expression of the agony and pain of life as experienced by blacks in America; yet, the very act and mode of articulation demonstrates a toughness that releases, exhilarates, and renews.

The blues singer evokes, matches, and intensifies the "blue" feeling of the listener in the act of singing the blues. Sterling Brown observed and recorded this in his poetry.

> Dey comes to hear Ma Rainey from de little river settlements
> From blackbottom cornrows and from lumber camps
> Dey stumble in de halls, jes' a-laughin' an' a-cacklin',
> Cheerin' lak roaring water, lak wind in river swamps.
> An' some jokers keep deir laughs a-goin' in de crowded aisles,
> An' some folk sits dere waiting wid deir aches an' miseries
> Till Ma comes out before dem a-smilin' gold-toofed smiles . . .[6]

Neither the intent nor the result is escape but, instead, the artistic expression of reality. According to Roosevelt Sykes, blues pianist,

> "Blues is like a doctor. A blues player . . . plays for the worried people. . . . See, they enjoy it. Like the doctor works from the outside of the body to the inside of the body. But the blues works on the insides of the inside."[7]

The aesthetic quality depends upon the singer's ability to express deep feelings.

> "You got to sing the blues with your soul. It looks like you hurt in the deep-down part of your heart. You really hurt when you sing the blues."[8]

The blues women expressed reality and enhanced the emotional impact of their experiences through the satire, irony, and drama of their individual performance styles. Variations in their experiences were often reflected in their treatment of themes. The underlying assumption is that content and style are an outgrowth of both the personal and professional experiences of these women. From these a new blues tradition evolved as the women incorporated existing practices—the break in the second half of each four bars of the first two lines of the standard twelve-bar blues; talking in breaks; improvising new verses for endless repetitions—into their own innovative styles. These women expanded the realm of blues in several ways. They wedded blues to jazz through the interpolation of vocal melodies with accompanying instrumental rhythmic and melodic improvisation. They retained the spontaneity of live blues performance within the constraints of the new recording technology—limited recording time, censored lyrics, arrangers and composers imposing their views, and unfamiliar studio musicians—through the use of dramatic vocal techniques, serious and comedic ad libs, and references to current events. They voiced the experiences of the city women while demonstrating a common bond with southern rural women, and with men. They altered nonblues songs such as "He Used to Be Your Man But He's My Man Now," "Give Me That Old Slow Drag," and "Daddy Your Mama Is Lonesome for You," to fit the blues format and to evoke the blues feeling, thus expanding the blues market for songwriters. Although most of the songs blues women sang were either composed or arranged by professional songwriters such as Clarence Williams, Chris Smith, Perry Bradford, and W. C. Handy, many wrote their own blues, too. They therefore were creative as well as interpretive artists. Among them were the country types such as Ma Rainey, city types, such as Bessie Smith, vaudeville-dance hall types, such as Ida Cox, and the sophisticated cabaret types, such as Alberta Hunter and Edith Wilson. Their vocal qualities ranged from light soprano to deep contralto, with varying degrees of soft, round, mellow tones to guttural, barrelhouse, razor-edged shouts. But all were blues singers, certified by the "millions of colored folks who [were] the principal buyers of 'blues' . . . written by born writers of 'blues' . . . sung by colored artists mostly girls whose training and natural sympathies enable[d] them to give an interpretation to 'blues' with such natural and telling effects."[9]

The southern country woman's life revolved around a peasant economy and was dependent upon the success or failure of crops. She was actively involved in sharecropping or tenant farming and worked in the fields with her family as a young child; she probably married in her early teens; she took in laundry or did domestic work; or moved to the city. Schooling was totally absent or ended after the primary grades. The early years of the blues women were also often spent in domestic or other service jobs. Hunter washed dishes in a whorehouse when she arrived in Chicago at age twelve; Wallace was a maid for a snakedancer in Texas; Lizzie Miles was a barmaid in New Orleans. According to Frazier, many southern black women's first exposure to town or city life was when they had temporary jobs as domestics. For the men, sawmills, turpentine, lumber, and road camps offered the first glimpse of town or city life. If they lived near the Mississippi River or the Gulf Coast, levee camps were a source of work.[10] Men who moved away from the plantations and farms often left their women behind. The southern country blues women understood the impact of crop failure, oppressive farm-owners, cheating company stores, and the drudgery of working from sunup to sundown to make ends meet. They could express the hurt of women whose men left to find work and never returned, or were itinerant lovers who moved on when the jobs ran out, or were serving time on a prison farm or chain gang. Bessie Smith captured the feeling in "Long Road."

> It's a long old road, but I'm gonna find the end;
> It's a long old road, but I'm gonna find the end;
> And when I get back I'm gonna shake hands with a friend.[11]

Southern working-class women from cities such as Memphis, Houston, New Orleans, and Louisville were often no better off than their rural counterparts. They were directly exposed to the day-to-day inequities of racial politics and its economic consequences. The only dependable and consistent work available for them was domestic service as long as they knew how to keep their mouths shut and stay in line. Some took advantage of the new freedom and went to work in the cafés, honky-tonks, and dance halls where men from the lumber camps, foundries, and mills spent their money. They made alliances with the men that were usually as temporary and tenuous as the jobs the men held. When abandoned a few resorted to streetwalking to earn their keep; others joined the throng of migrants who headed to northern towns and cities. Alberta Hunter's "I Got a Mind to Ramble" and Sippie Wallace's "Up the Country Blues" both address that experience.

The tough, brutal life of the northern city began to take its toll on many black women in the early years of the twentieth century. Their realities were crowded tenements, poverty, disease, unemployment, marital conflict, and general despair. The "loose" women that some blacks preached about were outnumbered by the widows, divorcées, and single women who found city life to be harsh and unrelenting in its physical and mental stress. Indeed, the post–World War I boom not only stimulated additional migration to cities by black women, it quickly pressed them into life in the "fast lane." Churches, social clubs, and fraternal societies blossomed alongside cabarets, whiskey joints, and brothels, and women were the mainstay of both types of institutions. Although complaints rose from church and temperance groups about the evils of alcohol, more blacks turned to whiskey for relief from social and emotional problems. The absence of family and community ties sometimes caused both men and women to move "from hand to hand" in Bessie Smith's words, straining marriages and relationships. The jealousy, discontent, and unhappiness created tensions that often erupted in domestic disturbances. Thus, jail and serving time are recurring themes in women's blues not only because of the bias in the legal system but because women in cities witnessed, were victims of, or sometimes resorted to violence to avenge mistreatment or infidelity. Women, at least in song, used violence, or the threat of violence, as one means of retaliation.

Therefore, the themes of women's blues lyrics are generally the same as those of the men's—infidelity, alienation, loneliness, despondency, death, poverty, injustice, love, and sex. But women responded to these concerns differently and dealt with certain themes more or less frequently. Some blues are a response to the hard times inflicted by society or nature. Flood blues by Rainey, Bessie Smith, and Wallace are a direct reaction to a natural phenomenon that wreaked havoc on thousands of poor rural southerners. Hard times for city and country folk are depicted not only in the prison blues, but in others that discuss unemployment, disease, and poverty. The current of morbidity that ripples through Spivey's "Blood Hound Blues" and "Red Lantern Blues" is also apparent in her "T.B. Blues" and "Dope Head Blues." She decries two problems that plagued the black community and castigates those who turned their backs on the victims. Her "New York Tombs," about the notorious prison, was written much later and continued to demonstrate the social consciousness of "T.B." and "Dope Head."[12]

Poverty was the omnipresent force which lurked in the black community, rural and urban, licking at the heels of those who were trying desperately to elude its stranglehold on their dreams. Bessie Smith's "Poor Man Blues" is an eloquent statement about the cruel irony of poverty in the land of riches. Though "Poor Man Blues" is post–World War I, its content is appropriate today.

> Please listen to my pleading, 'cause I can't stand these hard times long.

> Please listen to my pleading, 'cause I can't stand these hard times
> long.
> They'll make an honest man do things you know is wrong.

In the second stanza Smith reminds the listener that poor men served in the war and would do so again, if called, because they too are patriotic Americans.

> Poor man fought all the battles, poor man would fight again today,
> Poor man fought all the battles, poor man would fight again today,
> He would do anything you ask him in the name of the U.S.A.

Then, she challenges the rich to deny their exploitation of and dependence upon the labor and talent of the poor.

> Now the war is over, poor man must live the same as you,
> Now the war is over, poor man must live the same as you,
> If it wasn't for the poor man, Mr. Rich Man what would you do? [13]

There is no more powerful statement about the politics of poverty than in the concluding line.

Cox points the finger at Uncle Sam as the culprit who takes away her lover, husband, and "used to be" in "Uncle Sam Blues" and her source of income in "Pink Slip Blues." Both illustrate the tenuousness of life in the early days of the Depression although Franklin D. Roosevelt's New Deal programs such as the Works Projects Administration had offered a new hope for thousands of low-skilled, unemployed Americans. This and social welfare programs promised an avenue out of poverty, but for many the expectation was greater than the outcome. The dreaded cutoff notice—the pink slip—was the central idea in Cox's wry rendition of a common scene among the poor in the 1930s.

In the first and second stanzas of "Pink Slip Blues," Cox shows how the welfare check becomes the controlling force in the life of a poor person.

> One day every week I prop myself at my front door,
> One day every week I prop myself at my front door,
> And the police force couldn't move me 'fore that mailman blows.
>
> 'Cause a little white paper Uncle Sam has done addressed to me,
> 'Cause a little white paper Uncle Sam has done addressed to me,
> It meant one more week, one week of prosperity.
>
> But bad news got to spreading and my hair start to turning gray,
> But bad news got to spreading and my hair start to turning gray,
> 'Cause Uncle Sam started chopping, cutting thousands off the WPA.

The security of the weekly funds is ended and the person must go back to breadlines or begging to survive in a jobless world.

> Just a little pink slip in a long white envelope,
> Just a little pink slip in a long white envelope,
> 'Twas the end of my road, was the last ray of my only hope.
>
> After four long years, Uncle Sam done put me on the shelf,
> After four long years, Uncle Sam done put me on the shelf,
> 'Cause that little pink slip means you got to go for yourself.[14]

Uncle Sam personifies the men who control the quality of life for blacks in America, especially females. The paycheck is thus the sign of prosperity that can be taken away overnight. The ray of hope is dimmed by a pink slip: no more WPA job, no more money, no more prosperity. "Uncle Sam done put me on the shelf," could easily be translated as "my man or good daddy done put me on the shelf" that "means you got to go for yourself," which most black women expected was inevitable. Although the mixed meaning found in blues poetry is often attributed to attempts to disguise sexual connotations, in "Hard Times Blues," Cox employs metaphors to describe the stress and conflict arising from two losses, job and money, and lover and provider. The dilemma of poverty is more painful because her man is not there to give her money or solace.

> I never *seen* such a *real* hard time before,
> I never *seen* such a *real* hard time before,
> *The* wolf keeps walking *all* round my door.
>
> They *howl* all night and they *mourn* till the break of day,
> They *howl* all night and they *mourn* till the break of day,
> They seem to know my good man's gone away.
>
> I can't go outside to my grocery store,
> I can't go outside to my grocery store,
> I ain't got no money and my credit *don't* got no more.
>
> Won't somebody please, try 'n' find my man for me.
> Won't somebody please, try 'n' find my man for me.
> Tell him *I'm* broke and hungry, lonely as I can be.[15]

Note the stress words which capture the singer's feelings and verify their intensity and depth of despair. Such blues are timeless, not because of their musical uniqueness but because of the universality of their subject matter.

Most blues, however, express more personal, if still universal, themes. Love and sex, separately and together, occupy the greatest amount of attention but with varying intensity and seriousness. The tenuous nature of black male/female relationships lies at the core of blues literature. Lost love is universally agreed upon as the main

cause of the blues and it is a theme with seemingly endless variations. Interestingly, women usually do not joke about loss, and are
more likely to sing about their grief and its results: extreme depression, bad health, hallucinations and nightmares, suicide attempts,
or violence. There are basically two causes for the loss of the lover
sung about in women's blues—infidelity and death. Notable examples of loss due to death are the famous Graveyard series of blues
recorded by Ida Cox: "Graveyard Dream Blues," "New Graveyard
Dream Blues," "Coffin Blues," and "Death Letter Blues." These are
superbly drawn scenarios of a woman tortured by visions of her
lover's death or impending death. From the somber lyrics sung in
traditional twelve-bar blues structure emerge images of a distraught
woman unwilling to let go, even in the face of death. In "Death Letter Blues," the woman responds immediatley when summoned to
her dying lover's deathbed, a common scene for black women, even
today, as disease, overwork, drug addiction, or violence snatch their
men away prematurely.

> I received a letter that my man was dying,
> I received a letter that my man was dying,
> I caught the first train and went back home flying.

Having arrived too late she can only watch as his body is carried
away for burial.

> I followed my daddy to the burying ground,
> I followed my daddy to the burying ground,
> I watched the pallbearers slowly let him down.

With matter-of-fact resignation, born of the constant struggle with
fate, she accepts his departure with parting words of love, but her
last words suggest that she is prepared to move on with her life:

That was the last time I saw my daddy's face,
That was the last time I saw my daddy's face,
Mama loves you, sweet papa, but I just can't take your place.[16]

The anguish of a bereaved woman at her man's wake is vividly portrayed in the dirgelike "Coffin Blues." Overcome by grief she calls out,

Daddy, oh Daddy, won't you answer me please,
Daddy, oh Daddy, won't you answer me please,
All day I stood by your coffin, trying to give my poor heart ease.

Unwilling to accept the reality of her loss she resorts to tender caresses and whispers in an attempt to communicate beyond the boundaries of death.

I rubbed my hands over your head, and whispered in your ear,
I rubbed my hands over your head, and whispered in your ear,
And I wonder if you know that your mama's here.

Reflecting on the pledge of love for her man, she expresses the desire to join him in death.

You told me that you loved me and I believed what you said,
You told me that you loved me and I believed what you said,
And I wish that I could fall here across your coffin bed.[17]

On the other hand, "Graveyard Dream Blues" could well be interpreted as a nightmare deriving from a love affair rife with conflict and infidelity.

Blues on my mind, blues all 'round my head,
Blues on my mind, blues all 'round my head,
I had a dream last night, the man I love was dead.

Lord, I went to the graveyard, fell down on my knees,
Lord, I went to the graveyard, fell down on my knees,
I asked the gravedigger to give me back my good man, please.

The gravedigger may well be a metaphor for the "other woman" or for fate lurking in the shadows to snatch the lover away, because his refusal to return her lover implies that he has the power to do so if he chooses.

The gravedigger looked me in the eye,
The gravedigger looked me in the eye,
Said, "I'm sorry for you lady, your man said his last goodbye."

Refusing to believe her man is gone for good she is wretched with apprehension; relief floods through her being when she realizes it was a dream.

I was so worried, I wanted to scream,
I was so worried, I wanted to scream,
But when I woke up it was only a dream.[18]

Ironically, when the loss of a lover is due to betrayal or abandonment, then death is desired by the betrayed woman. "Death Sting Me Blues" by Sara Martin illustrates this theme in the final lines.

Blues, blues, blues, why did you bring trouble to me?
Blues, blues, blues, why did you bring trouble to me?
Oh, Death, please sting me and take me out of my misery.[19]

Other responses to abandonment and infidelity include depression, illness, flight, violent or nonviolent vengeance, invocation of the supernatural, and self-assertion. Bessie Smith's "Dying by the Hour" is the dramatic soliloquy of a woman whose depression about her man has driven her to promiscuity,

> It's an old story, every time it's a doggone man,
> It's an old story, every time it's a doggone man,
> But when that thing is on you, you just drift from hand to hand.

to contemplation of suicide and hell,

> I'd drink a bottle of acid, if it wouldn't burn me so
> I'd drink a bottle of acid, if it wouldn't burn me so
> And telephone the devil, that's the only place I'd go.

and extreme loss of weight,

> Once I weighed 200, I'm nothing but skin and bones.
> Once I weighed 200, I'm nothing but skin and bones.
> I would always laugh but it's nothing but a moan and groan.

until she loses grip on herself and no longer has a will to live.

> Lawd, I'm dying by the hour about that doggone man of mine,
> Lawd, I'm dying by the hour about that doggone man of mine,
> He said he didn't love me, that is why I'm dying and losing my
> mind.[20]

The progressive despondency portrayed so dramatically by Smith sometimes took a different direction. Similar lines, "I used to weigh 200," appear in "Take Him off My Mind" by Ida Cox, but she does not consider suicide as a solution to her distress. Rather she contemplates murder but loses heart "when [her] love comes down."

> I cried and I worried, all night lays and groan,
> I cried and I worried, all night lays and groan,
> I used to weigh 200, now I'm down to skin and bones.
>
> It's all about my man who has always kicked and dogged me 'round,
> It's all about my man who has always kicked and dogged me 'round,
> I tried my best to kill him but when I did my love comes down.[21]

Cox and Smith both transport the listener to the somber nether regions of the broken spirit. A sense of resignation hangs on each note, which seems to take every ounce of strength that the singer can muster. Yet each responds to the same dilemma quite differently—Smith depicts complete resignation and lack of self-control; whereas Cox is ambivalent, holding on to her sanity by making verbal threats.

"Doggone men," were the bane of many a woman's existence, and solace was sought through audacious schemes which included signifying, going off with other men, or using gypsy magic or supernatural powers.

> I've gone to the gypsy and begging on my bended knees,
> I've gone to the gypsy and begging on my bended knees,
> That man put something on me, Oh won't you take it off me please.
>
> Just fix him for me, gypsy, lay your money on the line,
> Just fix him for me, gypsy, lay your money on the line,
> Just fix him so he'll love me, but please take him off my mind.[22]

The distraught woman's request is ambiguous, for she asks the gypsy to take the lover off her mind while fixing him so he will love her.

The insoluble dilemma—the sweet pain of tormented love—is too good to let go completely.

"New Orleans Goofer Dust Blues" is a pithy lesson in the use of witchcraft for romantic security. The singer says, "Go to New Orleans, that's where you learn your stuff. / To keep your man now-a-days, / You got to use some goofer dust."[23] Louisiana was, and still is rich in the cultural mix that harbored and nurtured African voodoo, and the use of "goofer dust" was a commonly accepted remedy.

The strong belief that the supernatural had the power to affect love relationships underlies the examples above. In some cases, the blues are personified and are spoken of as having inherent powers which result in sickness, alcoholism, drug addiction, or death. Sara Martin's "Death Sting Me Blues" attributes "consumption of the heart," and her "uses of cocaine and whiskey" to the blues which "is like the devil" making her "hell-bound soon."

This supernatural persona is sometimes assigned to the blues to illustrate their power over the individual—to make you miserable; to haunt or to track you down; to aid you in getting your lover back; to enslave you. Bessie Smith's "In the House Blues" depicts the blues as a monstrous tormenter who disrupts her sleep and chases her about.

> Catch 'em, don't let them blues in here,
> Catch 'em, don't let them blues in here,
> They shakes me in my bed, can't set down in my chair.
>
> Oh, the blues has got me on the go,
> Oh, the blues has got me on the go,
> They runs around the house, in and out my front door.[24]

Similarly, Cox envisions the blues as a bearer of bad news each time they appear walking, talking, and smiling slyly.

Early this morning the blues came walkin' in my room,
Early this morning the blues came walkin' in my room,
I said, "Blues, please tell me what are you doing here so soon."

They looked at me and smiled but yet they refused to say,
They looked at me and smiled but yet they refused to say,
I came again and they turned and walked away.

After disturbing her and arousing anxiety as the blues always aim to do, they confirm her suspicion that she will lose her man.

The first thing they told me, "Your man you're going to lose."
The first thing they told me, "Your man you're going to lose."
At first I didn't believe it but I found out it was true.

Her final plea reminds the blues that they brought her pain and tears previously, and implicitly acknowledges that they are or will be a frequent visitor.

Blues, oh blues, you know you been here before,
Blues, oh blues, you know you been here before,
The last time you were here, you make me cry and walk the floor.[25]

Not only are the blues viewed as having physical attributes, which allow them to walk and run, talk to and shake the victim; but they can also predict the future and cause emotional reactions. They can even enslave the sufferer, according to Ma Rainey.

If I could break these chains and let my worried heart go free,
If I could break these chains and let my worried heart go free,
Well, it's too late now, the blues have made a slave of me.[26]

"Hoodoo Man Blues," "Spider Web Blues," "Red Lantern Blues," "Blood-Thirsty Blues," "Nightmare Blues," "Garter Snake Blues" are some of Spivey's blues with bloodcurdling, spooky images which call forth the conjurers, root doctors, and voodooism of southern black life. Yet they all deal with the conflict of torn love affairs or the aftermath of pain, as in "Blood Hound Blues," in which she describes how she poisoned her man, went to jail, escaped and was tracked by bloodhounds. The principle of this blues is vengeance by a woman who was abused: "Well, I know I done wrong, but he beat me and blacked my eye."[27] Spivey's "Blood Hound Blues" is typical of the blues that contain confessions of guilt and declarations of vindication and are a mixture of strength and weakness; the will to take corrective measures while admitting remorse or despair for the act committed.

> Well, I poisoned my man, I put it in his drinking cup,
> Well, I poisoned my man, I put it in his drinking cup,
> Well, it's easy to go to jail, but lawd, they sent me up.
>
> I know I've done wrong, but he beat me and blacked my eye,
> I know I've done wrong, but he beat me and blacked my eye,
> But, if the blood hounds don't get me, in the electric chair I'll die.[28]

The image of the vengeful woman who acted out her violence is often cast in a prison setting. "Court House Blues" by Clara Smith, "Sing Sing Prison" and "Jail House Blues" by Bessie Smith, and "Worried Jailhouse Blues" by Bertha "Chippie" Hill recount the horrid conditions of prison life and their toll on one's physical and mental well-being. Clara Smith considers a three-month sentence light compared to how the man she loved made her feel—ninety-nine years old. Though she was jailed "on account of one trifling man," the jurymen acquitted her.[29]

Bessie Smith unabashedly sang of killing her old man, and then made a bold plea for a fatal sentence in "Send Me to the Electric Chair." She describes in grisly detail how she "cut him with my barlow, I kicked him in his side, I stood there laughing over him while he wallowed round and died."[30] She begs the judge to "burn her" because she wants to reap what she sowed. This is a woman scorned who took the ultimate step with no regrets. Bessie Smith's own life was peppered with incidents of a violent nature, so the conviction she brought to this blues is authentic. She was known not to take any foolishness from anybody, male or female. In one fight with her husband she shot at him while he stood on the railroad tracks pleading his case. She and Clara Smith had words at a party in New York which allegedly ended with Bessie whipping Clara into submission.[31]

Mistreatment, whether philandering or physical abuse, is the source for many blues lyrics, and though actual violence to oneself or the perpetrator may result, it is more frequently threatened than carried out. In "Georgia Hound Blues," a womanizing, faithless mate is given fair warning by Cox. He is likened to a dog chasing after bitches in heat.

> You don't want no one woman, you don't do nothing but run around.
> You don't want no one woman, you don't do nothing but run around.
> And chase after wild women, just a Georgia hound.

She castigates him for his lack of discretion and denigrates the fast women who are the source of community gossip.

> Your love is like a radio, you are broadcasting everywhere,
> Your love is like a radio, you are broadcasting everywhere,
> You can locate the women clowning by listening in the air.

• •

10   COLUMBIA RECORDS NEWSPAPER AD FOR CLARA SMITH

Fed up, she warns him that she may kill him if he does not straighten up.

> Like a hound, you chase all night and you don't come home till
>   morn.
> Like a hound, you chase all night and you don't come home till
>   morn.
> Pretty daddy, the undertaker has got your last [chase] on.[32]

The hound, a familiar figure in southern life, was used for hunting coons, rabbits, and possums at night—a common occupation in the Georgia piney woods where Cox was born. During and after slavery the hounds' moonlight howls echoed as they chased their quarry— man or beast. By 1925 the radio was swiftly taking the place of the phonograph in American households, so it began to appear more and more in the lyrics of the music makers. And since blues singers also enjoyed the added popularity gained by their radio broadcasts, it was natural for their songs to incorporate advances in technology. The broadcasting simile, "your love is like a radio," refers to men's favorite locker room or barbershop sport—bragging about their con- quests and exploits of women.

Martin's "Got to Leave My Home Blues" voices a different reac- tion—that of a woman who is admittedly promiscuous. At first, all of the woman's abuse and violence are directed toward herself, as she describes her descent into degradation.

> I took morphine last night to ease my pain,
> If it hadn't a been for the doctor I'd been in my grave.
> I lost my job and almost lost my home,
> 'Cause I wouldn't let other women's men alone.

● ●

11   COLUMBIA RECORDS NEWSPAPER AD FOR BESSIE SMITH

Then she shifts to a positive, aggressive position, shakes off her depression, and decides to eliminate the cause of her blues—her man.

> Trials and tribulations are like a million pounds,
> They ain't nothin' to what it'll be when I run my good man down.
> I'm gonna shoot him and cut him just as long as I choose.
> He's the cause of my having them, "Got to Leave My Home Blues."[33]

Her remorse derives from the recognition that promiscuity could plunge her into a downward spiral. It is short-lived as she plots a vicious attack on the man whom she blames for her wayward conduct. This blues has a message for both women and men: it points out the dangers of infidelity for married women, while reminding men that two-timing can be hazardous to their health.

Sometimes the ordeal of coping with an adulterous mate, poverty, and overwork proved too debilitating for a woman to retain her inner strength and determination. Thus we have a group of blues that depict the weariness, depression, disillusionment, and quiet rage that seethe below the surface when a woman has reached the end of her rope. Some have torturous opening lines which lead gradually toward an optimistic closing, as if the act of expressing the feeling is cathartic. Lizzie Miles, for instance, sang "I Hate a Man Like You." In her cynical rendition, she gradually draws forth an image of a woman who accepts, with resignation, the sorry state of her marriage to a philandering gambler. This bragging, arrogant, woman-chaser causes more trouble for her than he is worth. The sweet talk that attracted her has soured and turned into the poison that incites her to recite a litany about his shiftless behavior.

> I hate a man like you, don't like the things you do,
> When I met you, I thought you was right,
> You married me and stayed out the first night.

She denounces him for gossiping about her,

> Just like a woman you're always carrying tales,
> Trying to make trouble, wanna get me in jail,
> Then you can't find no one to go my bail.
> Lawd, I hate a man like you.

and for gambling away all of his money, leaving the burden of their upkeep on her tired shoulders as a laundress.

> Walkin' around with a switch and a rod, shootin' dice, always playing cards,
> While I bring a pan from the white folks' yard.
> Lawd, I hate a man like you.

> ....

> Eatin' and drinkin', sittin' at the inn,
> Grinnin' in my face and winkin' at my friends,
> When my back is turned you're like a rooster at a hen,
> Oh, I hate a man like you.[34]

Enmity has replaced love in this bitter relationship, yet there is no indication of intent to leave or do violence; only contempt remains, binding her vengefully to the spiteful end.

Rather than wallow in the pathos of broken or abusive love affairs, some women sang about leaving. "Oh now I'm leaving you, / Someday you'll understand, / 'Cause why? I can't go on loving a mistreating man."[35] Martin reminds her lover how she played the "game of love . . . on the square" but because he thought he could find a good woman anywhere he "never meant [her] no good."[36] The style of this blues is typical of the cabaret type. Clara Smith put it more bluntly in "Mama's Gone, Goodbye." She was "aching mighty long" because he had "dogged [her] around" for years but she woke up to tell him what was on her mind.

"Every Dog Has His Day," according to Sippie Wallace, even though "Love . . . have made many a girl wish that they were dead." She advised the mistreater to ". . . go on Baby, I'm gonna let you have yo' way / 'Cause every dog must have his day."[37] Not one to hold still for shabby treatment, Wallace strips her man of all the luxuries she gave him before she packs up and goes "Up the Country." She broadcasts to the neighborhood what her plans are, humiliating him in the process. "Up the Country Blues" puts the man's business "in the street," as she calls

> Hey-ey, Mama, run tell your papa,
> Go tell your sister, run tell your auntie,
> That I'm going up the country, don't you wan-ta go-o?
> I need another husband to take me on my night time stroll . . .

She sets the stage for a long rap that will be scathing, while demonstrating her power to put the shoe on the other foot. She continues,

> When I was leaving, I left some folks a-grieving,
> I left my friends a-moaning, I left my man a-sighing,
> 'Cause he knew he had mistreat me and torn up all my clothes . . .
> I told him to give me that coat I bought him, that shirt I bought him,
>   those shoes I bought him, socks I bought him,
> 'Cause he knew he did not want me, he had no right to stall,
> I told him to pull off that hat I bought him and let his nappy head go
>   bald.[38]

The power word in a rap is one that clearly denigrates one's kin or looks. Wallace does both by calling "mama, papa, sister" and later makes derisive remarks about the lover's "nappy head," an absolute taboo during an era when blacks were striving to lighten their skin and straighten their hair so they could look more like whites. The object of such defamation probably wished he had been more discreet after this attack. Wallace captured a feeling experienced by many women—the desire for ultimate vengeance in a public arena. Under these circumstances, she would receive approval and support for this behavior and might even be joined by other women with a call-and-response chorus in a live performance.[39]

This is clearly an assertion of power and demonstrates that women began to use the blues as a positive means of retaliation. This tactic derives from a practice employed by African and Afro-Caribbean women to embarrass men who had either neglected or abused their women. Usually when black women "go public," it is to negotiate respect, asserts anthropologist Roger Abrahams. One of the situations in which "talking smart" routines develop in male-female relationships occurs when "the two participants are deeply involved" and the woman uses it to "produce strategic advantages and to modify the man's behavior."[40] This is the goal implicit in Wallace's lyrics in which the silent, suffering woman is replaced by a loud-talking mama, reared-back with one hand on her hip and with the other wagging a pointed finger vigorously as she denounces the two-timing dude. Ntozage Shange, Alice Walker, and Zora Neale Hurston employ this scenario as the pivotal point in a negative relationship between the heroine/protagonists and their abusive men. Going public is their declaration of independence. Blues of this nature communicated to women listeners that they were members of a sisterhood that did not have to tolerate mistreatment.

Unlike the audacious mood exhibited by Wallace, melancholia

pervades Clara Smith's version of "Freight Train Blues" as she contemplates her lover's mistreatment.

> I hate to hear that engine blow, boo-hoo!
> I hate to hear that engine blow, boo-hoo!
> Every time I hear it blowing I feel like riding too.

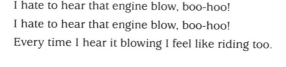

> I'm going away just to wear you off my mind,
> I'm going away just to wear you off my mind,
> And I may be gone for a doggone long, long time.

In the last stanza, Smith uses the traditional phrase, "I asked the brakeman let me ride," but when he refuses her the right to ride she retreats to her room.

> When a woman gets the blues, she goes to her room and hides,
> When a woman gets the blues, she goes to her room and hides,
> When a man gets the blues, he catches a freight train and rides.[41]

Thus, Smith's version points out the limitations on women's mobility as compared to men—women often have to conceal their pain and embarrassment behind closed doors or masked expressions.

Leaving a mistreating "daddy" was easier sung about than achieved, as indicated by the ambivalence expressed in Lottie Kimbrough's "Going Away Blues."

> I'm going away it won't be long . . .
> And then you know you must have done me wrong.

She loses her nerve and sobs:

> My heart aches so I can't be satisfied.
> I believe I'll take a train and ride,
> I believe I'll take a train and ride,
> 'Cause I miss my cruel daddy from my side.

Finally, she reveals the source of some of her misery.

> I've got Cadillac ways, got some super ideas.
> I can't see what brought me here . . .
> It must have been this new canned city beer.
> I'm lame and blind can't hardly see,
> My doggone daddy turned his back on me . . .[42]

We can deduce that alcohol was one of Kimbrough's devils, along with a thirst for the luxuries of high living in the city. It may well be that that combination clouded her judgment in the choice of men. The phrase, "lame and blind," may be alluding to venereal disease, another affliction that was rampant in northern cities.

Some women's blues acknowledged that their own infidelity was the cause of their troubles. In "Please Come Back and Love Me Like You Used to Do," Trixie Smith pledges to mend her wayward ways.

> Once I had a dear sweet daddy,
> But I didn't treat him right,
> So he left this town with Mandy Brown,
> That is why I'm blue tonight.
> So I'm leaving here today
> When I find him, he will hear me say,

> Please come back and love me like you used to do
> I think about you every day.
> You reap just what you sow in the sweet by 'n' by,
> And be sorry that you went away.

Although she makes the veiled threat that he may be sorry about leaving her, she quickly resorts to pleading for his return;

> Oh baby, I'm crazy, almost dead,
> I wish I had you here to hold my aching head.
> I want you back and honest, baby I'll be true,
> If you love me like you used to do.[43]

Sippie Wallace's "Mail Train Blues" is about a woman who is committed to traveling anywhere to find her man. In "K.C. Man's Blues," however, Clara Smith decides to stop roaming around, and wants to settle down with her K.C. Man who has white teeth, "two pretty gold crowns" (a sign of prosperity, as well as adornment popular among black men in those years), "poro hair" (a slicked back hairdo), and "coffee-color brown" skin. This man was the epitome of the high-stepping city dude who turned every woman's head when he glided down Hastings, State, or 33rd Street.[44]

Although she knows her man is in Chicago, Bessie Smith is too numbed by his departure to follow him.

> Blues on my brain, my tongue refused to talk,
> Blues on my brain, my tongue refused to talk,
> I would follow my daddy, but my feet refuses to walk.

She even faults the "mean old firemen," and "cruel old engineer" for the loss, thus displacing the blame in order to ease the pain of her man's walking out on her. Her threat of suicide is hurled at them since no one else is there.

> Big red headline, tomorrow's *Defender* news,
> Big red headline, tomorrow's *Defender* news,
> "Woman Dead Down Home with Those Chicago Blues!"
> I said blues.[45]

Other traveling blues expressed the nostalgia of women who were homesick or tired of struggling for survival in the city; or who just had a "mind to ramble." Trixie Smith's "Railroad Blues" is truly a classic among the hundreds of train blues extant, and perhaps her best recording. She is joyful as she anticipates her arrival in Alabama for a reunion with her man. The faint sounds of the train rumbling toward the station set goose bumps shivering—"let it get here, let it get here, don't let it stop now, please, not before I get on." Smith captures that feeling of tingly anticipation tinged with apprehension as she shouts

> Now if the train stays on the track I'm Alabama bound.
> Now if the train stays on the track I'm Alabama bound.
> Don't you hear that train coming, I'm Alabama bound.

Her elation abates temporarily when the sight of the train evokes the sad memory of her man's departure on an earlier train.

> Now, the train went by with my Papa on the inside,
> Now, the train went by with my Papa on the inside,
> Lawd, I couldn't do nothing but hang my head and cry.

The feeling quickly subsides as her ride on the Seaboard and Airline train becomes imminent.

If you ever take a trip on the Seaboard and Airline,
If you ever take a trip on the Seaboard and Airline,
'Cause if you ride that train it will satisfy your mind.[46]

The shuffling back and forth from place to place characterized the restlessness of a people who were seeking relief from poverty, alienation, and discrimination. Mothers and fathers warned their children about the dangers of city life, two-timing men, dishonest employers, gambling, and whiskey, but they went anyway. At about nine years of age, Bertha "Chippie" Hill went with a circus and ended up singing blues in rough houses around New York's wharf. The Pratt City she sang about in "Pratt City Blues" was not her birthplace but she convinces the listener that it was. In a fine traditional performance with Armstrong on cornet and Reuben Jones on piano, Hill demonstrates that she understands the nature of street life, a topic she sang about often. Her reason for traveling was to get away from a super-hot two-timer and to find good times on 18th Street, rather than in Sandusky [Ohio] where she had to hang her head in shame.

Get full of high-powered likker, it's down on 18th Street.
Get full of high-powered likker, it's down on 18th Street.
Going back to Pratt City, where it tastes nice and neat.[47]

Clara Smith's "L & N" Blues" not only illustrates the "rambling bug" that afflicted women, but also gives an implicit message about segregated travel when she has to switch from the Pullman to coach on the trains below the Mason-Dixon line.

• •

12   PARAMOUNT RECORDS NEWSPAPER AD FOR TRIXIE SMITH

Got the travelin' blues, gonna catch a train and ride,
Got the travelin' blues, gonna catch a train and ride,
When I ain't riding I ain't satisfied.

I'm a ramblin' woman, I've got a ramblin' mind,
I'm a ramblin' woman, I've got a ramblin' mind,
I'm gonna buy me a ticket and ease on down the line.

Mason-Dixon line is down where the South begins,
Mason-Dixon line is down where the South begins,
Gonna leave a Pullman and ride the L & N.[48]

The trains clickety-clacked down the East Coast from New York to Florida; from Chicago to Memphis, from Kansas City to Houston with numerous stops in between, winding their way in and out of some of this nation's most beautiful land—pretty little towns, greening tobacco farms, and railroad shanties—splitting the towns down the middle into a black-and-white checkerboard, exposing to its passengers the awful paradox of racism. Trains were the purveyors of hopeful black men and women who left the South for the "good life up North," or the North to go back home to friends and family "down South." They traveled with all their worldly goods in one battered suitcase or croaker sack, and a shoebox of tender, juicy fried chicken, biscuits and pork-chop sandwiches which added to the pungent aroma of warm bodies crowded in the coaches. Loud laughter and joking mixed with the cry of babies bounced to sleep by weary mothers as the train jostled its human cargo to its destination. And like Trixie, Clara, and Chippie they brought their hopes on board when they rode the train.

However, the cities, especially in the North, were not only symbols of hope; they were quagmires of human decay. As disease, alcoholism, drugs, and vice encroached on the black community, women introduced blues addressing these social concerns. Kimbrough's blues was not about an isolated case, for alcohol and dope and the diseases and afflictions that accompanied their use were just as destructive to women as to men. Bessie Smith's immortal "Gin Mill Blues" is probably the most famous. A recitation of the list of blues lyrics that discuss drinking, its causes and effects, could become a litany. The day-to-day struggle of black working-class people eventually turns into a depressive state in which alcohol is often sought as a pain reliever or "tonic." "My baby left me," "We had a fight," "My baby treats me mean," "My baby runs around," are recurrent phrases found in drinking blues sung by both women and men. Men sang about "Whiskey Headed Women," and "Juice Head Babies" and women sang about drinking to keep from worrying. Some boasted, others moaned. Margaret Johnson exhibits nonchalance about her habit in "Dead Drunk Blues." For her, drinking releases her from worry and frustration.

> Oh give me Houston, that's the place I crave,
> Oh give me Houston, that's the place I crave,
> So, when I'm dry, I can drink whiskey (just the same).
>
> Whiskey, whiskey, some folks' downfall,
> Whiskey, whiskey, some folks' downfall,
> But if I don't drink whiskey, I ain't no good at all.
>
> Lawd, can I get drunk papa, one mo', one mo' time?
> Lawd, can I get drunk papa, one mo', one mo' time?
> 'Cause when I get drunk, nothin' worries my mind.[49]

There are two paradoxes in this blues, typical of the alcoholic: one is the belief that whiskey is a problem for some people but not for her; and the second is the contradiction that a drink will improve performance, sharpen the senses, while erasing worry or dulling the pain.

There is no evidence that Houston was the best city for whiskey-loving fun nor that women there were more likely to resort to drink. It just happened to be one of the cities where the blues was the staple of musical fare. In those smoky, crowded rooms the smell of barbecue, beer, whiskey, and sweaty bodies mingled into a delicious aroma rich with life. Johnson's performance exudes the good feeling derived from that carefree environment of momentary release from the pressures of life. With every drink, lost love, lost job, or mistreatment faded further into the background. Ma Rainey sang, "Reeling and rocking drunk as I can be," a blues about going to K.C. with her Gatling gun to bring her man back home.[50] Alcohol blues were big sellers for Bessie Smith and her peers because many people could identify with the problem.[51]

"Dope Head Blues" by Spivey was the first blues to openly address the drug problem, which was creeping into the black community in the twenties. Marijuana, or reefer as it was called then, and cocaine were sometimes mentioned by entertainment reporters though not explicitly: "Such and such dropped by and left us with a package that kept us smiling."[52] Studio sessions often began with drinks for all before laying the sound on wax. Sammy Price recalled that J. Mayo Williams made sure that his singers had plenty of liquor to loosen them up.[53] Unfortunately, alcohol and drugs soon spread like gangrene through the black community, infecting men and women, young and old, and the blues world added addiction to its repertoire of themes.

"Hustlin' Woman Blues" by Memphis Minnie and Lil Johnson's "Scuffling Woman Blues" voiced the grief of prostitutes who cannot "make it" on the streets either because the police are constantly hounding them or the pimp is pressuring for some more money.[54] In other instances, women are singing about their roles as sex objects and workhorses, whom men control and manipulate. An early Rainey blues, "Hustlin' Blues" captures that desperation and violence.[55] Chippie Hill's version of the same sordid story begins with a benign dialogue between her and the rent man, spoken by Richard Jones, pianist. But when she begins to sing about standing on the corner till her feet get soaking wet, you are jerked into the steamy dangerous world of hustling tricks. Caught between the desire to get out of the "business" and the immediate need to obtain funds for rent, food, and the omnipresent pimp, the streetwalker is the loser to a mean system with the odds stacked against her.

> Got the streetwalking blues, ain't gonna walk the street no more,
> Got the streetwalking blues, ain't gonna walk the street no more,
> 'Cause the cops is getting bad and the dough is comin' slow.[56]

Sexual exploitation was not one-directional. Frazier observed that some of the homeless women sought associations with men simply to satisfy their desire for sex and companionship, but "younger more sophisticated types more adept at vice and crime . . . demand to be entertained by their daddies."[57] The more relaxed attitudes toward sex in the black working-class community was reflected in blues erotica. Women singers brought new twists to such blues as they exploited and expanded the allusions used for double entendre.

"My Man-of-War," a double play on words, pairs the image of the famous racehorse, Man-of-War (1919–1920) with World War I battlefield language to paint a torrid, erotic scenario of sexual maneuvers.

> My flat looks more like an armory,
> Takes his bugle when he calls me,
> At night he's drilling constantly,
> He's my man-of-war.

> When he advances, can't keep him back,
> So systematic is his attack,
> All my resistance is bound to crack,
> For my man-of-war.

. . . .

If I'm retreating, he goes around
   And gets me in the rear.
He keeps repeating a flank attack
   Till victory is near.

And when he turns his machine gun loose,
   Then I surrender, for there's no use,
He makes me throw up my flag of truce.
   He's my man-of-war.[58]

Some audiences expected raunchy lyrics and singers gave them what they wanted, from Rainey to Bessie Smith to Edith Wilson and Gladys Bentley. The difference was in degree just as with other themes: Wilson, Hunter, and Miles, for example, could use a feigned naiveté cultivated from their Paris cabaret experiences. However, they had originally emerged from the Chicago-New York cabaret scene, which preferred their spice less "refined." Rainey and Lucille Bogan responded to the demands of the tent show masses with raw, heavy-handed lyrics that were cleaned up for recordings.

A larger issue, often overlooked in such discussion, is how the women used these lyrics to project a new image of themselves as total beings with independent spirits. Garon, in his study of the psychological basis of blues poetry, points out the emergence of the black woman as a free-standing person who articulates the intent and desire to break away from sexual, as well as racial oppression.[59] "Tired As I Can Be" by Bessie Jackson, also known as Lucille Bogan, is an eloquent illustration of that theory.

   I'm a free-hearted women, I let you spend my dough
   And you never did win, you kept on asking for more.
   And now I'm tired, I ain't gonna do it no more.
   And when I have you this time you won't know where to go.

My house rent's due, they done put me outdoors
And here you riding 'round her, in a V-8 Ford.
I done got tired of your lowdown dirty ways
And your sister say you been dirty, dirty all your days.

. . . and now I'm tired, tired as I can be
And I'm going back South, to my used to be.[60]

The famous "Trouble in Mind Blues" as sung by Chippie Hill may begin with despair but the mood shifts to one of optimism as she gets going.

I'm alone every night and the lights are sinking low,
I've never had so much trouble in my life before.
My good man, he done quit me and there's talking all over town,
And I know my baby, you can't keep a good woman down.

And though suicide is mentioned, it is merely a fleeting thought because the confidence bred from coping with and successfully making it through myriad disappointments sustains her.

Now I'm blue, yes, I'm blue, but I won't be blue always,
Because the sun is going to shine in my back door someday.[61]

This optimistic audacity is a clear example of blues as life, identifying the source of the pain, acknowledging its effect, then taking a step to deal with it. In this instance, the blues is a purgative, or aesthetic therapy, as aptly described by black psychologists Alfred Pasteur and Ivory Toldson.[62] Hill captures the tone of the black woman who has grown up with the understanding that self-reliance is one of her most important tools for surviving in a male-dominated culture. In her rendition she articulates the anguish of a burdensome life, yet demonstrates that toughness of spirit which fuels the will to overcome despair and to wait for the better day that is on the horizon.

For some women self-reliance was not enough to fulfill their emotional and physical needs; distrust of men pushed some of them toward forms of antisocial behavior that isolated or alienated them from the group. As we have seen, violence was the most extreme of such reactions. Role reversal was another. Hence, the bragging, arrogant woman could fend for herself and make a fool of a man at the same time. Loving a man was for young women unschooled in the ways of the city. "I'll tell a king up on the throne, / That I don't love nobody, nobody under the sun, . . . so I don't have the blues," was advice given to the lovelorn in a dry, wry manner by Clara Smith, who changed from a loving woman to a vamping dame.[63] She doesn't "love nobody, need nobody, nor want nobody" and she wants the world to know that.

> . . . When I'm with a feller, it's simply for making a show.
> I keep a feller spending till his money's gone
> And tell him that he's nothing but a pure breed hog.
> I don't love nobody, so I don't have no blues.
>
> I let a feller take me all around the town
> And if he ask me for a kiss, I will knock him down.
> I don't love nobody, so I don't have the blues.[64]

Whether this declaration of cynicism should be taken literally is a matter of context. In a public arena the blues woman would receive an affirmative response from her audience because she had demonstrated that she was as bad as a man in mistreating a lover. For many of the women who identified with the singer and her song, however, that cynicism could give way to melancholia as memories of lost love or home and family welled up.[65] Another example of the same type of blues was Chippie Hill's "Charleston Blues," in which she puts down her old man in the female version of "Going to Chicago, sorry but I can't take you, / There's nothing in Chicago that a monkey-woman can do."

I'm going to Charleston, honey, but I can't take you,
I'm going down on King Street, baby, but I can't take you.
Now, it ain't nothing on King Street, baby, that a crazy guy like you
    can do.

I'm going back to the fish house, baby, and get me some shrimp,
I'm going back to the fish house, baby, and get me some shrimp,
I gotta feed, baby, two or three hungry old pimps.

Now, I knowed you baby, when you did not even know yourself,
Now, I knowed you baby, when you did not even known yourself,
Now, you trying to give me the jive, baby, but you got to help
    yourself.[66]

Not only does she leave him but she impugns his masculinity by implying that he cannot take care of a woman or himself. Another sweet papa who couldn't take care of business had to hit the bricks in Bertha Idaho's "I Don't Care Where You Take It." After a year of listening to sweet talk that was followed by empty-handed excuses, he is advised to prearrange his visits so as to avoid running into the woman's new man.

So, I don't care where you take it, sweet papa, just move it on out of
    here,
'Cause this ain't no filling station, or no parking space,
If you looking for sweet doings, papa, find yourself another parking
    place,
So, I don't care where you take it, sweet papa, just move it on out of
    here.[67]

Sex between men and women was not the only topic in women's sexual blues. Homosexuality, though generally frowned upon by the black community, was also sung about. The previously mentioned "Shave 'Em Dry," which had many versions by men and women, contains lines in the Rainey recording which may, according to Garon, refer to lesbianism. "Going downtown to spread the news / State Street women wearing brogan shoes / Eh-heh, daddy, let me shave 'em dry."[68] She also wrote and recorded "Prove It on Me," an explicit statement of her preference for women and willingness to be open about it.[69] Rainey's and Bessie Smith's episodes with women lovers are indicative of the independent stance they and other women blues singers took on issues of personal choice. By addressing the subject openly, they show other women that there are other options available—the same option that Shug, the blues woman, offers to Celie in a tender, powerful encounter in *The Color Purple.*

All of the sexual activities were not serious; many were fun and games, indulged in as diversions after long road-trips. Sex—with other women, young boys, whoever—could be found in the major cities where the women performed. Bertha Idaho's "Down on Pennsylvania Avenue" paints a vivid panorama of that famous Baltimore street, the center of night-time activities for blacks during the 1920s, 1930s, and 1940s. Showpeople, pimps, prostitutes (male and female), gamblers, and numbers runners rubbed elbows with black businessmen and women. It was the place to be after dark if you were looking for action on the "freaky side."

> I want to tell you about a street I know,
>> In the city of Baltimore.
> And every night about half past eight,
>> The broads that [are] strolling just won't wait.

> *Refrain: You'll find 'em every night on Pennsylvania Avenue.*

> Let's take a trip down to that cabaret,
>> Where they turn the night into day.
> Some freakish sights you'll surely see,
>> You can't tell the he's from the she's.

Now if you want good loving, and want it cheap,
   Just drop around about the middle of the week,
When the broads is broke and can't pay rent,
   Get good loving, boys, for fifteen cents.[70]

Mary Dixon's swaggering encounters with all types of men did not prepare her for the kind she confronted in "All Around Mama." The first stanza shows that she was amenable to variety in her choice of men and that she was open to all kinds of lovemaking. Refrain:

I've had men of all sizes, had 'em tall and lean
Had 'em short had 'em flabby, had 'em in between,
I'm an all around mama, I'm an all around mama,
I'm an all around mama, with an all around mind.

She expresses her delight in finding a young man who can satisfy her sexual appetite; but drunkenness clouds her memory of another one-night stand.

Had a boy, young and tender, treated me so fine,
Never had nothing else but that thing on his mind.
Met a man in the gin-mill, we drank gin so fast,
Took me home, I remember, I said, "Oh my, yes!"

She draws the line when an effeminate man approaches.

I met a man, was a butler, when he spoke I ran,
Was too mannish for a woman, too girlish for a man.
Had a man, a good old sweetback, said that I should know
Said he didn't do no loving lest he had some dough.[71]

Yet she ends up spending her money on a sweetback.

Women also employed the bragging, signifying language of males to boast of fine physical attributes and high-powered sexual ability. In these blues are found metaphors that liken automobiles, foods, weapons, trains, and animals to the sex act or genitals. The prurient nature of many of these blues led to a spate of community activities seeking to ban them. Black newspapers waged the battle against performers who included them in their repertoire and accused them of using lewd lyrics as a substitute for talent. This was clearly not the case because the best of the blues women sang sexual blues sometimes. Admittedly, some were openly lascivious and left little to the imagination. These red-hot mamas brag about sexual moves:

> Men, they call me oven, they say I'm red-hot
> Men, they call me oven, they say I'm red-hot
> I can strut my pudding, spread my grease with ease
> 'Cause I know my onions, that's why I always please.[72]

or instruct women on how to and where to have sex.

> Well, I'm goin' to Memphis, stop at [Satch's Hall]
> Gonna tell you women how to cock it on the wall.[73]

She orders the man to move on because he is not a good sex partner.

> Back your horse out my stable, back him out fast,
> I got another jockey, get yourself another mare.
> Now, you can't ride, honey, you can't ride this train,
> I'm the chief engineer, I'm gone run it like Stavin' Chain.[74]

Only the most naive would miss the sexual implications of Bessie Smith's "I need a little sugar in my bowl, I need a little hotdog between my roll."[75]

The fun of some of these blues comes from their wonderful play on words, such as the sportscar metaphor of Hill's "Sports Model

Mama." There is nothing sleazy nor sneaky in her bragging about her sexiness for this is a woman sure of herself and unashamed. Sex is her livelihood, hence her reference to daily "punctures"; and she claims that a small woman (sportscar) can do it as well as a large woman (limousine).

> I'm just a plain little sport, have punctures every day,
> I'm just a plain little sport, have punctures every day.
> You may want a limousine, but they puncture the same way.

She does not hastily make love but takes her time, even though she may be criticized by her streetwalking cohorts.

> I know you women don't like me because I speak my mind,
> I know you women don't like me because I speak my mind,
> I don't like to make speed, I'd rather take my time.

She finally brags about men's preference for her brand of lovemaking.

> When the men comes to buy you'll always hear them say,
> When the men comes to buy you'll always hear them say,
> Give me a sports model mama because they know the way.[76]

Not only does she demonstrate that she can satisfy a man just as well as a more expensive or classier woman (limousine), but she also puts potential rivals at bay. Cleo Gibson uses the same automobile metaphors in "I've Got a Ford Engine": ". . . Ford engine movements in my hips / 10,000 miles guaranteed / . . . You can have your Rolls Royce / Your Packard and such / Take a Ford engine car to do your stuff."[77]

In "Rolls Roycc Papa," Virginia Liston takes a different tack. She berates the man for his poor sexual performance with phrases like, "Your carburetor's rusty . . . your gas tank's empty . . . steering wheel wobbly."[78] Through these blues women called attention to the

CELEBRATED OKEH ARTISTS

Margaret Johnson

Eva Taylor

Sara Martin

Virginia Liston

fact that some of the problems in relationships with men stemmed from men's sexual incompetence or impotence. Throaty growls, coy expressions, and sensuous movements lent a torrid atmosphere to the performances of these blues, which were intended to "titillate," according to Edith Wilson.[79] Singing lewd or raunchy blues provided a form of release of pent-up feelings which were repressed by social norms that prohibited open discussion of sex.[80] Consequently, they were usually performed only at parties, midnight rambles, bawdy houses, or clubs.

Sexy attributes as a threat to other women and a lure for men were flaunted in "Mean Tight Mama," by Sara Martin; "Mighty Tight Woman," a Sippie Wallace classic; "All Around Mama" by Mary Dixon. An "all around mama" could have men of "all sizes, . . . tall and lean, . . . short, . . . flabby, . . . in between . . . young and tender."[81] "Tightness" alluded to the female's closely built vaginal and pelvic area, which supposedly enhanced sexual pleasure. Clara Smith cloaks the activities of a promiscuous woman in a veiled display of innocence and pure-hearted virtue in her version of "Kitchen Mechanic."

> Women talks about me and lies on me, calls me outta my name,
> They talks about me, lie about me, calls me outta my name.
> All their men come to see me just the same.
>
> I'm just a working girl, po' working gal, kitchen mechanic is what
>   they say,
> I'm just a working girl, po' working gal, kitchen mechanic is what
>   they say,
> But I'll have a honest dollar on that rainy day.[82]

• •

13   OKEH RECORDS BLUES SINGERS:
      MARGARET JOHNSON, EVA TAYLOR, SARA MARTIN,
      AND VIRGINIA LISTON

The dollar may be honest by the time the rainy day arrives but it will have to be laundered first, because the kitchen mechanic obviously is doing more than washing dishes.

Advice to other women is a staple among women's blues themes, especially how to handle your men. After her return to the stage in 1966, Sippie Wallace made "Women Be Wise, Don't Advertise Your Man," her theme song. The title and lyrics suggest that a good man is so rare, it is best for a woman who has one to keep quiet or someone will steal him. On the other hand, one should not invest all of one's affection in a single man, according to Clara Smith in "Every Woman's Blues."

> Don't ever let no one man worry yo' mind,
> Don't ever let no one man worry yo' mind,
> Just keep you four and five, mess up all the time.

> You can read you' hymnbook, read your Bible, read your history,
>   and spell on down,
> You can read my letters, but you sho' can't read my mind.
> When you think I'm crazy about you I'm leaving you all the time.[83]

Not only is this woman sexually independent, but she is smart enough to know that book learning is merely one source of wisdom when making personal decisions. She asserts control over her own mind and refuses to be intimidated by her lack of education, a ploy often used to create a feeling of inferiority.

The best example, thematically and stylistically, of this genre is Ida Cox's "Wild Women Don't Have the Blues." She expresses disgust for women who brag about "their fighting husbands and no-good friends" in one breath and then "sit around all day and moan, wondering why their wandering papas don't come home."[84] Her advice is counter to the prevailing norms in the black community—monoga-

mous relationships, fidelity, temperance, family, home, and health—
yet it illustrates the urge for self-determination and expression.

> I've got a disposition and a way of my own,
> When my man starts to kicking I let him find a new home,
> I get full of good liquor, walk the street all night,
> Go home and put my man out if he don't act right.
> Wild women don't worry,
> Wild women don't have the blues.

The implication is that since men cannot be depended upon to be
faithful, then a woman would be foolish to act like an angel in order
to keep one.

> You never get nothing by being an angel child,
> You'd better change your way an' get real wild.
> I wanta' tell you something, I wouldn't tell you no lie,
> Wild women are the only kind that ever get by.
> Wild women don't worry,
> Wild women don't have the blues.[85]

Women's blues in the 1920s were often composed by others, usually men, but they represented a distinctly female interpretation.
The choice of performing style, inflection, emphasis, and improvisation on certain aspects of the lyrics gave a perspective and expressiveness that had profound effect on their listeners. They introduced a new, different model of black women—more assertive, sexy,
sexually aware, independent, realistic, complex, alive. Though the
themes they addressed were universal, their renditions linked them
to other women who identified with the realities of which they sang.

"Up the Country . . ." and Still Singing the Blues: Sippie Wallace

He left home one morning just 'bout the dawn of day,
Now he [was] gone one morning just 'bout the dawn of day.
Some old long tall woman stole my man away.

So many days Lawd, I stole away and cried,
So many days Lawd, I stole away and cried,
Didn't have no blues but I just wasn't satisfied.
Shorty George is *the* only man I choose . . .

Texas-style blues singing and piano playing was introduced to an expanded audience when Okeh Records released Sippie Wallace's rendition of "Shorty George" in October 1923. For the first time, many blues lovers would hear the shouting wail that typified Wallace's vocal style and for which she had become known as the "Texas Nightingale" in her native state.

● ●

We cannot draw direct causal links from Wallace's childhood experiences at the turn of the century to the achievements of peak years as an artist from 1923 to 1927. Yet the events and encounters beginning within her family and neighborhood greatly influenced her public and private life and they continued to pervade her blues writing and performance until her death in 1986. Hers is a clear case of "the blues is life . . . the blues is art . . . is life." When Wallace said, "I sings the blues to comfort me on," she confirmed that the blues is an integral part of her life. When she declared that singing the blues "is my job," she acknowledged the blues as a source of livelihood. Her comment about trying to keep her blues compositions from sounding "churchy" indicates her recognition of the blues as a distinct art. The blues is an existential art form that provides a creative outlet and a catharsis for Wallace and her audience.[1]

Wallace's music-making is so bound up with her living that one cannot readily discern where the performer enters and the elderly matron exists or vice versa. In private conversations one would hear a confirmation of the values expressed on stage or in public. The charm and twinkling wit on stage were also manifested in the little pranks she played on her "children" and friends at home. Consequently, while her relationship with the music and lyrics evolved in the performance, her commentary on stage, in media settings, or in private conversation reveals an internal consistency that is often lacking in many performances. In contrast, Helen Humes, former singer with Count Basie's band, could sing a blues as well as or better than some of Wallace's contemporaries, but she emphatically stated that the blues was just another type of music to her no different than the ballads or pop tunes.[2] She did not identify with the blues as a source of personal expression or emotional outlet as Wallace did. Wallace's life story reveals some of the forces that shaped her as a person and performer—close family ties, low economic status, strong religious feelings, love of music.

• • •

Beulah Belle Thomas was born to George and Fanny Thomas on 1 November 1898 in Houston, Texas, a frontier town with a growing black population at the turn of the century. Cotton was still king on the large plantations that employed many of the blacks who migrated there from Louisiana and Mississippi.[3] Blacks were still heavily influenced by plantation rhythms—backbreaking work from sun-to-sun, Monday to Saturday, large gatherings for Saturday night frolics, and church all day Sunday. Those who worked in towns and cities were laborers or domestics, and among these were the Thomases, who had thirteen children. Wallace was the fourth child of the religious, hardworking couple who neither indulged in nor approved of the Saturday night "wang dangs" that spawned such blues notables as "Ragtime" Henry Thomas and "Blind Lemon" Jefferson. Though the elder Thomases did not live to see it, two of their sons, George Jr. and Hersal, and one of their daughters, Beulah, rose to stardom on the vaudeville circuit.

Beulah, nicknamed Sippie by her siblings, spent her preteen years singing and playing piano at the family church, Shiloh Baptist. It was there that she earned a certificate for singing from a Sunday school teacher. Although she had very little formal education beyond elementary school, her older brother George and sister Lillie encouraged her musical career. Under George's tutelage she began to learn the popular music her mother disdained. Wallace described how she began writing her own blues lyrics, too, with his coaching.

> You see, my brother wrote music, you know, and I used to always hang around him all the time. And my brother never did have no words and I used to hear the words, get the words from different women, you know, girls come around singing. I get the words, I put them down on a piece of paper, and I carry them in a room and learn them. And then by listening, then I learn how to put them together.[4]

Wallace's parents, like most good Baptists, would not counte-
nance the "devil's music" in their home and punished their children
if they were caught listening to it or playing it. They believed, as did
the mass of black working-class people, that the only music fit to
sing came from hymnals and church songbooks. The nonreligious
or anti-religious themes that emerged in slave seculars and eventually evolved into the work songs and the blues of southern blacks
were regarded, therefore, as "devil's music."[5] According to James
Cone, however, the blues reflect the same existential tensions as
spirituals in black people's search for truth in the reality of the black
experience. He contends that it is a mistake to attempt to interpret
black life without the commentary of both blues and spirituals since
they "flow from the same bedrock of experience."[6] Perhaps Wallace
(and her peers) intuitively realized this, because she and her brothers defied their parents' strict interpretation of what was vulgar and
what was acceptable.

By the time she was in her teens, she had succumbed to the
catchy rhythms of her brother's piano playing and joined him in his
creative efforts. When George Jr. went to New Orleans to pursue his
musical career in 1912, fifteen-year-old Sippie soon followed. In
New Orleans she met and married Frank Seals. This was a mistake,
caused by her youth and her inexperience with men:

> I've been the biggest fool in the world. I believe everything everybody
> said was true, you know. Just like if you'd say "I love you." Well, I got a
> little enough sense to believe that you love me. I ain't got no better
> sense than that. And mostly—and then when I first, you know, when I
> first married, I thought that you get a husband wasn't nobody going to
> have him but you. But that's the wrongest thing and it's the wrongest
> way to teach a child, 'cause can't no woman have a man by herself.
> Girl, you going to have help. I don't care how good you are, you going
> to have help. Then you couldn't have no husband by yourself, nohow.

So, my brother, me and him wrote "Adam and Eve Had the Blues." I got all mine [ideas], got them from the Bible . . . this is true facts. . . .

And Eve is the cause of all of us having the blues, child. Even little dogs have the blues, even little birds have the blues, even little bees, even everything has it. Everything been having trouble.[7]

"Adam and Eve Blues" probably evolved differently from the way that Wallace recalled it, but her recollection of the process by which her personal experiences evolved into song is true to life. Her blues links religious and secular ideas and reaffirms the belief that the blues is a universal experience.

When Adam and Eve was in the Garden of Eden
They didn't know till the good Lord walked out.
Eve turned around and soon she found out,
Yes, what it was all about.
Eve called her husband and she got close to her spouse.
She said, "Here's some fruit, eat it, it will make us fine."
She said, "Eat some fruit, the good Lord is gone."
Adam said, "Yeah, it won't take long."[8]

The broken marriage affected Wallace profoundly enough for her to pay tribute to her mother's admonitions about "keeping company" in the first blues she wrote, "Caldonia." It is interesting to see how Wallace used the noun, "mama," in this rendition sung at her home in 1975.

Oh Caldonia, you treat your mama mean,
Oh Caldonia, you treat your mama mean,
You don't trust her like she's no human being.

In the first stanza, "mama" refers to herself as she decries the inhumane treatment of a lover. However, the second stanza takes a curious turn as "mama's" advice about men is recalled. In stanza three the traditional "muddy waters" line is used as a lead into the third line, which reiterates the theme of family and spouse abuse, common to many blues.

> And if you had listened to what your mama said,
> And if you had listened to what your mama said,
> You would not been here having those blues today.
>
> You drink muddy water and you sleep in a hollow log.
> You drink muddy water and you sleep in a hollow log.
> And you treat all your family just like a dog.

She employed another traditional blues line, "I looked up on the mountains," for the transition from the general statement about the family to focus on the infidelity of her lover. The shift from remorse to anguish replays the admonition of her mother and acknowledges that "no woman have a man by herself."

> I looked up on the mountain, looked far as I could see,
> I looked up on the mountain, looked far as I could see,
> The woman had my daddy, Lord, and the blues had me.
>
> You can take my baby, but you sure can't keep him long.
> You can take my baby, but you sure can't keep him long.
> I got a new way of loving, you better believe you women can't
> catch on.[9]

The optimism of the last stanza is typical of many blues in its affirmation of the belief in one's ability to alter the chain of events affecting one's life. In this example, Wallace resorts to a boastful assertion of her sexual prowess as the tool for turning the tide. In so doing she cleverly accomplishes two goals in "Caldonia"—atonement for disobeying her mother, and resolution of her feelings of abandonment.

Sixty years later Wallace reminisced that "Mama didn't want me to go with boys . . . [but] I was a fool, anybody was all right with me. Just as long as it was a boy. Mama never let me receive company." [10]

Both parents had died by the time Wallace returned home around 1918 to live with her siblings. The stagestruck young woman could not forget her experiences in New Orleans's Storyville district where brother George's friends included King Oliver and the soon-to-be famous Louis Armstrong. Disappointment in love was overshadowed by the burning desire to dance and sing in one of the tent shows that visited Houston on the TOBA circuit.

The teeming crowds of black folk would gather on both sides of Houston's streets to watch the parade and hear the lively orchestras play the latest ragtime and marching tunes. Wallace figured that with her talent, she might get a chance to play or sing for one of the showpeople, so she and other budding musicians waited around all day hoping to be noticed. For many of these aspirants, the only jobs available were temporary—to help raise the tent, hawk tickets, or pass out handbills—and Sippie's first break was not any better. Wallace began her roadshow career as a maid and stage assistant to a Madame Dante, a snakedancer with Phillip's Reptile Show. As she described one of her experiences she could barely contain the laughter that bubbled inside.

> I was scared when I started waiting on her. See, my church name is Beulah and when the tent show came around the block from my house the show was so good they kept it there. So I used to play the blues down there because I knowed a girl who worked there. So when they got me to earn work on an opening chorus, you know, where you

dance, I couldn't dance so Madame Dante asked me to be her maid. I used to light her incense. I would do like this [she demonstrates a wiggle and hand movement] and back up, then light it. Then, she'd just do a butterfly dance and I'd go out there and get a great big snake named Cary. He was very long and big. So when Madame was all loosened up she'd motion for me to bring the cane basket with the snake, you know. And I was just as scared as I can be and I had that thing just like this here when one time out in the middle of the stage that old snake come sticking his head up and I let it fall. [She laughs heartily.] It was jumping all out that thing. Child, I let that thing go and I flew. I never will forget that.[11]

By mentioning her lack of dancing talent and her willingness to work as a maid, Wallace underscored two things: jobs on stage were scarce but much sought after, and domestic labor was a mainstay for black women, even in show business.[12] There was no bitterness in that compromise for Wallace because it brought her closer to her goal of becoming a performer. As Madame Dante's maid she began her travels around Texas, from Houston to Dallas to Galveston to Waco and all the little towns in between.

Wallace soon gained a reputation as the "Texas Nightingale" as she sang with small bands for picnics, dances, and holiday celebrations. From these she went with tent shows around Texas as a singer, not a maid.

Her first recordings revealed a seasoned performer who had learned her craft well. She owed much to her brother George, who was by this time a respected composer and music publisher in Chicago. He was on the recording staff of the W. W. Kimball Company's music roll division and director of his own orchestra when Wallace, Hociel Thomas (a niece who was also an aspiring blues singer), and Hersal Thomas, her baby brother, arrived to join him. He played a significant part in getting the trio going.

Hersal Thomas was a superb pianist who often accompanied his sister when she performed, although he was only thirteen or fourteen years old. His musical gifts included composition also, and his name was listed on sheet-music credits as well as on recordings. Sippie and George renewed their songwriting partnership to produce the popular "Shorty George" and "Underworld Blues." The musically talented Thomases, George, Sippie, and Hersal, quickly became famous in the recording field. George's "Muscle Shoals Blues" was a best-seller in 1922 but it did not match the popularity of Wallace's first recordings on the Okeh label, "Shorty George" and "Up the Country Blues." The Windy City had a new star. Her first recording purportedly sold 100,000 copies—quite a feat for a newcomer in a young field.

In just a few months, Wallace's portrait was featured in the ads for her recordings hailing the "Texas Nightingale" as one of General Phonograph Corporation's new race stars. The dignified portrait was often accompanied by "exceptionally high-type dialect, especially prepared to appeal to the colored race," according to a trade magazine for the phonograph industry.[13] Examples of that so-called "high-type dialect" appeared in a series of monthly full-page ads featuring each of the Okeh recording artists, Wallace among them.[14] General Phonograph was unabashedly pursuing the dollars from the "colored population" through the *Chicago Defender.* Employing dialect in that manner would be considered objectionable by most consumers today, but back then the ads were successful in selling Wallace's recordings. Fortunately, they did not use the obscene caricatures found in some ads.

Wallace's blues style is a mix of Southwestern rolling bass honky-tonk and Chicago shouting moan, a seductive brew that fit her personality. She had a strong, smooth voice and good articulation that pushed the words straight forward (a quality that blues pianist Sammy Price considers imperative to good singing).[15] Her ability to

THE FIVE'S

WORDS BY
Geo. W. Thomas

MUSIC BY
Hersal Thomas
and
Geo. W. Thomas

FEATURED BY
Lizzie Miles

Published for
Band and Orchestra

Published by
GEO. W. THOMAS & CO.
428 Bowen Ave., Chicago, Ill.

Player Piano Rolls and
Records Ready

shift moods within a song adds a dimension that is missing in singers such as Spivey and Mamie Smith. An unorthodox sense of timing and accentuation of words give her lyrics punch and tension. In the first verse of "Shorty George," for example, the third line has more weight because she drags out "tell" and "I" for emphasis and authenticity.

> I wrote a letter *and* mailed it by air,
> I wrote a letter and I mailed it in the air,
> You can *tell* by that, *I* got a man somewhere.[16]

The plaintive swoop in the last verse is a device Wallace used to wrench tears from the most ordinary melody. Her slide down a fourth on "Shorty" and up a fourth on "only man" gives a twist that ends that song with a dynamic surge of melodic emotion ("Shorty George is *the* ONLY MAN I choose").

"Shorty George" remains a Wallace classic after sixty years because of her distinctive phrasing, punctuated by those mournful slides and shifting moods. Eddie Heywood's stride piano set a loping pace to allow the vocal a full range of flexibility. When Wallace sang "Shorty George" in the 1980s, although age forced her to sing in a lower octave, she still used a singing shout that grabbed the listener and made him or her want to join in the call.

The contrast in mood of the second side of her inaugural recording, "Up the Country Blues," demonstrated that she could convey a broad spectrum of mood and feeling. No pleas here for "Shorty George." Instead we hear a wronged woman who does not stand by weeping and wringing her hands, but who ushers the mistreating two-timer out of her house and out of her life. The listener is convinced that her singing conveys her own manner of dealing with

• •

15   SHEET MUSIC COVER FOR "THE FIVE'S" BY
GEORGE THOMAS AND HERSAL THOMAS, BROTHERS
OF SIPPIE WALLACE

hurt and anger. Any woman who has been betrayed by a "sweet daddy" who spent her money while steadily two-timing her can identify with Wallace's answer to this dilemma.

In "Special Delivery Blues," with Louis Armstrong on cornet and Hersal on piano, Wallace portrays the scorned woman who is unwilling to accept the finality of rejection by her lover. The mellow rolling piano in the introduction is ably contrasted by Armstrong's crisp staccato notes. Hersal's use of tremolo chord progressions, which follow Wallace's ascending melodic line, builds each line to an intensity, which is relieved by Armstrong's brief broken phrases. She slides up a fourth on the last word of the first line in each stanza, imitating the piano roll, dragging out every ounce of melancholy from each word. The last line of each stanza releases the tension with an upbeat tempo and syncopated chord progressions.

> He said, "I'm leaving you, Baby. It almost breaks my hear-ar-art,"
> He said, "I'm leaving you, Baby. It almost breaks my heart.
> But remember sometimes that *the* best of friends must part."

> ....
>
> Hey, Mr. Mailman, Did you bring me any ne-e-ews?
> Mr. Mailman, Did you bring me any news?
> 'Cause if you didn't it will give me those "Special Delivery Blues." [17]

Wallace's vocal signature was stamped on many blues like these. Whether she was pleading with or lambasting her man, she employed the ascending melisma and the intervallic leaps to emphasize meaning and mood and to achieve a powerful effect.

● ●

16   OKEH RECORDS NEWSPAPER AD FOR
      SIPPIE WALLACE

Many of the ideas for her blues came out of her personal concerns. She repeatedly commented that she would just be "thinking it over in my mind, child, and it would just come to me to make a song about what was troubling me." The joy and satisfaction that grew out of the creative interaction she shared with her brothers is reflected in her exuberant renditions of "Shorty George" and "Up the Country Blues." But other occasions and relationships inspired her to write in a different mood. Among them were "Can Anybody Take Sweet Mama's Place?" and "He's the Cause of Me Being Blue" with Clarence Williams.

A very attractive, buxom young woman, Wallace had already remarried by the time she joined her brother in Chicago. Her second husband was Matthew Wallace, a dapper Houstonian whom she adored. Their union had to bear the strains of big city living and all of its temptations—unattached women, drinking, and gambling. For a while Matthew played a major role in the further development of his wife's career, serving as her manager and, on occasion, as master of ceremonies, and as co-author of a couple of her blues. As was typical for stage acts, he used dramatic gimmicks to introduce his wife, such as this one:

> The curtain would open and you wouldn't see nothing but this big record player, . . . you know, a Victrola. Then Matt, he would come out and open the door, don't you know, and then I would step out singing while Hersal was playing the piano. It was beautiful, child, you should of seen it.[18]

Unfortunately, Matt's penchant for gambling interfered with his effectiveness and eventually led to financial problems for the couple. Perhaps this is one of the reasons why Wallace said "A Gambler's Dream," written by Hersal, was one of her favorite blues. She remarked that every time she sang it she thought about her mother's admonitions. Ironically, it was her niece, Hociel, and not Sippie, who recorded it for Okeh in 1925.[19]

Her recording about gambling was "Jack of Diamonds Blues," which was issued in March 1926 along with "Special Delivery Blues." "Jack of Diamonds," written by Matt Wallace and Hersal Thomas and featuring Armstrong and Thomas, does not have her usual emotional impact or dynamic vocal flexibility. The tale is one of strife brought about by gambling fever and the strain it puts on a relationship.

> Jack of Diamonds, you appear to be my friend,
> Jack of Diamonds, you appear to be my friend,
> Gambling is going to be our end.

The use of a metaphor, Jack of Diamonds, rather than a name, conceals the gambler's real identity but reveals the deceptive behavior that soon becomes destructive.

> You stole all my money and cut up all my clothes,
> You stole all my money and cut up all my clothes,
> And you come home broke and tried to put me out of doors.

The frustration of trying unsuccessfully to please turns to resignation, and the blues ends by acknowledging the cruelty of her lover.

> There is nothing in this world I've found that that pleases you.

> I love Jack of Diamonds but he was a cruel man,
> I love Jack of Diamonds but he was a cruel man,
> He would play dice and cards and his game was old coon can.[20]

The promotion of Wallace as a recording artist in 1923 and 1924 enhanced her stage career as well. Soon she was a regular headliner on the TOBA circuit. Her life was busy with travel to the big cities on the route—Chicago, Oklahoma City, Dallas, Galveston, and her hometown, Houston. Always a lover of beautiful, fancy stage costumes, Wallace would wear feathers and sequined gowns, low-cut to emphasize her full-bosomed figure. Her pecan brown round face was accented by full lips and big, soft brown eyes, which were most expressive as she sang. And when she sang she could drain the listener emotionally, pleading to "Sweet Daddy"; lashing out at the "mistreater"; or teasing like an accomplished vamp. In between engagements she could be found in Okeh's studios in New York or Chicago. Wallace counted among her close friends blues singer Sara Martin and the comedy team, Butterbeans and Susie, all of whom were on the Okeh label at one time, and who served time on the TOBA. She entertained these and other show biz friends with fine dinners, and was the guest of many other friends as she traveled.

Meanwhile, Detroit had replaced Chicago as home base for her, Matt, Hociel, and Hersal. Both Hersal and Hociel had cut their own recordings by 1925, so the Thomases were a musical family of quite some note. They settled into an area on Detroit's Eastside, which was densely populated by blacks, Russian Jews, and Italians. Matt worked as a laborer when he could find work.[21]

The deaths of the three siblings who had been instrumental in the development of her career came unexpectedly during her peak years on stage. In 1925 she was summoned to the bedside of her dying older sister, Lillie, who had taught her how to sing as a child. Then, in June 1926, Hersal succumbed at sixteen to food poisoning. And in 1928, George Thomas's songwriting and publishing career ended suddenly when he was run down by a streetcar in Chicago, bringing an end to the brilliant trio's collaborations.[22]

In their years together, the talented brothers and sister had produced some solid winners in the blues field. "Bedroom Blues" was one of Wallace's best. Its theme is abandonment.

> I was thinking 'bout my sweet daddy, I mean all night long,
> I was thinking 'bout my sweet daddy, I mean all night long,
> 'Cause he left me here in this old lonesome home.

She is denied the relief of free-flowing tears to assuage her loneliness.

> Lawd, I tried to cry, but my tears refused to fall.
> Lawd, I tried to cry, but my tears refused to fall.
> I was all alone, no one to love at all.[23]

Wallace's initiative and push for a stage and recording career derived not only from her desire to make it big but also from the fact
that singing and playing were her only tools for making a living. Fortunately, she could better her existence while expressing herself
creatively. Her vivid, matter-of-fact style was an outgrowth of life on
the rugged road from poverty to prosperity. Still, her early religious
training tempered her behavior and served her well as she struggled
with career, family, and marital strife. She observed and disapproved of the sometimes irrational outbursts by Bessie Smith, Mamie
Smith, and Spivey when they drank too heavily and created scenes
at parties, but she acknowledged that she loved a good time, too.
When asked if the hard conditions of stage life may have caused
many of the performers to drink heavily, Wallace gave a forthright
answer that revealed her early upbringing.

> People just get besides theirselves, you know. They get an inch and
> take a foot. Because they made some heroes some people can make a
> "pure D ass" out of themselves, you know, hurt their own self. . . . I
> drank beer but I didn't act like a fool; I was not a party girl. I was a
> theatrical woman and loved it, but I knew how to act, you know.[24]

"Knowing how to carry yourself" was important to the Texas war-
bler who believed that proper manners gained respect from others.
She and most of her peers valued their personal integrity and did
not sell out in order to achieve their goals. Helen Humes used ex-
actly the same phrase when she spoke about her years on stage: "I

didn't have that [people talking about her], because . . . I knew how to carry myself in the right way."[25] Black mothers at all socioeconomic levels hammered that principle into their daughters as a means of developing self-respect and protecting their reputations. Wallace's mother was no different. Understanding this is critical to understanding the black woman blues singer, not just as a folk figure, but as an artist whose professional and personal standards dictated choice of material and manner of presentation.

Wallace could play the piano as well as sing so she was hired by local musicians for socials and club dates, a practice she continued in Detroit long after her blues recording career had ended in 1929. I queried Wallace about the attitudes of the men with whom she performed toward the women singers and pianists, because I wondered if they respected them and valued them as professional colleagues. She admitted that she was not readily accepted as a leader of a group, but she told the following story to illustrate that the deciding factors were getting bookings and being able to pay the players.

> It was my job. And then I asked them how much they charged, you know, and finally after I got them their first two jobs then they got to be my orchestra. And that time they wasn't getting but five dollars a man. It was that time when I first started "St. Louis Blues" and "Barrelhouse Man" and all. And they didn't want any kind of junky piece, you know, they didn't have no special song.[26]

Linda Dahl's discussion of the careers of Lil Hardin, Lovie Austin, and other women pianists confirms that the main ingredient for getting with a band and staying was ability.[27]

Although she was exploited by record producers, scouts, and songwriters, as were her blues-singing sisters, Wallace did not consider herself a victim. Perhaps her close relationship and collaboration with her brothers diminished any effect of male domination while nurturing the excitement and exhilaration of creating and making music with them on record and on stage. Unfortunately, she, like others, had no control over her written and recorded work in terms of royalty agreements.

Once she was recognized as a "hot" item on disc, she was pursued by the black male songwriters who depended on talent like hers to sell their songs. She was not naive about the exploitation of her talents or the cutthroat nature of the business. She knew she could get royalties for her compositions but she accepted the practice of being paid a flat fee for a recording. One might expect Wallace, since her brother was in the publishing business, would insist on royalties. On the other hand, she might have felt that the money was staying "in the family," since his livelihood was derived from the recording company's profits. Underlying all of her discussions about her appearances and recordings was a tacit trust and acceptance of the terms made by the "head people," as illustrated in the following remarks:

> When I sing in concerts now I just get a salary, no share in the gate receipts—that goes to the head people. When I make records they give me a contract but when I first started they was only paying one hundred dollars a record. Only unless you owned the song could you get royalty every few months. But if you didn't, somebody would pay you fifty dollars for singing and then the company would pay me fifty dollars to record it.[28]

Her acceptance of male control was not atypical behavior for a woman raised in a home that upheld traditional views of men and women. For Wallace the bold move was in her break away from her religion's sanction against women performing blues on stage. Although she did not exercise the option to assert herself in the management of her career as did some of her illustrious counterparts, such as Hunter, Wilson, Cox, and Spivey, she used her talent wisely and well.

Okeh boldly advertised Wallace as the "Texas Nightingale . . . one of the leading stars of the Race . . . with her high C blues wailing," an appropriate assessment of the talents and vocal style that led them to press at least forty-one sides while she was under contract between 1923 and 1927.[29] Eddie Heywood, Clarence Williams, Perry Bradford, Hersal Thomas, and Danny Wilson were pianists on various sides which also featured rising instrumentalists Louis Armstrong, Buddy Christian on banjo, and Sidney Bechet on clarinet.

An unexplained recording hiatus of two years was ended when she was put under contract in 1929 by RCA Victor Records. There, she made four sides but only two were issued, the popular "I'm a Mighty Tight Woman" and "You Gonna Need My Help." The 1926 Okeh recording of "Mighty Tight" had Cicero Thomas on cornet and Hersal on piano, but in 1929 Wallace accompanied herself on piano backed by Natty Dominique, cornet; Honoré Dutrey, trombone; and Johnny Dodds on clarinet. "Mighty Tight Woman," one of the few erotic blues recorded by Wallace, demonstrated her superb vocal phrasing and her pianistic abilities (and I wish they had been recorded more often). The delightful mixture of naive sweetness and vampish sensuality captures the spirit of the streetwise black woman, confident and independent, yet absurdly expecting real love.

> I come to you, sweet man, falling on my knees,
> I come to you, pretty papa, falling on my knees,
> I ask, if you ain't got nobody, kind daddy, take me please.

This blues illustrates the dynamics of black male-female relationships, as seen in the woman's feigned submissiveness followed by a brash display of sexual arrogance in the second and third stanzas:

> 'Cause I'm a mighty tight woman, I'm a real tight woman, I'm a jack-of-all trades.
> I can be your sweet woman, also be yo' slave.
> I can do things so good, till you will not [see yo' head].

If you're a married man, you ain't got no business here,
'Cause when you're out with me, I might make yo' wife shed tears,
'Cause I'm a mighty tight woman, and there is nothing that I fear.[30]

The final stanza shifts the mood from that of an abject groveling woman to one who is in total command.

The hint of morality that surfaces in the final verse points out the ambiguities that pervaded the mores of the black community. Wallace's inclusion of this particular blues in her repertoire reflects that same ambivalence. Her home training taught her to exercise restraint in her public behavior, yet this blues typifies the contradictions of externally imposed restraint versus internally driven passions and desires. A clue may lie in her interpretation of this song. In the recorded version, the voice is coyly sincere. Although it was one of the last records Wallace cut in the "blues decade," "Mighty Tight Woman" has not only remained a favorite of old-timers but has also become a hit with the present generation of blues lovers.

Wallace produced some noteworthy sides during her Okeh years, using subject matter that ranged from jealousy, mistreatment, and vengeance to skin color and natural disaster, all treated with equal verve and vigor. The twinkle of her eyes belied the vocal threats of physical revenge by a jilted love. The mournful wail drew sympathetic sighs from understanding listeners who identified with the tragedy of love gone cold.

Sippie Wallace's career suffered the same decline as that of her peers when the record industry faltered during the Depression. She had not developed versatility of style and repertoire as Wilson or Hunter did, so she could not gain employment as a comedienne or sultry chanteuse. Hers was a raw country-style talent well-suited to belting the blues but not to sweet mellow ballads, and Detroit was a blues city not a Cotton Club town. She lacked the training and experience to change, and sorely missed the guidance of her brother, George, at this critical point in her career. Without him she had no songwriting partner to inspire her and to put her musical ideas on paper. Chicago and New York songwriters who could get work were no longer writing blues but rather the fast-paced show or revue tunes.

Wallace's stage bookings dwindled and finally petered out. By 1932 she had slipped into obscurity along with many of her other singing sisters. Her husband, family, and church became the focal points of her life. In the 1940s she became the guardian of Hociel's orphaned daughters. Her installation as a nurse in her church brought her joy and satisfaction, as did her work with the choir.

It was to church music that she turned her songwriting and piano-playing abilities for the next three decades. Her return to the roots of her musical tree nurtured her creativity. Conversations about "her" church and "her" choir sparkled with ardor.

> I hear a good number at church and I play. Here I got a little old choir. My choir—I write any kind of song I want and let them sing, you know. Now this is something I tried but they won't learn them. They want to learn. They want to learn, but they can't. Now your key is important, too. When I got my certificate for singing our teacher said, "Learn your key and anybody can play for you if you know your key." And so all I got to do is say play me so and so in G or play me such a number in F or in B or something like that. Like when I sang "Precious Lord," now that was in G, I mean, F. See? [Plays.] Now I got to play it in the anthem. Now here's the anthem part. Ain't it good? Now here's "The Lord Is My Shepherd." Ain't that pretty? Uh-huh.[31]

During that session in 1975 Sippie played and sang several religious songs she had written for her choir, interlacing the songs with comments. She introduced each one by saying, "Now here's something I like."

I said the good Lord wasn't able to give me rest after all my labor.
All your tears you'll turn to smiles up to heaven after a while.
When I sit down at his knees I know my journey will be complete.
I need rest, rest on my journey, Lord, and never tire.
I need rest, I need rest, rest for my journey, Lord, and never tire, oh
    after a while.
I need rest, rest for my journey, Lord, after a while, after a while.[32]

She explained her feelings about the church and her music, the
spirituals and blues, in the following manner:

> I shout sometime, it feels so good. Because I mostly do blues for jobs.
> But for my heart it's at church. That's why I make it to church all the
> time. Everytime I go I always ask can I sing the spirituals.[33]

Wallace, the blues singer, might have remained obscure for the
rest of her life, except for an occasional club date in Detroit. For
more than twenty years, she issued just two recordings. In 1945
Mercury Records released the great "Bedroom Blues." Backed by Albert Ammons, piano, and his Rhythm Kings (which included Artie
Starks, clarinet; Lonnie Johnson, guitar; and John Lindsay, bass), she
proved, without a doubt, that her voice and style had not diminished over the years. Although the recording was excellent, the
blues audience had already shifted its attention to the Chicago and
Memphis sound. Bebop, swing, rhythm and blues were all struggling for the attention of the listening public, so her record did not
sell and she slipped back into obscurity. The next recording on Detroit's Fine Arts label, in 1959, suffered the same anonymity but it
must have convinced her friend, Spivey, to keep urging her to come
out of "retirement" and try the folk-blues festival circuit that was
sweeping the country.[34] As a result, Wallace went to Europe in 1966
and captivated a new, younger generation of blues enthusiasts.
    The Storyville recording of her Copenhagen performance dem-

onstrated that the second coming of Sippie Wallace was long over-due. With Roosevelt Sykes and Little Brother Montgomery sharing the piano, she presented new renditions of her old classics, "Trouble Everywhere I Roam," "Shorty George Blues," "Special Delivery" and "I'm a Mighty Tight Woman," and introduced "Women Be Wise, Don't Advertise Your Man." One reviewer wrote: "Visiting Europe in 1966, Sippie Wallace astonished by the breadth of her singing and a delivery recalling Bessie Smith."[35] He commented that the remakes with Montgomery and Sykes in Denmark were of "exceptional merit."

Bathed by the spotlight of Lincoln Center's Avery Fisher Hall, Wallace at eighty could still evoke some of the deepest emotions as she sang the blues. The pathos that came through her voice could be matched only by the expression on her face; and any listener, whether a novice or longtime blues lover, could identify with those feelings as she closed her eyes and sang. What was left of the once vibrant, strong, steady voice was a husky talking-singing sound, but the loss of vocal flexibility was made up for by the expressiveness she put into each word, each phrase. The famous plaintive slide could still be heard, although in a much lower register. There was no mistaking that what she sang about she had experienced, yet she still had a ready smile and that good-natured sense of humor that often made herself the butt of a joke. No one could doubt that Wallace understood the deepest meaning of the blues. Wallace's career spanned more than sixty years, yet there was a freshness every time she sang. Though the fingers trembled and missed some notes when she attempted to accompany herself, she dauntlessly con-tinued—delivering a soul-touching "Precious Lord Take My Hand" or a rousing "Women Be Wise."

When this generously built woman, who looked like the typical huggable grandmother, welcomed visitors into her modest home in

• •

17 SIPPIE WALLACE AT THE ANN ARBOR FOLK AND
BLUES FESTIVAL IN 1976

a quiet Detroit neighborhood, a broad, gap-toothed grin spread over her face. She needed no prodding to sit down at the piano and sing whatever was requested, and before you knew it your soul was touched by the warmth of Wallace's gospel or blues songs. You empathized strongly with her sorrow, exuberance, or humor as she sang one song after another, many of them her own compositions. Everyone who knew Beulah "Sippie" Thomas Wallace loved her. Jolly, and candid when chatting with new acquaintances as with old friends, she was serious about her music twenty-four hours a day. She was charming, flippant, wise, and sometimes naive, but always sincere and honest. Her warmth, her sincerity, and deep religious sense came through when she was singing the blues, for she cared deeply about communicating with her listeners and wanted to share her feelings with every one of them.

Her religious and family values still had a great influence on her attitude toward the blues and the propriety of her stage career when she was in her eighties.

> I wanted to be a blues singer, because another girl wanted to be a blues singer. I wanted to be a blues singer like she was. But I don't know why, because I always was in church.[36]

Over and over, she expressed concern about violating church doctrine when she talked about continuing to sing the blues professionally while serving as pianist for her church in Detroit. The clearcut decisiveness of her youth had been replaced by a sense of guilt. The essence of her ambivalence came through when she remarked that she was trying to stop playing and singing the blues but that everybody wanted her to keep on. When asked why she wished to stop, she replied, "Because I play for the church, you know." She felt that if she performed in other places besides the church someone from her congregation might hear her and she wouldn't want people to get the wrong impression. She felt that playing for the church and still singing the blues was wrong, unless it was someone's job; then it was all right, but she was still uncomfortable because her pastor or some church member might not like the idea. She settled the matter by saying, "Suppose this wasn't nothing but a job, you see, you try to make good of everything you do."[37] Wallace could not stop singing the blues and live.

Without skipping a beat, and sure that she had dealt with the issue satisfactorily, she stopped talking, turned to her piano, and moaned through one of the dozens of songs she had penned in recent years.

> Yesterday, I saw you leave,
> I laughed and sang,
> I wouldn't grieve.
> But after my laughter came tears.
>
> I told my friends,
> I didn't care,
> I laughed about the whole affair.
> But after my laughter came tears.
>
> My pride kept me from showing you,
> That I was blue.
> Oh, but by myself,
> Don't nobody know what I've gone through.
>
> My lips don't feel,
> My heart's in pain.
> I made believe, but never again,
> 'Cause after my laughter came tears.

18   SIPPIE WALLACE AT HER HOME IN DETROIT IN 1977

19   (*Overleaf*) SIPPIE WALLACE AND LITTLE BROTHER
            MONTGOMERY IN CONCERT, BALTIMORE, 1978

With a heavy sigh she said, "Lord, that singing worry me so, when my husband died, girl. I've been a lonesome soul." She finally admitted that she not only sang the blues because it was a job but because it "helped to comfort me on." Wallace quickly began talking about the new songs she was writing and how everything she wrote "end up in church. I end up 'churchy' sure as you walk."[38] This disturbed her because she believed that there must be some distinction between what she composed as a blues and what she composed as a church song. She used a simple device: "to keep it from ending up like a church song I got to play it fast, not slow, like it should go."[39] It is often difficult to distinguish between the music of the church and the blues, because both come from a well of deep personal feelings—one toward a spiritual being, the other toward a human being.[40] Wallace and many other blues singers such as her contemporaries Spivey, Cox, and Martin and, more recently, Sister Rosetta Tharpe, Aretha Franklin, and Mavis Staples, demonstrated that the boundary between the two fluctuates.

A small notepad filled with her ideas for new hymns and blues was always close at hand, evidence of Wallace's continuing creativity. The ups and downs in her stage career did not diminish her capacity and desire to produce new music. The church and its rich musical heritage continued to provide the inspiration for her creative output over the thirty or so years that she was absent from the stage.

Wallace's retirement from her position as church musician in 1980, along with a resurgence of singing engagements, assuaged her internal conflict about the blues and the church. And although crippling arthritis hampered her piano-playing, and a minor stroke had left her speech slightly slurred, neither of these handicaps diminished her performances. She was sought after as a performer in clubs in the Detroit area, and at major blues concerts in Washington, New York, and Boston. Her appearance on NBC-TV's "Today"

show in 1983 demonstrated that she was enjoying every minute of her rejuvenated career. Detroit honored her with a special Sippie Wallace Day that featured a blues concert. She was cherished as a local treasure, and she and other outstanding Michigan women were inducted into the Michigan Hall of Fame with a lavish dinner and ceremony in October 1983. She appeared on local and national television, grand as ever in her wide-brimmed hats with ostrich plumes, singing the blues with a joy that she could barely contain. Her delivery still had vigor and style, and her audiences, though fifty to sixty years younger than she, responded with cheers, laughter, and prolonged applause. Her program freely mixed the blues and church songs as the spirit moved her. In recent recordings, there is that same depth of feeling and her inimitable phrasing, spiced with a combination of zest and flirtation. Her last album was nominated for a 1983 Grammy award. "A Mighty Tight Woman" is no longer a museum piece but a hearty manifesto of female assertiveness.

The Texas Nightingale continued to perform until shortly before her death. To the astonishment of many, she accepted an engagement to appear at blues concerts in Germany and Denmark in the spring of 1986, just six months prior to her passing. She was widely acclaimed for those performances, which were videotaped and recorded.[41]

In numerous ways, Wallace was the archetypal woman blues singer—gutsy, yet tender; bereft, but not downtrodden; disappointed, yet hopeful; long on talent, short on funds; legendary, but not widely acclaimed; exploited, but not resentful; independent, yet vulnerable. Her life story is not resplendent with dramatic events that capture the imagination—a bronze Cinderella whom Prince Charming rescued from drudgery and cruelty. Instead, it might be considered quite pedestrian except for her musical talent; it did not save her from toil and grief but did enable her to communicate her feelings about life's triumphs and disasters.

Her music is a wonderful admixture that reflects her personal and artistic perspectives. By dint of extremely hard work, often under stressful conditions, she coped with life and retained a sense of her personal integrity. She sat on stage, regal in a beaded chiffon dress, large hat, and lace gloves, and created her personal picture of the world by utilizing her lusty vocal talents and keen insights. She sang for her living, that was her job; and she believed that when she sang she provided her listeners with information about her life that might help them to come to grips with their own lives.

Sippie Wallace died on her eighty-eighth birthday, 1 November 1986.

I Have Killed My Man

Bloodthirsty Woman Confesses!

"You can just lie down and let me walk." He was the only man I ever loved! Yes! I killed my man—a low-down, good-for-nothin' fellow.

"I told him BLOOD was in my eye—still he wouldn't listen to me. 'Stead of givin' him SUGAR I put my KNIFE in him!

"I am a mighty mean woman and won't stand for no back-talk."

And now there is a terrible, slinking hoodoo that creeps after this woman wherever she goes and lets her feel the touch of cold, clammy hands. Soul and body are being racked by BLOOD THIRSTY BLUES!

Never Seen So Much Blood

"I've never seen so much blood! Blood—blood! Don't you see all that blood?"

Oh! You are filled with pity for this blood thirsty woman whose soul is in such TORMENT! There comes before her vision the terrible sight of the man she loved. There he is—dead upon the floor—and he welters in his blood. The red fangs of vengeance drove her into a mad people. But when the toll was taken there came to her tortured mind NO REMORSE!

NOW YOU CAN HEAR THAT SUFFERING HEART SOBBING OUT ITS STORY OF WOE.

Oh, you whose hearts are tender—listen and thrill to the tale of BLOOD THIRSTY BLUES! Okeh Record No. 8531.

One More Sniffle

Here she is with "DOPE HEAD BLUES." There's nothin' that little brown lady don't think the cat's. And how she feels! Just like a lovin' rooster. And then, "Som-go-get my aeroplane, and drive it to my door. Win's that fellow?" are all 'stupid'! That's the Prince of Wales. And he sure has got me worried!

"I'll just take one more snif' and that will get me all in Jail."

LISTEN TO WHAT DOPE HEAD BLUES makes one woman see, feel and hear. Okeh record No. 8531.

EXTRA!

The story with all its horrors is sung by

Victoria Spivey
(*Exclusive Okeh Artist*)

on

Okeh Record No. 8531

A Record That Groans With Tragedy

Only 75c

Ask for . . .

8531 { Blood-Thirsty Blues
Dope Head Blues

Sung by VICTORIA SPIVEY
with Guitar Accompaniment

RACE OKeh RECORDS
ELECTRIC

OKEH PHONOGRAPH CORPORATION   25 West 45th Street, New York, N. Y.

Blues Was Her Business: Victoria Spivey

I caught the No. 12 but the man laid down and died,
I caught the No. 12 but the man laid down and died,
Hurt me so bad, I hung my head and cried.

Victoria Spivey was barely twenty when she penned and recorded "No. 12, Let Me Roam," for the Okeh label in 1927. She captured the mood of a distraught woman who boarded the No. 12 train to go see her man, only to find him dead. Spivey continued to write, sing, and play blues like "No. 12" for over fifty, fruitful, exciting musical years because "blues was her business." She exorcised the bluest of feelings with her famous moaning, groaning, finger-popping style that made her singing unique. Her influence can be heard in the recordings of Dinah Washington, Esther Phillips, and Patti LaBelle. In fact,

• •

20   OKEH RECORDS NEWSPAPER AD FOR VICTORIA
      SPIVEY'S "BLOOD-THIRSTY BLUES" AND "DOPE
      HEAD BLUES"

Spivey once remarked that Dinah Washington "carved me"—the highest compliment one blues singer could pay to another.[1]

"Vickie," as she referred to herself in some of her compositions, used personal experiences as the raw subject matter for her songs. Her voice had a distinctive nasal quality quite different from Sippie Wallace's rich, open sound and Edith Wilson's mellow, lilting tones. Her forceful, hard-edged style was punctuated with moans that she called her "tiger squall" and that became her signature on the more than one hundred sides she recorded from 1926 to the mid-1960s. Although a latecomer on the 1920s recording scene she had a strong impact and soon gained attention with her rowdy, sometimes harsh lyrics that reflected her Texas blues background.[2] Her past reveals some of the factors that shaped her development as a musician. Personal ambition and drive sustained her career for over fifty years.

Vickie's parents, Grant and Addie Spivey, were descendants of slaves who had migrated to Texas in search of the better life promised in the Emancipation Proclamation. Grant's father reputedly acquired great land holdings in both Texas and Louisiana but, as with many blacks, he was financially unable to retain them for the benefit of his children. So, in search of work to support their family, young Grant and Addie migrated from Galveston to Houston, Texas, at the turn of the nineteenth century. It was there that Victoria, born 15 October 1906, developed her lifelong love for music amidst the sounds of the string bands in which her family played, vaudeville shows, and silent movies.[3] Her mother's singing of the semi-classical songs which she loved, as well as the religious music of her church, was a part of the heritage that the spunky little girl absorbed as she began shaping her own musical future.

Addie Spivey was widowed when Grant was killed accidentally while working as a laborer. Although Vickie was only seven years old at the time, she was so affected by her relationship with her father that the memories of him were expressed in two songs she wrote several decades later.

Mrs. Spivey managed her children with a firm hand, yet she was wise enough to give Vickie the flexibility she needed when she expressed her desire to play piano in some of the less reputable places in Houston. Before she reached her teens she had maneuvered herself into a job as pianist at the Lincoln Theatre in Houston. A friend had told her of the opening and she convinced the manager to hire her without letting him know that she could not read music. She managed to keep up the masquerade by going to a store and listening to the latest hits so she could memorize them and learn them on her piano. This trick was soon discovered and she lost her job.[4]

Undaunted, she moved on to playing anywhere she could find a job—bordellos, whiskey joints, and picnics—with her brother, Willie, who played blues piano, serving as her chaperone.[5] This was a concession to her mother who did not readily approve of the atmosphere to which her daughter was being exposed. But her goal was not to be merely a piano player in a whorehouse for the rest of her life. This ambitious young woman had her eyes on a much brighter, more exciting career on stage.

Spivey haunted the music halls when Ida Cox and other greats appeared. She listened with fascination to the recordings of Mamie Smith, Sara Martin, and Ma Rainey. String and jug bands took on a new significance when Rainey was up front with her fabulous jewels and deep warm voice groaning about the woes of love. The satin-swathed bronze goddess, Cox, was her idol, inspiring Spivey to press on with a blues career.

As Spivey continued performing in Houston, Galveston, and other west Texas towns, she quickly became a sensation in her own right.

By 1918, she had acquired a firm grip on the blues style from her association with Texas blues pianists and singers, Robert and John Calvin, and Henry "Lazy Daddy" Fillmore.[6] During that period they were engaged for gay houses by "landladies" and for whiskey joints and picnics. Called "Little Mama" and "Vickie" during that time, she also played in the "bloody 5th Ward" in Houston, pumping out her version of the notorious "Ma Grinder Blues," a dirty dozen blues.[7] The loping boogie-woogie beat of Texas blues evolved from this environment through the fingers and voices of "Blind Lemon" Jefferson, Sippie Wallace, Hersal Thomas, Joe Pullum, and Spivey, who added her own special twist when she performed. Her first encounter with the famed Blind Lemon was at a house party in Galveston where she was engaged. He sat in for her while she took a break and impressed her with his blues: they "were so full of soul."[8] She recalled fondly the many nights she and Blind Lemon worked the houses and picnics.

> Lemon and myself continued meeting at house parties where we would give one another much-needed intermissions. What a pleasure! It got so good that the landladies would try to hire both of us at the same time. We did it when we could and loved it. . . . The more money the house lady made the more we made—although we never worked the joints under ten dollars per night, no perhaps, but per night. Plus stacks of those Bo dollars [silver dollars] which people would lay as tips across the piano board, plus all you could fool the public that you could drink.[9]

Purportedly, it was during one of those house party performances that Spivey was heard by Cox, who was so impressed that Cox encouraged her to come with her show.[10] But for a reason long gone from memory, Cox left without Spivey, much to her disappointment.

Nevertheless, dauntless and determined, she followed the advice and encouragement of her brothers and went to St. Louis in quest of her own recording opportunities.

Approaching twenty, this veteran singer-pianist with almost ten years of show business experience set out to sell her own composition for a recording with Jesse Johnson, who owned the leading record store in St. Louis and was a talent scout for Okeh Records. Fortunately, Johnson, husband of Edith Johnson, who later recorded blues also, responded to Spivey's talent and not her pushiness. The startling result was the successful rendition of her famous "Black Snake Blues," released in July 1926.[11]

The audacious Spivey was now established on the recording scene for many years to come. Even the advertisements for these first issues were unusual for they used only her photograph, no gimmicks or stereotypes. There she was with a big smile, her face framed by close-cropped hair, one arm raised in the air, the other on her hip, as if she were saying, "Hello, World, I'm your new blues star." In the next two years she wrote and recorded no fewer than thirty-eight blues for the Okeh label in St. Louis and New York.

The famous "Black Snake" was even more successful for Blind Lemon Jefferson than for Spivey. For Spivey this was a terrible blow, leading her to claim Jefferson had stolen her song. Decades later she would write:

> We were buddies . . . until I heard his recording of "Black Snake Moan" on Paramount which came out some months after my original "Black Snake Blues" on Okeh. It was so much like [it], including the moan. I was really angry for a while knowing that Lemon and myself were like brother and sister in our jobs. . . . John Erby and myself met Lemon in St. Louis and we straightened the matter out.[12]

The dispute was settled for friendship's sake. It is likely that both artists had a rightful claim to their individual versions of this blues, whose lyrics and melody were a part of the folk literature. As was the custom in the environments where the country blues evolved, melodies and lyrics were used by many singers in a locale. Lines and even whole verses "traveled" from one song to another, as performers adapted them to their special style and circumstances. Spivey noted herself that everyone in the west Texas clique performed versions of the "Ma Grinder," which probably was the source for her "Organ Grinder Blues." The key to recognition as an outstanding artist was unique improvisation upon and soulful renditions of material that was common to many. Spivey distinguished her style with her "tiger squalls" and an additional four bars at the end of the traditional twelve-bar format.[13]

On the heels of "Black Snake Blues," "Spider Web Blues," and "Dirty Woman Blues," came the "Arkansas Road Blues," a superb country-style blues with John Erby on piano and Lonnie Johnson on guitar. The moaning which was soon recognized as her musical signature was punctuated by a fine interplay between Erby and Johnson.

> I got my train sack and now I'm going back.
> Because, I got those Arkansas Blues.
> But I ain't gonna travel this big road by m m-m-m-m, by myself,
> But I ain't gonna travel this big road by m m-m-m-m, by myself,
> If I don't take my baby, I sure won't have nobody else.
>
> But when he were arrested and put in that mean ole m-m-m-m,
>   mean ole jail,
> But when he were arrested and put in that mean ole m-m-m-m,
>   mean ole jail,
> I were the only person to try and go his bail.

Hey-ey, hey-ey, hey-ey, hey-ey, aa-ah
Hey, whyn't you let me know,
Daddy, if you don't want me, they are plenty more.[14]

In this rendition Spivey's unusual vibrato captures the mood aptly. She slides easily from words into moans and back—a vocal device found in religious singing throughout the South from slavery times—illustrating a bereft and miserable woman mourning over a lost lover.

Spivey lived in Moberley, Missouri, a town near St. Louis, with her older sister Elton, a vaudeville singer known as the "Za-Zu Girl," in the latter half of the 1920s. There she was inspired to write the "Arkansas Road Blues" to express the feelings of separation from family and professional companions. "No. 12, Let Me Roam" and the chilling "TB Blues" were also penned while she served as a staff songwriter for the St. Louis Music Company. The No. 12 train that ran through Moberly thus became the subject of another traveling blues.[15] Johnson's guitar and Erby's piano backed Spivey's harsh country vocals laced with moans and groans. This was one of Spivey's best compositions and recordings.

I caught the No. 12 but the man laid down and died,
I caught the No. 12 but the man laid down and died,
Hurt me so bad, I hung my head and cried.

I asked the conductor had he seen my man,
I asked the conductor had he seen my man,
He said, "Lady, I'm only a conductor on this train."

As in many blues, the emphasis shifts from losing the lover to re-membering him as "the best." Finally, the last stanza indicates a change: a mixture of determination to keep going and nostalgia about the past relationship.

She said, "You can get a man in the East, a man in the West,"
She said, "You can get a man in the East, a man in the West,"
But she don't know, his love was the best.

I kept on riding, rode to the end of the line.
I kept on riding, rode to the end of the line.
Everybody left me in the station, left me crying.[16]

"TB Blues," the more memorable of the two, gained fame as other artists performed it in later years. Urban living with congested, shabby housing carried the constant threat of tuberculosis, influenza, pneumonia, and diphtheria. Spivey had seen a childhood friend succumb to the ravages of TB and immortalized the feelings of ostracism and abandonment in "TB Blues." Memphis Slim's rendition on the Spivey label is inspired, slow, mellow urban blues at its best, with rippling piano accompaniment, spiked throughout by spoken ad libs. Dispute about the origins of this blues prompted another article by Spivey in her column, claiming others had stolen the idea from her.[17]

Spivey moved into other performing areas when the blues market showed signs of decline. While she was in New York for recording sessions with Porter Grainger, the prolific blues composer-pianist convinced her to try the musical stage in the production of *Hits and Bits from Africana,* a revue of songs and dances from a show starring Ethel Waters which had just folded on Broadway. She was heralded as the "Newest Star" by the *Pittsburgh Courier* upon her opening at the Lincoln Theatre in New York in November 1927.[18] Other members of the cast included a young comedienne, Jackie Mabley, who would become internationally famous in later years, and actress Lottie Gee. The show was a smash so the backers agreed to its hitting the road, with Philadelphia as the first stop. It was so well received there that the road manager could not resist the temptation of heisting the receipts and skipping town, thus ending Spivey's first major stage venture.[19]

In the same period between late 1927 and early 1928, Spivey's seeming obsession with eerie subjects pervaded her next releases, "Garter Snakes Blues," "Blood-Thirsty Blues," "Red Lantern Blues," Dope Head Blues," "Murder in the First Degree," and "Nightmare Blues." These gruesome topics had not been presented in this manner before, so she was gambling with public taste when they were issued. The promotions pictured a horned devil-woman strangling her man, and lanterns moving on spindly legs as they glowed with fiendish grins. "Victoria Spivey has been seein' things that will make your blood run cold . . . lanterns moving' from hole to hole . . . curdlin' groans and piercin' screams!"[20] The text keyed on clammy hands, voodoo, and prisons. "Dope Head Blues" was significant in that it was concerned with the hallucinations and disorientation connected with sniffing cocaine, a topic that had not been addressed in blues before this time. A decade later, cocaine or "happy dust" as it was called, was used by Sporting Life to torment and tempt Bess in George Gershwin's *Porgy and Bess.*

For some reason, probably related to the market, Spivey's next releases shifted from the pathos and torment of these blues to the lighthearted but decidedly erotic "Organ Grinder Blues," "My Handy Man," and "The New Black Snake Blues."[21] There is no doubt that she is discussing the sexual prowess of her man in "Organ Grinder Blues":

> Grind it north . . . grind it east and west,
> When you grind it slow I like it best.

. . . .

You don't have to pass your hat no more,
You're the grinder I been waiting for.[22]

The brittle voice contrasts with a delicate, lazy orchestration. Such notables as King Oliver, Clarence Williams, and Eddie Lang were in the band. The grinding abrasive quality of Spivey's voice is perfect against the playful wah-wahing of horns and the steady strides of the piano and guitar. This delightful musical juxtaposition heightens the eroticism of the lyrics.

Subsequent duets with Lonnie Johnson, such as "Furniture Man," "Toothache Blues" and "You Done Lost Your Good Thing," were light fare of little musical value. The inimitable Clarence Williams played piano on these issues, which are humorous and laden with double entendres. The pornographic lyrics are probably the only reason they were issued.

Spivey made her screen debut in 1929 in King Vidor's pioneer musical production, *Hallelujah,* which was touted as the "first all-Race film drama in history."[23] The story was a typical tale of the Negro in the South with cotton fields, spirituals, blues: the whole works. Spivey had a minor role as "Missy Rose," a slave girl. Her ability to bring authenticity to anything she attempted paid off for her in *Hallelujah,* for she was hailed by critics as a screen find. A feature article quoted her remarks: "Grit, pure grit, is the thing that counts in trying to get ahead."[24] While *Hallelujah* was being filmed Spivey married Reuben Floyd, a trumpeter, who was a member of the cast. The short-lived marriage ended in divorce.

She went to RCA Victor in the latter part of 1929 in search of better recording opportunities. This relationship was brief but it produced some fairly strong sides with Luis Russell and his band, including the spine-tingling "Blood Hound Blues" and emotionally taut "Moaning Blues." With her usual assertiveness she also inveigled a contract for her sister Addie, known as "Sweet Pease." The gamble paid off, for "Sweet Pease" had four sides released: "Day-Breaking Blues," "Heart-Breaking Blues," "Leaving You Baby," and "Longing for Home."[25]

The decline of the recording industry did not bring a halt to Spivey's singing career. She moved to Chicago in 1930 and teamed up with other blues musicians, such as "Tampa Red," "Georgia Tom" Dorsey, the rising "Memphis Minnie," and "Washboard Sam."[26] There she recorded several numbers on Vocalion and Decca. About 1931, with dogged determination, Spivey took off across the country as featured singer with a band she had organized, the Hunter Serenaders, which included Reuben Floyd, trumpet; Joe Jones, drums; and Ben Webster, tenor saxophone. Vickie and this group played in Canada, the Midwest, and eventually, the East Coast.[27] Her early experiences in Texas stood her in good stead, for she adapted quickly to the change in public demands. Tough-minded, able to stand her ground with anyone, she lived well during a time when many black entertainers were down on their luck.[28]

Spivey had a flair for good business management, which she put to use to obtain bookings in a variety of roles. After a few months as featured singer with the Hunter Serenaders, during which period she recorded with them, she appeared as a single with revues throughout the Midwest. One of these was "A Family affair which included her sisters (Leona, 'Sweet Pease,' and Elton, the 'Za-Zu Girl'), and her brother Sam."[29] She toured Oklahoma and Texas as the star of the Dallas *Tan Town Topics in 1933*. In the following year Spivey met, and became manager of a fantastic Harlem "hot" dancer, Billy Adams. They soon became marital partners and developed an exciting dance-comedy act that attracted the attention of Olsen and

Johnson, producers of musical revues on Broadway. Subsequently, they became one of the featured acts in Olsen and Johnson's *Hellza-poppin* revue, which was on Joe Glaser's booking circuits.[30] During this period, Spivey also performed in the company of such stellar musicians as Louis Armstrong and Bessie Smith.

Having decided early on to make the greatest demands on herself as an artist, Spivey worked at it constantly. When others, such as Bessie Smith, who may have started with a greater natural talent, were having difficulty adjusting to the Depression and its effects on black entertainers, Spivey made adjustments but not compromises. She dished out the blues in a newer swinging version in her record-ings of the latter half of the 1930s. "TB Got Me Blues" came out with a vamping piano and a hot trumpet reminiscent of Armstrong. The pathos, missing here, is replaced by a cynical tone expressing dis-dain for fair-weather friends.[31]

"Detroit Moan" is probably the best of the sides she made on the Vocalion label in 1936 and 1937. The hard-edged, incisive wail still had a chilling effect, something only Spivey was able to achieve on a continuing basis.

> Detroit's a cold, cold place and I ain't got a dime to my name,
> Detroit's a cold, cold place and I ain't got a dime to my name,
> I would go to the poorhouse, but Lord, you know I'm ashamed.

• •

21   OKEH RECORDS NEWSPAPER AD FOR VICTORIA
SPIVEY'S "NEW BLACK SNAKE BLUES"

> I got to leave Detroit if I have to flag number 94,
> I got to leave Detroit if I have to flag number 94,
> And if I ever get back home, I ain't never coming to Detroit no
>   more.[32]

This blues, said to be one of Spivey's favorites, was adapted to suit the locales where she performed; the title was changed to "Philadelphia Moan" on the occasion of a folk festival there and "Brattleboro Moan" when she sang at a coffeehouse in Vermont.[33]

By 1940, the enterprising woman had again organized her own band and begun touring under her own steam. She worked for the Balaban and Katz shows briefly in the 1940s, then left the entertainment scene after she and Adams split up. Subsequently, the long, slinky, satin gowns were replaced by ordinary street clothes as she turned to church for fulfillment. The boogie-woogie piano gave way to the organ and choir loft in the Brooklyn church where she served for about fifteen years.

In the late 1950s, one of her fans, Leonard Kunstadt, met her through a mutual friend. What developed was an unorthodox liaison between a young white jazz-lover and an aging blues queen that lasted until her death, and had an enormous impact on the blues scene for the next two decades. Kunstadt gave Spivey the incentive to take interest in her music again. She began appearing locally at Gudes's Folk City in New York and was picked up by the promoters of the increasingly popular folk festivals featuring blues artists. Her renewed spirit energized Spivey enough for her to set up her own music company, through which she produced and issued her own recordings. These included the reissue of some of her earliest works on *The Victoria Spivey Recorded Legacy of the Blues.*[34]

Whether critics considered her first or second string was less important than her urge to preserve a significant era in American music history.[35]

Spivey also used her company to promote "old-timers" who were good but who had become "has-beens." These albums are gems when she allows the other musicians to sing or play, since most of her work sounds redundant and often relies on raunchiness instead of invention. Lucille Hegamin's rendition of "No. 12" (mentioned earlier) is excellent, and "He May Be Your Man," is a throwback to the 1920s with its vaudevillian slides and brassiness. In fact, Hegamin's voice is bigger, more powerful, and more convincing than it was forty years earlier. Buddy Tate on tenor sax, Eddie Barefield, alto sax and clarinet, along with piano, bass, and drums, provide a swinging ensemble that drives the music ahead. Hannah Sylvester is the jewel of this set, though, with her mellow voice and snappy timing that rocks through Spivey's "Mr. Cob," "A Basket of Blues," "Big Black Limousine," and "Hey, Big Texas."[36] Subsequent albums featured Lonnie Johnson, one of Spivey's 1920s collaborators, Little Brother Montgomery, and Peter "Memphis Slim" Chatman on *The Queen and Her Knights;* Big Joe Williams, Roosevelt Sykes, and Johnson on *Three Kings and the Queen;* the young John Hammond, "Sugar Blue," Bill Dicey, Mark Ross, young Bob Dylan on harp, and the inimitable Bukka White on *Spivey's Blues Cavalcade.* The collection is a blues lover's bonanza.

Riding the wave of renewed interest in the blues by young people in the United States and Europe, Spivey, by now called Queen Vee, went to Europe with the American Folk Blues Festival in the fall of 1963. She dazzled the crowd in her red gown as she sang "TB Blues," "Grant Spivey," and "Black Snake," and played the piano and ukulele.[37]

It was the success and exhilaration of her experiences with the folk festivals that prompted her to contact her lifelong friend, Sippie

Wallace, and urge her to join the movement in 1965. She and Wallace also appeared together at a few festivals.[38] For the blues fans who had the opportunity to hear the Texas Nightingale and the Texas Moaner on the same bill, Wallace's shouting wail juxtaposed to Spivey's nasal moaning must have been a rare treat. The raw power of the southwestern blues sound was molded into two unique styles by these artists—Wallace's focused on a rounder more open-throated sound; Spivey's was brittle and nasal, especially suited for the subject matter she preferred. The friendship was sustained by frequent calls and letters until Spivey's death from a chronic liver ailment in October 1976.

It is ironic that an artist capable of recognizing and fostering the talents of young and old blues performers was not aware of what was trite or mediocre in her own compositions and performances. Nevertheless, Spivey perceived herself as the queen and carried herself with regal bearing on stage or off, wherever she held court with admirers. New York was her kingdom; she could still be found in the cabarets and clubs of Greenwich Village being entertained or entertaining during the 1970s. Having a ball was what life was all about for Spivey, so glamourous clothes and lively partying were her kind of action.

Alcoholism became a problem, and sometimes she vented her temper on anyone in her presence, no expletives deleted, but people liked her anyway. One reason was her generosity; she was always helping someone in show biz.[39] Her last major stage appearance was in a benefit she organized to raise funds for the ailing Mamie Smith in 1963. Although many performers appeared, Spivey, the queen, reigned supreme in her gold lamé gown—a veritable, finger-popping, dancing live wire having a ball, at age sixty.[40]

Blues were her business and Victoria Spivey devoted nearly sixty years of life to their development and promotion. She may not have been the queen but she surely was a crown princess. Her devotion to the blues inspired her to compose hundreds of songs, to seek out the best artists to perform with and to write about. She lived up to her words—

> The Blues is life and life is the Blues. It covers from the first cry of a newborn to the last gasp of a dying man. It's the very existence.[41]

6

"He Used to Be Your Man . . ."
But He's Edith Wilson's Now

He's crazy 'bout my loving and likes my jelly roll
I want to tell you and keep you told,
I'm little and lanky and built for speed,
I got all that a good woman needs.
He used to be your man but he's my man now.

By 1920, Perry Bradford had scored many more blues and vaudeville tunes since "Crazy Blues" had skyrocketed Mamie Smith to fame. On the side, "Mule" Bradford (so-called because he admittedly was stubborn) had been dabbling in writing for stage revues. For *Put and Take,* a revue that featured Mamie Smith, he wrote both music and lyrics. But a squabble between Bradford and Smith resulted in Mamie's leaving the show, to be replaced by Edith Wilson in early 1921. Her good looks, coupled with a classy act, must have attracted the "Mule," because he wanted her to record some of his blues, too.[1]

• •

22   EDITH WILSON PUBLICITY PHOTOGRAPH, c. 1930s

Put and Take reopened at Town Hall in New York and attracted talent scouts from Columbia, who found Wilson's singing to their liking. Hers was a finger-snapping swinging style that the "Saturday night revelers" danced to, to chase the blues away. She was brought into their studios on 13 September 1921 to record Bradford's "Nervous Blues," backed by Johnny Dunn and the Jazz Hounds. On 15 September she cut "Vampin' Liza Jane" and launched Columbia's entry into the race records market. It is interesting to note the apparent similarities between Wilson's and Smith's beginnings in the big time. Both struck Bradford as good talent to sell his songs. Both had vaudeville or cabaret experience with not only blues numbers, but also ballads, ditties, and some humorous tunes. Both were physically attractive, light complexioned, and charming. Their voices were light and torchy, not rich and rough-edged like the voices of Ma Rainey, Bessie Smith, and Clara Smith; in Wilson's or Mamie Smith's singing there is more sauciness or teasing as the voice quavers, sighs, and glides.

Wilson was a singer who sang rather than emoted; she enjoyed what her voice could do and did it. A blues song was a song, not her life story. There was weakness at the top of the range but a pleasing natural quality. Her supple mezzo-soprano voice was at its best in torchy blues (six-bar verse with refrain) rather than the traditional twelve or sixteen-bar blues sung by Bessie or Clara Smith. Although the lack of gripping emotional intensity led most critics to discount her as a blues singer, Wilson's singing satisfied the type of audiences for whom she sang—whites who frequented "sophisticated" Harlem cabarets run by the underworld mobsters. Perhaps the Okeh and Columbia scouts were attracted to qualities close to those of popular white singers such as Mildred Bailey. These qualities also fit the prevailing taste for the musical revues with both black and white audiences.

Noble Sissle and Eubie Blake's *Shuffle Along* hit Broadway in

1921 and set a precedent for musicals. No longer were bits and pieces of varying quality thrown together and characterized as a musical. *Shuffle Along,* with a book, music, and lyrics written especially for the show, had a cohesiveness not previously seen in black stage revues. Broadway had a new winner and blacks another opportunity for displaying their multitude of talents. Into this rich milieu came lovely Edith Wilson with all the requisites for stardom— beauty, great vocal talent, a flair for acting, charm, ambition, and a devilish sense of humor.

She worked hard and continuously to broaden her repertoire of songs, languages, and comedy routines in order to gain entry into musical revues, nightclubs here and abroad, and eventually films. Soon she earned star status in many of the black musical revues of the twenties. Her saucy, torchy blues renditions were juxtaposed with comedy skits and hot dance routines starring the legendary Florence Mills. Wilson's blues singing was often the only kind heard by the many whites and upwardly mobile blacks who attended the Broadway theaters and Harlem clubs such as Connie's Inn and the Plantation Inn. Her polished, upbeat versions of the blues transcended the race market and even traveled abroad.

Edith Goodall Wilson was born 6 September 1896 in Louisville, Kentucky, one of three children of Susan Jones Goodall, housekeeper, and Hundley Goodall, teacher.[2] They lived in a quiet neighborhood of neat cottages and well-kept yards.

> I lived in a row of seven cottages, just alike, you know. Everybody was friendly with each other, and if they got vegetables and got too many, somebody would say, "Hey, you want some string beans?" and give you some, or give you a head of cabbage.[3]

Take It Cause It's All Yours

By Gus Horsely

EDITH WILSON AND ORIGINAL JAZZ HOUNDS

Get This Number For Your Phonograph on Columbia Record No. A-3634

PUBLISHED BY

Perry Bradford

MUSIC PUB. CO.

1547 Broadway, N. Y. C.

PRINTED IN U. S. A.

Children played and studied together under the watchful eyes of all the adults on the block. Wilson's parents worked, but two aunts, one who lived with them and another who lived a few houses away, supervised them. Her aunt "stayed at home, took care of everybody, of the home and us kids, you know." Besides family,

> in the same block, you see, there were people. And everybody was friendly, and all the kids on the street played together. Everybody looked after everybody. "Miss So and So, will you notice Edith til I come back?" She not only noticed, she kept her eye on you. That happened in so many places in Louisville, until I think that was the reason [it was easier to raise kids].[4]

The church was the center of social activities in the community and nurtured young black talent.

> I was baptized when I was eleven. And we had choirs and meetings and we had to go to the library. . . . There were programs and recitals in churches and clubs. All those kinds of things are still going on there [Louisville]. And look at "Buck and Bubbles" from Louisville [showing a picture of the performers]. Oh, yes, when I got the picture they were little kids.
>
> They used to have little kids give shows and have all of them do different things, and all like that. Because I've been singing since I was two years old.[5]

"Buck and Bubbles" eventually became a highly acclaimed tap dancing comedy team. They were only two of the many talented

• •

23   SHEET MUSIC COVER FOR "TAKE IT CAUSE IT'S ALL YOURS," FEATURING EDITH WILSON AND THE ORIGINAL JAZZ HOUNDS

youngsters who thrived in the rich cultural environment in which Wilson was nurtured. Dickie Wells, jazz trombonist; Jonah Jones, trumpeter; John Wickley and his orchestra; and Elmo Dunn, drummer, were among the fine instrumentalists who hailed from the Derby City. Additionally, Louisville produced four outstanding female blues singers—Wilson, Helen Humes, Edmonia Henderson, and Sara Martin. Wilson credits Martin as one of the main influences on her career choice. Since Martin was about five or six years older than Wilson, she was already on stage by the time Wilson heard of her.

> I can't remember anybody much that was in show business that went to school with me, although Jonah [Jones] I knew because he lived around the corner from me. But not any of those people went into show business. Sara Martin did. But she started to make records, you know, and you see, I left Louisville so young . . .
>
> I didn't know [Sara Martin] very good, but I knew about her because she was singing back in Louisville, you know, about then. And the reason I knew about her at all is when I started to learn songs, this boy, Jimmy Clark, and his brother, Joe Clark, put on shows and Jimmy played piano. Well, they had people come over to their house and rehearse, and I used to go play with his sister, and I'd hear these people rehearsing, and that's how I heard Sara. And I used to go in after they left and imitate them, you know, singing songs and stuff. And that's how come I got started in the business, really, because Jimmy said to me, "You sound good, come in and let me get you a key." And I went in and he got me the key to songs, so after that, why, he used to come and ask me to sing.
>
> Then they were going to put on a show down at White City Park, and Joe was going to put the show on, so he asked me, "Will your mother let you work? If so, we'll take you down to work in the show with us."[6]

Jimmy Clark's question about her mother's approval illustrates black attitudes about the activities of young people, especially females. Wilson's parents were no exception. There was also a doting grandfather retired from the army after serving for years as Gen. Ulysses S. Grant's personal chef. (Wilson claimed that her great-grandfather was a vice president of the United States.) She remembers him as quite a character who lavished his daughters and grandchildren with goodies and clothing every payday.

> Why, he would come with shoes for whoever looked like they needed a pair. He knew everybody's size. And he'd come in with maybe two chickens, two rabbits, some flour and so on. He'd have his arms full. And I used to laugh, because he used to stumble on the top step, cabbages and rolls and things would fly every way. Yes, my grandfather was kind of over the whole thing [a patriarch].[7]

Another incident illustrates the regard in which good manners and proper behavior were held in that community. As small children often do, Wilson developed a liking for a neighbor who made delicious baked goods, cakes and cookies.

> I'd say, "Hardaway, got any cake?" through the fence to her. She wrapped pieces of cake and things, handed it over the fence to me, and I'd say, "Thank you." But when Mrs. Hardaway come around to our house—she was a real ugly woman, and you know how kids are. And [my mother would] say, "Give Hardaway a kiss." I said, "Uh-uh," and backed off, you know. So my mother said, "The idea of you eating her cake," and told me to give her a kiss. And so I just [spit] and my mother didn't wait to get a strap. We had a coal scuttle with a little shovel in it, and she grabbed my dress and made herself a handle [holding the dress tight] and she shovelled me up with the shovel and I took one of the worst whippings I ever got for being like that. "Long

as you live, don't you ever do anything like that because you don't like the looks of a person. What makes you think you look so much better than anybody else?" Oh, my mother just laid me out. And I was a kid, so that's the sort of thinking that prevailed, you know. And I think that when they would do something, they certainly got punished for it. And it made better people, I think.[8]

Wilson's parents wanted their two daughters and son to get as much education as possible while also learning to be courteous and helpful. School and church programs gave each child a chance to sing, play an instrument, or recite as parents looked on with pride. Sacrifices were made to pay for extra lessons: "[The people in the neighborhood] were all after something to help themselves."

Everybody who had children [would try to get them music lessons]. . . . There used to be a . . . teacher, maybe for fifty cents a lesson, would give them music. So of course, like, if you're living in the Bronx and there's four or five families in that block, why those families all would do little things for each other, and all the kids would want to go. And there's always somebody trying to learn something to advance themselves.[9]

Wilson and her peers were fully aware of the expectations of family, friends, and neighbors regarding appropriate behavior. So Jimmy and Joe Clark were not about to incur the wrath of Susan and Hundley Goodall by encouraging their daughter to participate in any activity of which they did not approve. How did the thirteen-year-old Edith manage to continue singing with the Clarks? By doing what most thirteen-year-olds would do—figuring out a story, lying, and saying a lot of prayers—not to get caught. She told the Clarks her mother did not mind and proceeded to plot her strategy.

I had learned the songs, and I was afraid to ask my mother, so I started to do lessons with a girlfriend of mine who lived just on the next block. And I told my mother if I wasn't home when she went to bed I would be over there, but I'd be home soon. And she went to bed two or three nights and didn't notice.

The youngster thought that her scheme was successful, but she misjudged her mother's watchfulness.

One night she had to go to the bathroom; she came into the room and I wasn't in the bed and it was nearly eleven o'clock! So the next day she said I could never go out no more. And so I went out in the woodshed and started crying because she was upsetting my plans, you know, I couldn't go out in the streets. And she said, "You're not quite thirteen years old, you think you can go in the street, nasty little pup. I can't have that. Working! What can you be doing? Working! At night?" And I said, "Yes, Mama, in a show. Jimmy and Joe Clark have a show down in White City and I was working in it." So she said, "Put your clothes on and I'm going to take you down and see what you do." [10]

A terrified youngster hurriedly dressed while fears of punishment and embarrassment streamed through her mind. As she walked, Susan Goodall was preparing a speech with which to castigate the Clark boys for misleading her young daughter. Neither mother nor daughter could have foreseen the results—mother expecting to end the matter right there, and daughter, hoping against hope, that a miracle would change her mother's mind. Wilson was breathless as she related what happened.

So we got down there; they wouldn't let us in because [my mother] didn't have a pass. So they sent for the manager, and the manager came and brought her a pass and he took her in and told her, "Come on in and look and see. This girl is a natural. She was born for what she's doing, and she's going to do it. If she has this much perseverance already, regardless of what happens here, she's going to do it. So you would do much better to go stay with her and watch over her and see what she's doing, because she's got natural-born talent."

Every night, nearly, when I'd sing my song I'd stop the show, so that give him the courage to tell her that I had too much on the ball for her to stop me. He said, "Because maybe she'll run off from you and you won't know where she is." So anyhow she waited until I got through and said, "Come on, we're going to walk home." While we were walking she said, "I don't understand this." And I said, "Well, I like it. And I make more money than you." She was working for a family and didn't make but seven dollars a week and I was going to make thirty-five dollars that week. I said, "I make enough money that I can buy clothes for me and my brother to go back to school." She said, "But will you promise me that you'll go back to school?" And I did, but I didn't stay long.[11]

Thirty-five dollars a week would add a lot to the income of the average American household in 1910 and even more so to a black one. Wilson also pandered to her mother's desire to see her educated when she promised to return to school. Eventually, she reneged on her promise because the excitement of the stage was too powerful for her to resist. Her destiny was firmly cast when Mrs. Goodall acquiesced to her singing ambitions. At the age of twelve or thirteen Wilson had already demonstrated a maturity and practicality that stood her well in the future.

When World War I ended, among the troops returning home were several fine musicians, including the already famous James Reese Europe and Will Vodery, as well as an unknown pianist, Danny Wilson. Though he was little known at the time, his piano playing took him from Charleston, South Carolina, to Louisville, where he and his sister, Lena, performed on the same bill as the young Edith Goodall. He backed his sister's singing with a mean piano, playing vamps, strides, and syncopated rags. Lena befriended Edith, took her under her wing, and helped her with her songs. When the Wilsons left for Chicago, Lena told Edith to drop in to see her the next time she visited her aunt who lived there. Edith soon finagled a visit so she could spend more time with Lena and Danny rehearsing songs. Danny played and encouraged them to learn many kinds of songs, not just the blues. Since he had trained at a conservatory in Charleston, he was a good teacher. When Danny was asked to travel with an orchestra to Milwaukee, Lena decided to leave the show. Danny had been walking Edith home every evening after the three of them had finished their rehearsals. She recounted those days this way:

> I used to go there to see [Lena] and then go back to my aunt's. I'd stay till about dark, and he'd say, "You have no business going out there to walk by yourself," and Lena would say, "You take her home." So he'd take me home and we used to walk and talk and everything. And that's how we got together.
>
> His band left for Milwaukee and Lena stayed here [Chicago] and entertained in a nightclub. So then after he left he said he had gotten so used to walking with me every day, he wanted me to walk the rest of my life with him. [12]

Susan Goodall must have expected this to happen because she arranged for Edith to stay in Milwaukee with her friend, Mrs. Warren, while Edith and Danny made arrangements to be married.

By the time they were married, the couple had developed a solid musical alliance. With Lena, they formed a trio and performed in small clubs and cabarets in Chicago. Chicago was teeming with black stage talent as the postwar boom sent another migratory wave of blacks to the cities. The Southside had the Pekin and Sunset cafés, the Monogram and Grand theaters, the Dreamland dance hall, and numerous smaller spots. Several artists were beginning their rise to stardom. Lucille Hegamin and Alberta Hunter charmed many a crowd at the Dreamland with their crooning songs and luscious looks. Louis Armstrong and King Oliver blasted their cornets with new rhythms and wails, while Lil Hardin and Lovie Austin proved that women pianists and composers could play with the best jazz musicians around.

Danny Wilson knew that it was a tough business so he gave his wife the professional training that enabled her to compete. "My husband made me learn all kinds of songs. Not to be no blues singer, be a singer. He made me learn 'I'm Always Chasing Rainbows' and like that."[13] That training gave the trio the reputation it needed to move out of the small-time cabarets in Chicago to Thomas's club in Washington, D.C. in early 1921. From there they went to Rafe's Paradise in Atlantic City and then to New York City where they encountered the already famous Perry Bradford.

Columbia hired Edith Wilson to record for them in September 1921. Johnny Dunn and the Original Jazz Hounds backed her, and Danny was at the piano on several of the early Columbia sides. Her recordings reveal a mature performer with immense poise and professionalism. "Nervous Blues" does not send the listener moaning and groaning, but tapping and finger-snapping. Her creole-type yodel on "Nervous Blues" and "Wicked Blues" add an unusual and unexpected twist to otherwise undistinguished lyrics and melodies.

> Now, I've got the wicked blues,
> Since my baby went away.
> If I thought he loved me too,
> I would've asked him to stay.
>
> I'll buy a gun long as my right arm,
> Shoot everybody done me any wrong
> Now, I am all confused, 'cause I got the wicked blues.

Ee yoo, ee yoo, ee yoo, ee yoo.
Now I've got the wicked blues, etc.[14]

Thus began Wilson's recording career as a single.

Shortly after "Nervous Blues" and "Vampin' Liza Jane" were released, she hit the road on the TOBA circuit.[15] Billed as "Queen of
the Blues," Wilson worked the big theaters such as the Standard in
Philadelphia. Bradford supplied the songs and the backup of the
"Original Jazz Hounds." In fact, the first recording ads stated, "You
all know the Original Jazz Hounds formerly with Mamie Smith, on
the Okeh. Well, they were with Edith. And Johnny Dunn, that sensa-
tional cornet player that knows just what to do with Jazz and Blues
and how to cook it to make it taste nice."[16]

The lyrics, rhythm, and style of "Nervous Blues," "Vampin' Liza
Jane," and "Old Time Blues" are typical of Bradford's upbeat dance
tunes. They were all used in *Put and Take*. That probably accounts for
Wilson's highly charged renditions. Images of fast-stepping chorus
girls emerge when one listens to "Old Time Blues." The instrumental work between Dunn, Garvin Bushnell on clarinet, and Dope Andrews on trombone, does fairly cook as they bounce the improvised
melodies among themselves. The trombone melodies slide up and
down between a rapid-fire staccato from the cornet, and, underneath it all, the bouncy rhythms of John Mitchell's banjo and Danny
Wilson's piano sizzle. These tunes as originally sung and played are
danceable, cheery, and just plain fun.

For Wilson, they were a medium in which to perform. If the public enjoyed them she sang them. Only when the lyrics were extremely raunchy or distasteful, she said, did she draw the line—as
she once did when performing in Atlantic City.

> . . . we were working there, and the girls who sang the double en-
> tendre songs went off for some new club opening, and they over-
> stayed their time. And so these people liked these dirty songs, the

Try This On Your Piano

Nervous Blues

By PERRY BRADFORD
Writer of: Crazy Blues

Chorus

You can nev-er tell, — whats on a fel-lows mind may be lov-in and he's quit-tin all the time Tell me hon-ey Ba - by I would like to know, Let me know why you treat me so gee I'm ner-vos — And I'm all — con-

For Sale By All Dealers

girls used to open their legs and put it on the table and pick up money with it. And of course, I was disgusted about it. And so I told the owner I don't sing these kinds of songs and do these kinds of things. So this night, a lot of people came in the club and he said, "Well, these girls are nice and they don't sing those songs, these are my pretty girls." When the other girls came back someone told them what the manager said. I overheard them telling him he didn't need us because we couldn't keep the crowd. So I told my husband, "Give him notice." We beat him to the punch and quit.[17]

Time may have clouded Wilson's recollection, as well as her perception of her earlier work, because several of her recordings, such as "He May Be Your Man" and "My Handy Man" use the typical double entendre lyrics.

> He don't perform his duties like he used to do,
> He never holds my ashes 'less I tell him to.
> Before he hardly gets to work, he says he's through.
> My Handy Man ain't handy no more.[18]

She, Josephine Beatty [Alberta Hunter], Josie Miles, and Mattie Hite were noted for their ribald lyrics, according to Paul Oliver.[19] Such songs were Wilson's specialty when she opened at the Cotton Club in 1925. She did comedy skits in addition to performing the "adult songs" which were a must in the club's format.[20]

Columbia produced no more than thirty-two Wilson recordings, of which only twenty-six were issued. "Mammy, I'm Thinking of You" is the epitome of the blackface minstrel song, down to "darkies picking cotton" in a monologue recited in the middle of the record-

• •

24   EXCERPT FROM THE SCORE OF PERRY BRAD-
      FORD'S "NERVOUS BLUES"

ing. Selections like these were still in the repertoire of most vaudeville singers, as were the use of blackface, bandannas, and plantations in production numbers, and Wilson did not exhibit any greater
race consciousness than most of the performers of her era. The dilemma for many performers in the early 1920s, as well as today, was
the need to draw large audiences by presenting material that was
appealing to both blacks and whites. The race records were aimed
toward Blacks, but the musical revues were directed toward whites.
The music, costumes, skits, and dances, therefore, often catered to
whites' tastes for plantation stereotypes.

One of Wilson's first stage triumphs came in a revue set in "The
Dixieland Plantation Room" of the refurbished Winter Garden, a
Broadway theater that was the former home of the Folies Bergère.
Lou Selwyn and Lew Leslie staged scenes of a Mississippi steamboat
landing with a cotton field in the background bordered with water-
melons, cut and whole on the vine. The material was created by
Russell Robinson, Roy Turk, and Perry Bradford. Entertainment
entirely by "colored artists" featured Edith Wilson and the Jazz
Hounds, the Strut Payne Quartette, Chappelle and Stinette, and
Florence Mills and U.S. "Kid" Thompson of the *Shuffle Along* show.
Admission was on a membership basis with a two-dollar cover
charge. The food served matched the scenery—Southern dishes
were featured.[21] This show was so popular that it moved to Harlem's
Lafayette Theatre for a few weeks. Mills became a star in her own
right after "The Plantation Revue," and quickly moved to top billing
over Wilson.

During this very active period in 1922, Wilson cut most of the
sides issued by Columbia. Because her stage success was building
rapidly, she did not seem especially concerned about her recording
career. She remembered why she took it so matter-of-factly, however, as she explained the financial arrangements she chose for
herself.

Old Perry Bradford, I was hired by him. And I got 125 [dollars] to make the record. And, of course, in that time it was a lot of money. . . . [22]

I worked here, worked there, so I didn't sign up with anybody that was going to guarantee me. . . . The man who had Louis Armstrong, he tried to get me to sign with him and I wouldn't sign up with nobody, because I might get $250 for this job, and another man over here, he'd give $350. . . . I didn't know how long this show was going to last, so I'd just go working for a show because I'm contracted to work for the show and when that closed down, I'm through with them. [23]

In retrospect, the money Wilson earned at Columbia, a mere $3,250, was peanuts compared to the royalties that Bradford and other composers received for their songs; on the other hand, $125 was a large sum for a few hours' work at that time. To her credit, Wilson was eager to learn and willing to strive for a professional performance.

"The Plantation Revue" gave Wilson the opportunity to develop her skills as a comedienne and she polished them to near perfection. She subsequently appeared at Connie's Inn, the Lafayette Theatre, the Lincoln Theatre, and other New York cabarets in a variety of song and comedy skits. By 1923, "The Plantation Revue," rewritten and restyled into the musical comedy *Dover Street to Dixie* and starring Florence Mills, was booked for Europe. Mills, the darling of Broadway, headed a cast of singers, dancers, and comedians. Wilson was featured in slapstick comedy skits, as well as solo and duo vocal numbers. Wilson was cast as a combative wife in one comedy skit and sang an up-tempo blues in another scene. The cast was showered with accolades by Londoners, who were enamored of black music and entertainment. Parties were thrown by members of the London social set for the cast and other black entertainers working in England. Jazz music and black showpeople were quickly becoming de rigueur in Europe. Wilson's swinging blues style was great accompaniment for dancing the fox-trot and other hot dances which Irene and Vernon Castle had introduced to Europe's upper class just before the war.

Skin color was a major factor in the selection of females for singing and dancing roles in the revues that went on Broadway and the West End or to the fancy clubs like Connie's Inn and the Cotton Club. "High yaller" was a badge of beauty blacks valued. Those who were not born with it used cosmetics to whiten up. Wilson and Mills both were fair-skinned and the subject of speculation in London. As reported in the black press, the specter of racism haunted these and other artists in subtle ways.

> London, England. So great a success has Florence Mills created here in the musical comedy, "Dover Street to Dixie," that her reviewer . . . decided she is not colored. He adds, "To call them Negro would not in this case be correct, though perhaps a few members of Vodery's clever Plantation Orchestra show the pure characteristics of the race. Certainly Florence Mills and Edith Wilson and the "Dixie Vamps" in particular could easily pass in any Southern European country without being recognized as belonging to the aborigine race of Africa, which is so rapidly and rightly emancipating itself to the higher levels of Caucasian culture." [24]

On her return to the States in 1924, Wilson was featured in the "Club Alabam Revue" at the Lafayette Theatre in New York. The revue had attracted a wide audience at the Broadway cabaret of the same name before moving to the Lafayette for a two-week run. Fletcher Henderson and his orchestra had been playing for the revue at the Club Alabam and moved with it to the theater. This show was the beginning of Wilson's partnership with "Doc" Straine, a dancer who had already built a reputation as the male half of another comedy team on the vaudeville circuit. They continued their stage alliance for two years, garnering good press as a comedy team. J. A. "Billboard" Jackson praised " . . . Edith Wilson, the girl who with 'Doc' Straine has presented vaudeville with one of the few hit team acts of the season. She is singing at the Cotton Club, and taking an occasional fling into a metropolitan vaudeville date, when the price is right."[25] Her philosophy on business transactions is revealed again in that phrase "when the price is right." She asserted her independence and kept her career on track by seizing the opportunities which not only gave her good salaries but also favorable exposure. She signed on as a single at the Cotton Club, but also worked as part of a team when it proved profitable. She and "Doc" Straine eventually took their act on the road a few times during 1924–25, appearing at the Strand Theatre, Philadelphia; the Palace, in Pittsfield, Massachusetts; the Koppin, Detroit; the Orpheum, Boston; and the State Theatre, Chicago; as well as New York City theaters.[26]

Although the bulk of her Columbia output occurred in 1921–22, prior to her London engagement, she resumed recording with them in 1924. The band personnel had changed somewhat to include Elmer Chambers, cornet; Teddy Nixon, trombone; Don Redman, clarinet; Fletcher Henderson, piano; and Charlie Dixon, banjo. She later recorded two sides with "Doc" Straine, "It's Gonna Be a Cold, Cold Winter" and "There'll Be Some Changes Made."[27] They were her last on the Columbia label. By that time Bessie Smith and Clara Smith were Columbia's big drawing cards with a more traditional type of blues singing that attracted a large segment of the race market, whereas Wilson's stylized cabaret singing appealed to the moneyed, predominantly white patrons who frequented the Broadway houses. White singers such as Mildred Bailey and Blossom Seeley, however, were the choice of record companies for the white record buyer.

● ●

25   (*Overleaf*) INTERIOR OF CONNIE'S INN IN HARLEM

Wilson astutely followed her husband's earlier advice about acquiring versatility and worked toward that goal. It paid off during that decade because she remained active in both vaudeville and musical revues. She opened with Florence Mills in a new Lew Leslie production, *Dixie to Broadway*. The Bill Vodery band backed the cast, which included "Bass" Lawson, Billy Mills, Henry Winfrey, and "Slow Kid" Thompson, Mills's dancer husband.[28] *Blackbirds,* another musical revue starring Mills, went abroad in 1926, playing in Paris and London. Wilson was reported to be a big drawing card when they played the London Pavilion Theatre; yet, she had to confront problems with her contract and on stage. In one incident she claimed that Leslie was not fair with her casting or placement.

> When we went to London, Florence had signed up with Leslie and I wouldn't sign nothing. And she was getting a guarantee of $1,000 a week at that time. Why, I wasn't getting anything like that, so anyhow, when I got there on opening night, the first night the critics come and everything, I got ready to go on, and my number had been taken out. I was singing "He May Be Your Man" then. So I was furious. So I went to Mr. Leslie and told him, "Give me my passport!" They took your passports up, you know. I said, "Give me my passport and fare home. There was no need for me to come over here if I couldn't be seen by the critics. I have just as much right to be seen as any of these other people in this show. You didn't need me for that, you don't need me for nothing! Anybody here can be what else I was doing." I raised sand.[29]

Note that her concern was about her singing, not about the comedy routines. She perceived herself as Edith Wilson, vocalist, not a "singing comedienne," as she was portrayed by the Columbia record company and other promoters. She expected her reviews to be based mainly on her singing, not on her skits, which "anybody here can do." She reacted strongly when that image was threatened. The control of her career had to be in her hands even though she used materials that others selected for her.

Despite those unpleasant moments, Wilson enjoyed performing in *Blackbirds,* which ran from June 1926 through January 1927. As was the custom, many parties were given to fête the cast. One was thrown by Mills at the home of a wealthy British bachelor, Guy Robson. The highlight of the affair was a brief musical program by cast members. Mills and Ivan Browning began with "Love Will Find a Way" from the Sissle and Blake hit *Shuffle Along.* Negro spirituals by a trio were followed by Wilson's two numbers, which "rocked the house"; a recitation and songs from *Blackbirds* by Ada Ward, and finally specialty numbers by Layton and Johnstone. Among the guests was Lena Wilson, who had left her Greenwich Village cabaret act to join Edith.[30] When the show closed Wilson remained abroad to perform in several European cities. Paris adored her and she responded by quickly learning French songs to include in her program. As with Josephine Baker and Alberta Hunter, Paris welcomed the "colored chanteuse" with her naughty lyrics and impertinent humor.

Back in New York, Wilson worked as a single at Loew's State Theatre and the Cotton Club. The Cotton Club, which by then was nicknamed "Club Richman of Harlem" was featuring Ada Ward, the "colored Sophie Tucker," and Wilson, both late of *Blackbirds.* By then Duke Ellington's was established as the house band, with weekly broadcasts on the CBS radio network. On some of these Wilson sang. Though she had no hit records, she was being heard by a large radio audience.

In the Big Apple, "Club Richman," and Connie's Inn had blacks who imitated whites who imitated blacks; Sophie Tucker and Frankie Masters's Orchestra imitated blacks for white audiences at Chicago's Tivoli; and Jules Bledsoe, Alberta Hunter, and Paul Robeson acted as southern blacks in *Showboat* for whites in London.[31] The whole scenario was a twentieth-century version of the minstrelsy farce of the nineteenth century except that this time blacks were gaining more experience and exposure. Also, there was a large black audience to which they could turn for revalidation.

Wilson, like many of the entertainers who earned their living in a white world, reaffirmed their allegiance to the black community by performing in black theaters as frequently as possible or in benefit performances for various charitable causes. One such show raised funds for a home for indigent performers. A star-studded slate appeared—Ted Lewis; "Buck and Bubbles"; Fess Williams and His Royal Flush Orchestra from the famous Savoy Ballroom; Charles Gilpin, Shelton Brooks, and the Hall Johnson Singers; Fletcher Henderson, Edith Wilson, and Ada Ward from the Cotton Club; Leonard Harper and his Connie's Inn Revue; Will Marion Cook, Joe Jordan, and Tim Brynm as conductors; and Eddie Cantor, Jack Osterman, and Jack Pearl as masters of ceremonies.

Another benefit gala that presented the cream of the New York stage, both black and white, was the big NAACP All-Star Concert, 17 December 1929, at the Forrest Theatre. Clifton Webb, Alberta Hunter, Duke Ellington, George Gershwin, Clara Smith, Beatrice Lillie, and Edith Wilson were only a few of the galaxy of stage and screen stars. Mayor Jimmy Walker, James Weldon Johnson, J. Rosamond Johnson, Mary White Ovington, Dr. Adam Clayton Powell, Sr., and the Paul Robesons were among the luminaries in the audience. Wilson probably sang only one or two numbers at those affairs but her sincere concern for helping those less fortunate than she eventually led her into full-time work for charitable causes in the late 1940s.[32]

In 1928, she performed with Sam Wooding's Orchestra in the Creole Revels musical at the Lafayette Theatre. Later that year they toured Europe under the title Sam Wooding's "Chocolate Kiddies" in *The Black Revue*. Wilson remained in Paris as a single for a while, appearing at Chez Florence Jones Cabaret.[33] Tragedy struck while

she was abroad when her husband, Danny, back in the States, became fatally ill with tuberculosis. At the time of his illness he was
collaborating with Andy Razaf on some songs. Death came at the
end of a day full of work and partying with friends. Fortunately,
Lena and her husband were still living in New York so when the
young widow went back there, they comforted her.[34]

Wilson returned to Connie's Inn in a starring role in *Hot Chocolates,* which later moved to Broadway's Hudson Theatre and great
success. After five months it was still going strong with a lively cast
featuring "Baby" Cox, Jazzlips Richardson, and Louis Armstrong.
When the Roseland Ballroom celebrated its tenth anniversary in
September 1929, the revue cast participated in the evening's entertainment.[35] That year, Wilson, Armstrong, and Thomas "Fats" Waller
were billed as "The Thousand Pounds of Harmony" in *Hot Chocolates.*[36] One of Wilson's numbers was Waller's "What Did I Do to Be
So Black and Blue," which she recorded on the Brunswick Label.
That was the only recording she cut for them. In fact, three record-
ings in 1930 on the RCA Victor label with Bubber Miley and his
Mileage Makers were her last until a 1972 album with Eubie Blake.

The waning of the recording industry's quest for blues singers
during the 1920s did not adversely affect Wilson's career because
she had steadily developed herself as a stage artist. Her ability to
adapt quickly to new trends kept her going throughout the Depression. When big bands became popular in cabarets, she was right
there with the popular songs at her command. As might be expected, less money flowed into the productions staged in the early
1930s and their quality declined as a result. *Hot Rhythm* was one of
those disasters that attempted to profit from the tried and true for-
mula of the "colored revue." It opened to poor notices: "an average
Harlem cabaret floor transported to a downtown theater without
much success. . . . All [numbers] of which have been used . . . so
many times . . . that they are no longer novel."[37] Robert Littel of the
New York World summed it up this way: "Negro music and dancing

have had an enormous effect on our song and dance shows. Yet
most of these Colored revues . . . are in turn reflecting not the native Negro product, but the white Broadway reflection of it, which
may be one reason why . . . shows like 'Hot Rhythm' are also so
stale . . . and imitative and unattractive."[38] Once more black stage
folk were caught in a creative bind because they did not control the
pursestrings. In their efforts to appeal to white theater patrons they
fell into the trap of mediocrity, and the only profiters were Broadway producers trying to make a fast buck.

Survival was the key word for Wilson. She created her own revue,
which had a brief run at New York's Alhambra Theatre in 1930.[39] She
sailed again for Europe and had a successful engagement at Paris'
"L'Ange Blue." The Montparnasse club welcomed the beauty with
the velvet tones and dancing feet.[40] The smoky dimlit cabaret, the
haunt of many Americans abroad, was a perfect backdrop for her
renditions of French love songs and American popular songs.

The big bands were reviving the cabarets and ballrooms in Harlem
by the time Wilson returned to New York. The economy was looking
more hopeful as Roosevelt implemented his New Deal. Black play-
wrights, poets, and actors found new opportunities through the Fed-
eral Theatre and Writers' projects and the black community saw a
return of many of its fine artists to stages within its own boundaries.
Connie's Inn, Small's Paradise, the Lenox Inn, and the Cotton Club
still gave variety shows but the centerpiece now was usually a big
band such as those of Duke Ellington, Cab Calloway, Chick Webb,
Andy Kirk, Tiny Bradshaw, or Billy Bailey and her Chicago Rhythm
Girls.[41]

In between engagements at some of the night spots Wilson signed
on with more revues, which received mixed notices.

New York Sees 1932 Edition [of *Shuffle Along*]
And Raves Second Time[42]

OLD CAST BACK WITH NEW SHOW

You'll like "Shuffle Along" as it is offered at the Illinois theatre. . . . but you'll hardly rave over it as you did ten years ago. . . . The chorus is good and so is Miss Wilson but, all told, the singing is just so-so.[43]

Although she did well, the shows were not as exciting. They just exploited talent such as Wilson's without designing a good book and score and paying for a good cast and production.

"Hummin" Sam shuffled into town . . . and ere this review is in print more than likely will have passed like John Henry "down the line" and away from the New Yorker theatre where it first saw the light of Broadway. . . . It aped everything that was bad in the theater that white folks do. . . . It miscast and misdirected what secondhand ideas it had. . . . It was . . . not Broadway material, and would have languished even at the Lafayette in friendly hands.[44]

The era of the fabulous black revue had ended and so had the careers of most of their casts—no more money for "shuffling darkies," plantation jokes, and boisterous skits. Wilson battled to keep her career afloat by grabbing every legitimate offer that she felt qualified to fill, but it was tough for black entertainers to find work outside the black community. When Lew Leslie tried his hand at another edition of *Blackbirds,* away she flew with the troupe to Europe. *Play Bill Theatre World,* February 1935, cited *Blackbirds of 1935* as the Play of the Month at the London Coliseum. Wilson was said to be "a prime favorite of earlier coloured revues, . . . a tower of strength on the comedy side."[45] After a breathing spell of a few months in Chicago she was back in Harlem at the Apollo Theatre, trucking and singing. Except for intermittent appearances with bands such as Sissle's and Calloway's, she found steady employment elusive. Finally, Broadway began to close ranks against black performers. The big bands of Sissle, Calloway, Basie, and others were losing ground to Benny Goodman, Artie Shaw, and Paul Whiteman. Fletcher Henderson was moved from Benny Goodman's bandstand as pianist to the background as arranger. Wilson was one of the losers also, when her appearance at Billy Rose's Diamond Horseshoe with Sissle was cancelled in favor of an all-white cast. Offered a stint on the West Coast, she took it.[46] Wilson, Hegamin, Spivey, and Waters were among the few blues singers who ventured beyond the Midwest during that time.

For the first time, Los Angeles would see those sparkling eyes and that mischievous smile as she sang one of her favorites, "He May Be Your Man, But He Comes to See Me Sometimes." She worked the Orpheum and Bert Levy circuits while out west, covering Los Angeles, San Francisco, Denver, Seattle, Salt Lake City, and some cities in Canada.[47] The press hailed her as "a blues singer of international reputation . . . one of the leading lights in Lew Leslie's *Blackbirds*."[48]

At this juncture in the 1940s, her career took on an added dimension when she obtained a few minor film roles. Fluency in other languages was an achievement of which Wilson was very proud and she expressed great disappointment when the role she had in *To Have and Have Not,* the Bacall-Bogart classic, was deleted.

> I had a small part in *To Have and Have Not* because I could speak French, you know. But after they finished making the movie they cut out my scenes and put it in English.[49]

Other acting roles were on radio in the notoriously stereotypical *Amos and Andy* as Kingfish's mother-in-law and in *The Great Gildersleeve;* and as the voice of "Aunt Jemima" on the Breakfast Club show.[50]

By the end of the 1940s Edith had shifted most of her time and energy to the Aunt Jemima role. She retired from the stage and toured the United States raising funds for charities with Quaker Oats's "Aunt Jemima" Pancakes. Although many blacks criticized her for her portrayal of what some perceived as a negative "mammy" stereotype, Wilson did not agree. As in earlier years, she saw it as just another job and a role to play, not a depiction of herself or anybody else. She happily donned her bandanna, white blouse, big checkered skirt and apron, and sang and flipped pancakes from coast-to-coast, raising upwards of three million dollars. She also trained other women for the role. Pressure from civil rights groups caused the Quaker Oats company to halt the Aunt Jemima appearances in 1965. Wilson's contract with the pancake company ended a year later.[51] She herself insisted that her work accomplished more good than she was given credit for.[52]

Millard Wilson was one of the many people she met while living on the West Coast. They were married in 1947 and enjoyed a comfortable loving relationship until her death in 1981. Moving back to Chicago in the fifties, Wilson became active in civic and cultural activities. She was an active member of the Chicago chapter of the National Association of Negro Musicians, guest artist for Annual Black History programs in local churches and community organizations, and a member of the Friday Jazz Club.

In the 1960s, the blues and folk revival presented new opportunities for Wilson, so she came out of semiretirement to sing again. Her voice was smoky and deeper, tempered by time and age with elegant shading and phrasing. She was in much demand at major folk festivals throughout the 1970s and never disappointed her young audiences. They wanted blues; she sang them: "My Handy Man Ain't Handy No More," "He May Be Your Man," "Frankie," "Rules and Regulations, Signed Razor Jim," and more. She often updated some of the lyrics to squeeze laughs from the crowd but she never compromised the quality of her performances.

Poor health slowed her down in the latter part of the 1970s but did not stop her because she had two driving ambitions—to sing until she could not sing anymore and to build a home for indigent showpeople. She fervently said:

> I want to have a place where I can have musicians and entertainers, something like they were my children, to enjoy a home. [This woman] said "I came by to see you, because I've seen you on the air and I just loved you . . . here's my card, I'm going to talk to my husband and I would like to have a surprise for you when you come over tomorrow." Next morning when I got up my boss called and asked if I was going and I said "Yes, I'm going. Take me, aren't you?"
>
> So we went over to her home, and she said, "We have some property down here and after you said you would like to do to help people, I told my husband I would like to give you some of this property." She had gone down and paid the taxes, and paid up anything that was due on it, and they gave me the title clear free.[53]

Wilson explained how she hoped to get other musicians to help her finance her project.

> Count Basie and different others once said when they played in Miami they would come down and give me a day's work there and if they have some time off they'll train in the school. And with this little thing in the center, where I'll rent the stores out, that will keep me in money to help pay bills.
>
> Star Haven, that is the name. The builders already know what I

want to call it. I hope I live long enough to see it finished and see it accomplish what I would like to have for us performers. Like some girl who's been in show business all the time, who, when winter comes can't stay in the cold, that she could come and spend two months with us.[54]

Two phrases—"us performers" and "some girl who's been in show business all the time"—reveal the source of her inspiration and her identification with others like herself who were still working but would need a haven for rest and rejuvenation.

At eighty-one Wilson was still crediting her versatility for her success, but she was not boastful about it.

I'm very thankful that I had as much success as I did have, and it hasn't died out yet. Because I'm more thankful now because of my age. Everybody else is floundering out, or forgotten entirely. And I still get write-ups and things like that.

All the musicians, say the veterans . . . we meet every Friday afternoon at noon and have a little jazz session. Then seven or eight will play and so on, and the emcee will see me and I'll do a number. And I've gotten jobs out of that.

I've worked with different bands, all over, . . . I go around several places around town and I get a job here and a job there. I work every week or so. As long as I'm able to walk, I can sing, and I intend to do that.[55]

Backed by a jazz combo with "Little Brother" Montgomery at the piano, she romped through some blues and jazz classics on her 1976 album on Delmark Records with an ease that belied her age. The mischievousness was still there in a voice that was mellow and darker. In the late 1970s that elegant older lady, clad in purple chiffon with matching turban, sang blues and ballads in a Chicago

Northside lounge as often as they called her, thoroughly enjoying herself just like the patrons. In 1978, she sparkled in red lace and rhinestones, exchanging repartee with "Little Brother" as they conducted a workshop for enthralled university students. This, despite the need for a pacemaker to aid her ailing heart. She told the students what the blues meant but made it clear that she did not just sing the blues, she sang beautiful songs, whatever appealed to her: "Smoke Gets in Your Eyes," or "St. Louis Blues."[56]

When we compare Wilson's and Wallace's careers, we can discern how race subtly shaped their development as artists and, subsequently, their success over time. Black audiences and record buyers were the mainstay for Wallace, but Wilson could attract both blacks and whites in her cabaret and revue appearances. Whereas Wallace's live performances were mainly solo, not as a part of an act or revue, Wilson's varied. Also, Wallace toured on the TOBA, which emphasized black acts for black audiences; Wilson switched to the Keith and Orpheum circuits, which booked into more white than black theaters.

The contrast in the life styles and vocal styles of the two women is evident in their approach to their music and the avenues they pursued in the mid and later years of their careers. These held true when they worked together as artists-in-residence at the University of Maryland in 1978. Wallace's directness and earthiness when she sang and spoke to the students led many of them to gather around her to talk about life as if she were their grandmother. Wilson was just as warm and open as Wallace, but she was also very conscious of how she chose her words when responding to questions or comments. To the students she was an artist, not the grandmother next door. These characteristics were a part of their performances also when they presented a joint concert with Montgomery at the piano—Wallace singing from the deepest parts of her soul, Wilson entertaining with voice, eyes, hands, and even a few quick dance steps. The concert was not only remarkable but equally moving as both performed with the assurance of veteran performers.

The 1980 Newport Jazz Festival honored her, Sippie Wallace, and other blues singers; and she responded with "He May Be Your Man" and brought the house down.[57] Edith Wilson came to prominence in the "classic" blues era but she outlived it and sang as long as she could walk. She died of a brain tumor in March 1981. Star Haven, unrealized, will have to wait for another dedicated dreamer.

To the World's greatest ~~par~~
meaning everybody's dar~~
"Jerry"
Sincerely "Alberta"

She's Got a Mind to Ramble: Alberta Hunter

I got a mind to ramble but I don't know where to go.
Yes, I got a mind to ramble, ooo, but I don't know where to go.
If I'm lucky enough to leave here, I sho' ain't coming back no mo'!

Folks, I ain't got a crying penny, my poor feet are on the ground.
And if I ever want to be somebody I sho' got to leave this town.

Finger-popping, toe-tapping, and no time for foolishness! She stood tall, all five feet, two inches of her, put her hands on her hips, and belted out "I Got a Mind to Ramble" and the audience was convinced that no grass grew under her feet. Attractively attired in a stylish dress, with brightly painted nails and big dangling earrings, "Alberta 'Grandmama' of the Blues" defied age just as a spacecraft defies gravity.[1] The eighty-two-year-old singer enraptured a crowd of worshippers as she effortlessly moved from blues to French cabaret songs, or to an old favorite like "Love Will Find a Way" from Sissle and Blake's *Shuffle Along*. She was peppy and flip, rolling her

• •

eyes in a mocking manner, ad-libbing between lines, having a ball every minute. The Cookery in Greenwich Village was her temple, and the priestess resided over the evening's activities with the finesse derived from a lifetime of "rambling"—moving on to bigger and better things.

Alberta Hunter was the epitome of the cabaret singer of the late 1910s and 1920s, suave, attractive, body draped in satin, and singing songs that ranged from the sultry and smoldering to the ribald. Her sophisticated, swinging, bold style bristled with the assertiveness of a liberated city woman. It was a wonderful mixture of vaudeville brass, plaintive blues, and danceable fox-trots. Her voice had a rich quavering quality that bordered on a cry, especially at the top. She paid close attention to the vocal and emotional elements in her lyrics, which she delivered with crisp enunciation, punctuated on occasion with spoken ad libs like, "Play that thing, all right now, ye-es." Her ability to shift moods easily from the blues to a dance tune to an ingenue rendition such as "Sugar" by Fats Waller, was the hallmark of her versatility as an artist. She made over one hundred recordings on various labels including Black Swan, Paramount, Okeh, RCA Victor, Columbia, Prestige, and Riverside. On the Harmograph, Silvertone, Gennett, Buddy, and Puritan labels she recorded under various psuedonyms: May Alix, Helen Roberts, Josephine Beatty, or Alberta Prime.[2] Her experiences in the cabarets of Chicago and New York, and later, Europe, helped build her career to include recordings, musicals, plays, radio, and some film work. Hunter performed continuously from about 1912 until a self-imposed hiatus in the mid-fifties, followed by the triumphant comeback described above in 1977 at the age of eighty-two.

Hunter was born 1 April 1895, one of the four children of Laura and Charles Hunter of Memphis. Her earliest experiences with music were in elementary school.[3] Around 1907, she ran away to Chicago, where she eventually began singing professionally. Many accounts of Hunter's childhood adventures appeared in magazines and news-papers when she returned to an active singing career at age eighty-two. Though there is minor disagreement over the details, there is a consistency between the 1970s versions and stories that appeared twenty years earlier.[4]

An active, precocious youngster, Hunter was not unique in her desire to travel and see the world beyond Memphis. Black children were going to school in large numbers for the first time and were sensitive to the changes affecting their elders. The concept of unre-stricted travel and opportunities "up North" appealed to youngsters like her. At age eleven, Hunter concluded that Chicago would pro-vide all that for her if she could just find a way to get there.

If I'm lucky enough to leave here, I sho' ain't coming back no mo'.[5]

Hunter was an enterprising, self-confident youngster who loved to sing and received encouraging comments from family and friends. Judging from her height as an adult she must have been tiny for her age, but she made up for height in courage. She learned the songs her grandmother sang, or those she heard on the popular piano rolls found in many stores. One day on her way to the store with fifteen cents to purchase bread, she met her schoolteacher, Mrs. Florida Cummings-Elgerton. As they walked and talked, the older woman invited Alberta to go with her to Chicago. Hunter's eyes lit up and wheels began spinning in her head.

I got a mind to ramble but I don't know where to go.[6]

Now she had a destination. She had heard her mother mention that singers could earn ten dollars a week in Chicago. And here was Mrs. Cummings going to that wonderful city! Supposedly, the teacher had a child's pass that was not going to be used and told Alberta she could ride on it if her mother gave permission. As might be expected, the fifteen cents, the bread, and the truth were immediately forgotten, for Alberta had only one thought,

> If I ever want to be somebody, I sho' got to leave this town.[7]

She made a swift run around the corner and waited long enough to convince the teacher that she was obtaining her mother's approval for the trip. After the appropriate amount of time had elapsed, she sped back to the station, eager to begin her journey to fortune and fame. She left behind her widowed mother, two sisters, and her grandmother, who said Alberta was born to be a wanderer.[8] An unwitting Mrs. Cummings had in the tiny package seated next to her on the train a future international star.

Quick-witted, adventurous, perseverant, and spunky describe the enterprising youngster who arrived in Chicago with no one awaiting her. As she and Mrs. Cummings boarded a streetcar heading for the Southside she had to figure out where Helen Winston, a friend of her mother, lived. Alberta gazed out the windows, her eyes searching furtively for the Winston address. Fate was with her: she spied the number and jauntily hopped down from the car waving goodbye to Mrs. Cummings and her husband. Little did they know that she was arriving unexpected. But Helen Winston welcomed the girl, gave her lodging, and helped her find a job. She peeled potatoes for Winston's employer, earning six dollars a week plus room and board. Her family did not locate her for about two years, but then they decided to let her stay.

At age fifteen, Hunter tried to find a job as a singer by giving her age as eighteen. On their days off, Winston and Hunter went from one place to another, and the pert youngster would warble "Where the River Shannon Flows." Much to her chagrin, the proprietors would hustle them out with admonitions about her age and the trouble it would bring if the police found out. Theirs was a valid concern because Chicago was plagued with the problems arising from very young girls being hired to sing and play in brothels and sleazy clubs.

Finally, Winston and Hunter contrived a costume that disguised her age more effectively and they made the rounds again. Dago Frank's, a hangout for prostitutes and pimps, was reportedly seeking a singer. Just before she landed on her ear once more, the black pianist convinced Dago Frank's manager to give her at least a tryout. They did, and she was hired. Hunter worked there for better than a year, 1912–13, and then moved to Hugh Hoskins' "a sporting house for high-class Black con men," according to Hunter.[9] The friends she remembered at Hoskins included Tack Annie, a professional pickpocket, who "took me under her wing and taught me how to dress," and Zella Hunter, a pianist, who helped her learn a new song every day.[10] She worked at a string of clubs of that ilk including two years at the Hoskins Club, then the Deluxe Café, the Paradise Gardens, the Pekin Theatre Cabaret; and at two of Chicago's leading cabarets, the Elite 2 and the Panama Club, which was also a stepping stone in Ada "Bricktop" Smith's and Florence Mills's careers. These clubs were fashioned after the European cafés and saloons, with rich furnishings and polished bars, lavish foods, and continuous entertainment by bands like King Oliver's, comedy acts, and women singers who moved from table to table spurring customers to spend on drink, food, and other favors.[11]

Hunter was in much demand on the cabaret scene in Chicago. The luxurious Dreamland Café became a mecca for the moneyed crowd and a showplace for black talent. She was the featured soloist there for nearly five years, enjoying a highly favorable press as the years passed. No longer a brash, ambitious kid, she had become a sophisticated, ambitious woman. The Dreamland was frequented by the brightest and the best of white show biz, including Al Jolson, Sophie Tucker, and Eddie Cantor, who drank in every word of the

phrasing and style of Hunter's performances. They copied and prof-
ited from her unabashedly, but she was not fazed by that. By then
she was composing her own songs, although she admitted that she
did not read music. Her most famous composition, "Down-Hearted
Blues," was transcribed for her by pianist-composer Lovie Austin, who obtained a copyright to protect the hit.[12] "Down-Hearted
Blues" became identified with Bessie Smith. Never to be outdone,
Hunter kept on writing, singing, and when lucky, recording her own
compositions.

Early photos reveal Hunter as a petite brown beauty with wide-
set eyes in an almost perfect oval face. Tack Annie's lessons on dress
served her well because she was always smartly dressed on stage
and off. The stylish men and women who danced on the glass floor
of the Dreamland provided an endless fashion show for the singer
to emulate. As the band played above her on a raised platform, the
diminutive singer kept her audience captivated with her swinging
blues or torchy ballads, such as "Bring Back the Joys," her first recording, issued by the Black Swan company in early 1921. She was
backed by a group that included Fletcher Henderson. "Bring Back
the Joys" was typical of the dance-hall songs, suitable for the fox-
trot, that were popular among white clubgoers. Hunter had a full-
bodied contralto voice and her diction was superb even when she
sang songs in dialect. Those assets made the Black Swan issues very
listenable. Only four sides were recorded for Black Swan—little
competition for the Okeh and Columbia issues of Mamie Smith and
Edith Wilson, numerically, but qualitatively they were fine heralds
of a rising star.

Paramount picked her up in July 1922 and issued more than
thirty-five sides in less than two years, many of which were her own
compositions. In addition to "Down-Hearted Blues," outstanding
numbers included "You Shall Reap Just What You Sow," and "Chirping the Blues." "Chirping" was the standard twelve-bar blues which

also incorporated some lines from traditional country blues, to which Hunter had added her own twist with the resolution in the third line.

> Well, I'm worried now but I won't be worried long.
> Well, I'm worried now but I won't be worried long.
> It takes a worried woman to chirp this worried song.[13]

Singing to the piano playing of Henderson, Hunter demonstrates an upbeat style that speaks to the topic but emphasizes the rhythmic pulse of the music. The voice interplays with the piano to create an unbroken line from start to finish. Typical of her early recordings, there is not a building up of intensity, but a relaxed lilt. Style and beat were as important as lyrics to her performance. A 1961 version of "Chirping" with Buster Bailey's Blues Busters employed Sydney de Paris, trumpet; Buster on clarinet; J. C. Higginbotham, trombone; Cliff Jackson, piano; and Zutty Singleton, drums. The swing again emerges as the focus rather than the subtext as Buster, Sydney, and J. C. ripple in and out between Alberta's vocals with flourishes that contrast with her straightforward phrasing.[14]

She was hailed as the "Prima Donna of Blues Singers" by Paramount, which ran ads featuring the text of a particular blues and her picture.[15] Along with singers like Wilson and Lucille Hegamin, she brought the blues to a wider audience by polishing them up and presenting them as highly listenable dance songs. She was a more experienced artist than Wilson by the time she made her first recordings so they had fewer weak vocal spots than the early Wilson's do; and she did not rely on special vocal effects like wails, moans, or yodels.

Hunter appeared in Moss and Frye's *Dumb Luck* in Stanford, Connecticut, in the fall of 1922, and returned to the Dreamland off and on during the next year. Her big stage break came in 1923 when

27   LUCILLE HEGAMIN PUBLICITY PHOTOGRAPH

she was called to replace Bessie Smith in *How Come?* at Harlem's Apollo Theatre. Her performance was called an instantaneous hit. "America's most blasé theatre patrons promptly added their commendations to that of the Paramount and Black Swan record customers; and to the long since familiar approval of colored patrons of the better type cabarets, where this marvelous singing gift was first disclosed to the public . . . this young product of Memphis public schools who never had a music lesson . . . sings with a wonderful natural [tone], has a clarity of voice, a mellowness of tone, a clear pronunciation, all blended."[16] The reference to the "blasé patrons" denotes how white theatergoers were viewed by some black entertainment critics, so their enthusiastic response to her first appearance was noteworthy. The show played for five weeks at the Apollo before closing; it was so well received that it moved uptown to the Lafayette for five more weeks, then went on the road, booked at both black and white houses.[17] The Gayety, a burlesque house in Baltimore, ran the show to sellout crowds for nine days with notices that stated that Hunter "shone . . . in a manner that stamps her as the queen of the 'Blues' warblers."[18] From Baltimore the show went to upstate New York and later to Detroit's Schubert Michigan Theatre. She left the company there and returned to the New York cabaret circuit.[19]

She was probably receiving better than $125 a week while on the road so her return may have been for recording dates at Paramount. "Experience Blues" and "Sad 'n' Lonely Blues" were two more of her creations waxed in 1923.

Her genius flowed from a mixture of musical talent and the powerful, complex experiences she had had as a young black woman. The characters met in her adolescent years left indelible images from which to draw for her lyrics. In that extralegal society, she learned quickly how to fend for herself—when to hang in there and not be pushed around, and when to pack up and move on. That pattern was reflected in her manner of singing as well. She communicated with the audience intimately on one level but warned it to keep its distance because "I don't take no mess"; yet this was usually coupled with a wry sense of humor. The mixed message tantalized and seduced audiences—black and white, uptown and downtown. She could belt out the blues with the best of the blues sisters and she could sing a ballad that pleased the nightclub and theater crowds.

Meanwhile, "Down-Hearted Blues" was creating its own following as each new recorded version appeared—Bessie Smith on Columbia, Eva Taylor on Okeh, and Monette Moore on Paramount.[20] The tune was destined to be a favorite with blues singers for many years. In her rendition Hunter sang it with the passion that Albert Murray called "stomping the blues."[21] In a 1961 version, rather than moaning and groaning, she shouts it out with threats of retribution. It begins with the anger of a pious woman who uses a Bible quote to admonish her lover:

> Lawd, he mistreated me and drove me from his door,
> Yes, he mistreated me and drove me from his door.
> Ah, but the good book says, you got to reap just what you sow.
>
> I ain't never loved but three men in my life,
> I ain't never loved but three men in my life,
> 'Twas my father, my brother, and the man that wrecked my life.

By the last stanza, we hear a streetwise mama who is not given to mourning over men and who is used to getting what she wants.

> Got the world in a jug, stopper right here in my hand,
> Got the world in a jug, stopper right here in my hand,
> And if you want it, sweet papa, you got to come under my
>   command.[22]

The audacious, pert singer was called "The Brightest Blues Star of the Race," "A Wondergirl! And how she does her stuff. She whines the meaning'est, moanin'est, groanin'est Blues you've ever heard. A genius, she writes her own!"[23]

In March 1924, Hunter's version of "Old-Fashioned Love" from Miller and Lyles's *Runnin' Wild* was issued by Paramount and marketed as a sentimental love song. She later sang the number at a benefit for the NAACP which also featured the *Runnin' Wild* company. She tried the musical comedy bit again with the *Struttin' Time* company but was stranded after six disastrous weeks on the road.[24] Back she went to New York and the clubs and cabarets. By the end of the year she had left Paramount to record on the Biltmore label under the pseudonym Alberta Prime, with Duke Ellington's band. During the same period she recorded on the Gennett label as Josephine Beatty with Louis Armstrong and the Red Onion Jazz Babies. Armstrong's group was a perfect match for her lusty rendition of "Texas Moaner Blues." His cornet and Buster Bailey's clarinet punctuate the break in the vocal line with fluid ripples and muted wails.[25]

"Nobody Knows the Way I Feel This Mornin'" is probably some of her finest blues singing in the style of Bessie Smith and Clara Smith—open, unembellished, focused on feeling rather than pulse or tempo, deeply simpatico and emotionally expressive. Armstrong; Sidney Bechet, clarinet; Charlic Irvis, trombone; Lil Hardin Armstrong, piano; and Buddy Christian, banjo, give her a mellow sultry backing that makes you want to "scream and cry" with her as she berates her man between doleful groans. The sixteen-bar blues uses a refrain line to emphasize and reiterate the feeling of defeat and resignation, "Nobody knows the way I feel this mornin', this mornin'."[26] Every woman who has gone to bed tired, disgusted, and screaming mad because she was fed up with excuses, excuses, excuses and has prayed or hoped that tonight he will come home sober and on time, only to awake at dawn to find herself alone, knows that feeling.

"Early in the Morning" contrasts sharply with the agony and isolation of "Nobody Knows" in mood and setting. Stylistically it confirms Hunter's claim that Sophie Tucker "borrowed" heavily from her because it has the bluesy barrelhouse swing that characterizes Tucker's rendition of "Won't You Come Home, Bill Bailey?" Hunter said that one night "Al Jolson came to hear me do 'St. Louis Blues,' Sophie Tucker sent her maid, Belle, for me to come to her dressing room and teach her songs, but I never would go, so her piano player would come over and listen and get everything down."[27] She has said, however, that Tucker was a singer she admired. The most reasonable explanation is that they influenced each other—Tucker sought the rhythms, emotional expressiveness, and black dialectic inflections and Hunter learned stage presence and the use of sexy innuendoes from Tucker. As most artists did in that era of improvisational performance, they were constantly incorporating new ideas and techniques into their acts. In the integrated setting of places like the Dreamland there was constant borrowing, stealing, or co-optation of style, content, and material.

Less than five years after her first recording, Hunter had emerged as a bona fide star of cabaret and vaudeville. She imprinted blues and popular songs with her brand and brought to the stage a glamour that was sleek and sophisticated. She was not everyone's little darling like Florence Mills, nor a saucy, plump comedienne like Edith Wilson; nor did she spangle and sparkle laden with beads like Mamie Smith. Hunter understood what showmanship was and put her most into every performance. When a show did not meet her standards she felt no obligation and "rambled on." In 1925, Hunter set her own standards by forming her own act, "Syncopation de Luxe."[28] Using a pianist and dancer, she booked into small cabarets and set them rocking with her singing and dancing. The favorable response earned her a spot on an eighteen-act bill at the swanky Waldorf Astoria. Hers was the only black act.[29] Later she toured the East and the West on the Keith-Orpheum circuit.[30]

Upon her return from the West Coast in late 1925, Hunter signed with the Okeh label, which announced her first issues with a half-page ad sporting her now-famous profile with short, sleekly bobbed hair. "Take That Thing Away" and "Your Jelly Roll Is Good" were two

Perry Bradford entries, which, from the titles, fit the double entendre genre of blues records popular by then. Approximately sixteen sides came from her work with Okeh, most accompanied by
Bradford's Mean Four, with Bradford at the piano.[31]

With a new partner, Samuel Bailey, she returned to the Keith circuit in 1926, making short runs between New York and Chicago.
One of those dry spells in Chicago gave her enough time to develop
a relationship with a handsome waiter, Willard Saxbe Townsend.
They married but she "got a mind to ramble" and sailed to Europe
only a few weeks after the honeymoon. Telling about it in 1979, she
chuckled, saying she "did him a favor" and "made a man out of him.
He went to Canada, got two degrees, helped organize the redcaps'
unions and was the only Negro on the C.I.O. board. . . . That man
needed a wife, not a Marco Polo like me. I wasn't fixing to settle
down and give up my career."[32]

She had switched labels again, this time to RCA Victor, and produced two memorable sides with the legendary "Fats" Waller on the
organ: "Sugar" and "Beale Street Blues."[33] These sweet, syrupy vocals give a glimpse of Hunter's versatile song styling—nowhere is
there a hint of the hardened blues mama who threatens to lay her
man in his grave. Instead she is purring, cajoling, and reminiscing
about her sweet baby or about Memphis's famous street where the
blues was king.

When Hunter went to Europe in 1927 she carried a bagful of
know-how and a bodyful of nerve and verve. Her first European engagements were in hotels in London, Nice, and Monte Carlo, playing
to the peripatetic international set.[34] Paris appealed to Hunter with
its high fashion, exciting nightlife, and exuberant response to black
entertainers. Work offers were not immediately forthcoming but she
was not worried because she had survived in rougher situations. So
she endured the delays due to the labor permit problems that
plagued her and other American artists who sought active employment.[35] In the interim she attended concerts, went sightseeing, and
studied the language. Always one to keep abreast professionally,

Hunter prepared herself so she could be ready to accept a good offer. A few weeks later she appeared in Monte Carlo and then in London's Hippodrome. When Paul Robeson opened *Show Boat* to a raving success at London's Drury Lane Theatre,[36] Hunter got the supporting role, Queenie, but her labor permit expired; this caused brief difficulties until she was granted an extension. She gained recognition as an oustanding member of the cast.[37]

Vacationing, studying, or performing in Europe was quite fashionable among blacks during the latter half of the twenties. Foreign correspondents for the black press kept their American readers abreast of the doings at parties, concerts, and elsewhere. The artists themselves often served as overseas reporters, so firsthand accounts were often self-promoting. Ivan Browning, a member of the *Show Boat* cast, occasionally served as a columnist for the *Chicago Defender;* his feature, "Across the Pond," was a mixture of society news and stage reviews. A typical news item gave a detailed account of an elaborate party given by the Paul Robesons in honor of the Carl Van Vechtens, then told of visiting Afro-Americans and performances in the area. Among those who received plaudits for fine work were the Fisk Jubilee Singers, Noble Sissle, and Hunter, who was said to be studying French in preparation for the French production of *Show Boat.*[38] The production was never realized, however, so when the show closed at Drury Lane in 1929 she went back to the Paris nightspots that featured black entertainers: the Cotton Club, the Grande Carte, and Chez Florence Jones Cabaret.[39] She had been called the most popular "colored American woman artist in Europe since Florence Mills. . . . Socially, she is quite the vogue here [London], and has been highly entertained."[40]

In Paris and London Alberta endeared herself to admirers by singing their favorite songs, jazz tunes, an occasional blues, and the popular hits from *Show Boat.*[41] Nearly two years of shuttling between the two cities finally wore her down and she sailed home in May 1929. One of the first moves she made was from RCA Victor to Columbia, but they released only two sides. Fortunately, her stage career was so well established that she did not suffer from her relatively low recording output. Wall Street's crash probably affected her employment opportunities, just as it did those of other performers, but she did not give up. Instead she formed another trio with two young male dancers and obtained bookings in and around New York for a few weeks. When the Grand Terrace Gardens in her beloved Chicago beckoned, she went back for a short run.[42]

The small clubs and cabarets remained open, so the versatile song-and-dance routines that Hunter had developed over the years kept her active. Radio opportunities opened for her when Small's Paradise began broadcasting its floor shows in the early 1930s. Those shows were the first in a long line to come. She sang and danced in revues up and down the East Coast for nearly four years, returning on occasion to Harlem and the Lafayette, the Alhambra, Harlem Opera House, and Connie's Inn.[43] A new year, 1933, found her abroad again but this time, after briefly replacing Josephine Baker at the Casino de Paris, she moved beyond the London-Paris corridor, playing clubs in Amsterdam and Copenhagen.[44] Her fluency in languages made her popular everywhere she performed. Broadcasts from London and Copenhagen cabarets also featured her singing.[45] She appeared regularly in The Hague's Tabaris Café, Copenhagen's National-Scala, Athens's Femina Music Hall, and London's top pubs.[46] Everywhere she was acclaimed for her blues and her jazzy dancing. Her friend, Roy de Coverley, overseas reporter for the *Chicago Defender,* wrote these lines from Copenhagen:

> . . . later that evening came her première. She was nervous. She had been told, and truthfully, that Copenhagen critics were the most stringent in Europe. I was with her . . . before her first appearance and she was almost frantic about her pianist. He didn't have that swing. She was to appear first in the bar. . . . Her entrance caused a murmur of admiration. You know a brown girl does look wonderful in white satin, if she can wear clothes. And Alberta can . . .

"Two Tickets to Georgia!" Dark brown voice with velvet overtone. Rhythm. Brown eyes flashing, dark red mouth smiling. White satin body swaying to the beat . . . White faces . . . softening . . . as the magic of a singing Negro girl and Negro music take possession of them. Applause. She had done it.[47]

Hunter's singing style and stage presence were enhanced by the Parisian haute couture fashions she wore so well. Her recognition of the prevailing tastes was revealed in her choice of svelte rather than sparkling, bangled attire.

Broadcasts with the Jack Johnson Band from the Dorchester Hotel in London were added to Hunter's list of firsts during 1934, along with a film *Radio Parade of 1934,* also produced in England.[48] She returned to New York briefly in 1936, appearing with Louis Armstrong at Connie's Inn. The Middle East, Egypt, and Russia were added to her itinerary by 1935 and 1936, and when the Cotton Club revue went abroad in 1937, she was the star of the show.[49] Probably the juiciest news item about her during those years was the front-page story announcing Hunter's rumored engagement to a purported English nobleman, Baron Sommery Gade. Much ado about the planned nuptials was made in the papers for a brief period, but the fuss died out. Since no further mention was made of it by columnists nor by Hunter, evidently the marriage never took place.[50]

As fascism under Hitler and Mussolini progressed in Europe, Hunter found herself battling discrimination abroad as well as at home. Some of the singers who were abroad at the time left France and Italy and went to England; others, like Hunter, returned home.

Chicago welcomed her return in 1938. She sang with the Henry Levine Orchestra in "The Alberta Hunter Show" on WFZ, WEAF, and WOR radio for the next two years.[51] Never one to pass up new experiences, she tried her hand at serious drama in *Mamba's Daughters* with Ethel Waters in the starring role. The rumblings of war in Europe may have curtailed Hunter's travel abroad but it did not slow her pace. Her broadcasts over WJZ and WOR, New York, and occasional recording sessions on Decca and Bluebird filled in the lean spots during the years just before the United States entered World War II.

Hunter was one of many black stage stars who appeared in the 1940 World's Fair Negro Day gala concert; among them were Benny Carter, James P. Johnson, Eubie Blake, W. C. Handy, Margaret Bonds, and Maxine Sullivan. As a member of the committee of "Negro Actors Who Have Appeared in England," Hunter assisted with the group's benefit to raise funds for a mobile kitchen to feed citizens in the London war zone. The dwindling nightlife in Harlem forced Hunter to return to Chicago's Southside and to Detroit for performing opportunities. This time she emphasized the blues in her sets while plugging her European experience for promotional purposes.[52]

The war did not cramp Hunter's style for long and in 1944 her roving spirit sent her to serve in a USO troup in the European war zone. The diminutive dynamo, nearly fifty years old, captivated G.I.'s just as she had won over Europeans a decade earlier. A high point in her USO career was a command performance for Gen. Dwight D. Eisenhower and Soviet Marshal G. K. Zhukov on 10 June 1945 in Frankfurt, Germany. She and a sextet performed popular tunes of that day: "G.I. Jive," "Straighten Up and Fly Right," and "Deep in the Heart of Texas." Her sense of adventure came forth in a letter to her friend George Hoefer, as she described the places, people, and happenings during that period. She said that the general had called her and personally requested that she sing seven of his favorite songs. While in Nuremberg she ran into Floyd Smith, guitarist with Andy Kirk's band, and also visited Hitler's hideout and autographed his table. She witnessed the Russian takeover in Linz, Austria, and was "impressed by the site [*sic*] of the school where the peace terms were signed. . . . GIs are a wonderful audience . . . I'm singing plenty of blues for them."[53]

• • •

Hunter's zest for life and bright personality were magnetic, attracting friends wherever she traveled. Among them were the Robesons, Charles and Etta Moten Barnett, Mabel Mercer, Duke Ellington, and Eubie Blake, one of her earliest show-biz partners. But she withdrew from the glamour and glitter of that world after World War II to care for her ailing mother in Harlem. After her mother's death, the feisty little woman enrolled, at age fifty-nine, in a practical nursing course, earned her certificate, and worked for the next twenty years in a New York City hospital. She had lied about her age as a youngster; now she lied about it for reverse reasons, and began a new career at an age when most people retired. Many times during that period friends urged her to perform again but she stoutly refused, saying her life was dedicated to helping others.

In spring 1977, Ms. Hunter was "retiring" again, this time from her nursing career, at eighty-one. Sharp-witted as ever, she was busily trying to get better royalties for her early blues, "Down-Hearted Blues," "Chirping the Blues," and "You Shall Reap Just What You Sow." Recalling how Lovie Austin helped her, she said Lovie had sent an affidavit disclaiming copyright ownership.[54]

Although she insisted she would not perform again, it was only a few months before she made news in the entertainment world as the red-hot blues singer returning to the stage. Moving at a pace that would exhaust someone half her age, Hunter was writing songs again, appearing regularly in Greenwich Village, making the rounds of the TV talk shows, and loving every minute of it. Ironically, a Greenwich Village place called Edson's Hot Feet Club had been one of her mainstays for engagements fifty years earlier. Hunter had always prided herself on appealing to a cosmopolitan rather than a black audience, even to claiming according to John Hammond, that she had never played in Harlem (the record speaks for itself). One thing is sure, she became an important force in the revival of interest in the blues, and Hammond concurred with my opinion that she sang them with deeper, gutsier feeling in her comeback period than in her early years. He considered her to be a better musician than Eubie Blake even though Blake was more prolific, because Hunter was not locked into one idiom.[55]

According to Bobby Short, Alberta Hunter fought hard for everything with an inner drive that aimed toward success.[56] There should be little wonder then that she was able to achieve so much almost single-handedly. Hammond, then at Columbia Records, and Barney Josephson, owner of The Cookery, recognized this and facilitated her phenomenal creative output when she returned to the stage in 1977. In the short span of six years, she wrote the soundtrack for the film *Remember My Name,* recorded an album of new and old blues, *The Glory of Alberta Hunter,* supervised reissues of her 1930s recordings and her 1934 London broadcasts, and appeared frequently on commercial and public television while maintaining a long-running engagement at The Cookery.[57] Her "Amtrak Blues" is a fitting update to the theme of one she had written sixty years earlier, "I Got a Mind to Ramble."

In her 1980s performances and recordings, Hunter's delivery was still characterized by snappy rhythm and saucy repartee. The voice was big, vibrant, surprisingly flexible for one her age, and richly textured. She worked to her audience with confidence and they responded eagerly. Her blues sound was fine and mellow or low-down and gutsy, demonstrating Alberta's versatility. The stage and spotlight brought her back to renewed fame and glory, her love, her life. If she ever had the blues (and who has not), she sang them right into the ground and kept on moving until her death in the summer of 1984.

I got a mind to ramble but I don't know where to go . . .

Conclusion

This is the essence of the blues woman—autonomous, indomitable, versatile, ambitious, industrious, and sensuous.

> I have my own way of doing things, . . . you may not like it, but still, somebody else will. That's the way I feel about that. But I try to develop every song I sing, I do it my way.[1]

That need to "do it my way" was the driving force of the blues queens who rode the Toby time, worked in theaters, tents, cabarets, dives, and dance halls to foster their careers. They sometimes paid a heavy toll for their right to be heard and seen but their determination, fueled by a creative impulse, kept them going. For a brief decade, they achieved unprecedented popularity among black entertainers and audiences, while transforming a folk tradition to popular art.

We have had a closeup of four of these stars whose singing and life styles illustrate the versatility and variety of classic blues per-

• •

formance. Just as Bessie Smith, Mamie Smith, Wallace, Spivey, Hunter, and Wilson represented different approaches and styles of blues, so did many others whose careers ended or popularity faded at the close of the decade of the blues women. They all contributed to the formation and establishment of a blues tradition that was much broader and more complex; that incorporated a wider spectrum of styles and perspectives than those in the earlier years of tent show and vaudeville blues singers.

As with all popular music, regional tastes influenced the demand for one or another artist. Thus, Ma Rainey and Chippie Hall appealed to the masses of working-class people in the South and Midwest more than in the big cities of the East. Those who incorporated comedy and vaudeville routines into their acts, such as Ida Cox, Sara Martin, and Mamie Smith, attracted a slightly more sophisticated theater audience. Singers such as Wilson, Lucille Hegamin, Hunter, and Lizzie Miles purposely directed themselves to the cabaret set who were upwardly mobile and had money and time for extravagant leisure activities. The multitude of singers and listeners in each group created a vast market, and the record companies catered to it, heralding a new "queen," "moaner," or "nightingale," every month from 1922 to 1924.

Dozens of singers paraded on the recording scene during the blues decade—which is surely what the 1920s can be called. At no time before or since has there been as much attention concentrated on the idiom either in sheer recording output, live performances, or creative composition and arrangement. Only a few women, however, had enough artistry and professionalism to attain and sustain a superior career. These, undoubtedly, earned their place in the annals of American popular music. And although blues lovers who knew them and their music have individual favorites, most will agree that Sammy Price, who performed with several of the queens, speaks for everyone in his choice of the Queen Mother of the blues.

> Well, I think that Bessie, of all blues singers, was perhaps the queen
> . . . the greatest blues singer, female that I ever heard . . . Bessie
> Smith was popular from the beginning.[2]

John Hammond, Sippie Wallace, Thomas Dorsey, and even casual observers concurred. But each of them had other favorites: Hammond said Rosa Henderson was a superb singer; Price preferred Ida Cox; Wallace said she liked Mamie Smith. Price stated the obvious concerning the variations in taste, "Let's remember now, when you were a singer you could be popular in Philadelphia, and nobody ever heard of you in San Antonio, Texas."

More important than any ranking system, which would be rife with problems of validity and reliability, is what the blues women contributed to American popular culture. Emerging from southern backgrounds rich in religious and folk music traditions, they were able to capture in song the sensibilities of black women—North and South—who struggled daily for physical, psychological, and spiritual balance. They did this by calling forth the demons that plagued women and exorcising them in public. Alienation, sex and sexuality, tortured love, loneliness, hard times, marginality, were addressed with an openness that had not previously existed.

The blues women accomplished this with their unique flair for dramatizing their texts and performances. They introduced and refined vocal strategies that gave the lyrics added power. Some of these were instrumentality, voices growling and sliding like trombones, or wailing and piercing like clarinets; unexpected word stress; vocal breaks in antiphony with the accompaniment; syncopated phrasing; unlimited improvisation on repetitious refrains or phrases. These innovations, in tandem with the talented instrumentalists who accompanied the blues women, advanced the development of vocal and instrumental jazz.

Of equal significance, because they were such prominent public figures, the blues women presented alternative models of attitude and behavior for black women during the 1920s. They demonstrated that black women could be financially independent, outspoken, and physically attractive. They dressed to emphasize their symbolic importance to their audiences. The queens, regal in their satins, laces, sequins and beads, and feather boas trailing from their bronze or peaches-and-cream shoulders, wore tiaras that sparkled in the lights. The queens held court in dusty little tents, in plush city cabarets, in crowded theaters, in dance halls, and wherever else their loyal subjects would flock to pay homage. They rode in fine limousines, in special railroad cars, and in whatever was available, to carry them from country to town to city and back, singing as they went. The queens filled the hearts and souls of their subjects with joy and laughter and renewed their spirits with the love and hope that came from a deep well of faith and will to endure.

Appendixes

Other Blues Singers

Ida Cox, "The Uncrowned Queen of the Blues"

Ida Cox, whose Raisin' Cain Company toured TOBA from Chicago to Oklahoma City, from Houston and Dallas to Birmingham, Atlanta, Baltimore, Norfolk, and Philadelphia, was a premier blues singer, whose plain, robust, yet mellow style blended the country tradition with the sophisticated city elements. She was billed as "The Uncrowned Queen of the Blues" by Paramount Records, and deservedly so.

Born Ida Prather in 1896 in Toccoa, Georgia, and raised in nearby Cedartown, Cox's musical experiences began in the African Methodist Episcopal Church she attended.[1] She ran away from home at fourteen to tour with a minstrel show in the "pickaninny" role which was typical at the turn of the century. In a 1940 interview, she stated "I began my theatrical career as a comedienne back in 1915. . . . The next year I was taught how to sing torch songs . . . we called them blues back in those days."[2]

• •

Cox had roadshow experience with the Florida Orange Blossom Minstrels, the Silas Green Show, and the Rabbit Foot Minstrels. By 1922, she was an established professional billed as a single in the TOBA weekly listings of show schedules.[3] She recorded seventy-eight titles for Paramount from September 1923 to October 1929.

Although Paramount claimed to have Cox under an exclusive contract, she recorded for both the Harmograph and Silvertone labels simultaneously, using the pseudonyms Julia Powers, Jane Smith, Velma Bradley, and Kate Lewis.[4] Lovie Austin and her Serenaders accompanied Cox on the early recordings, producing some excellent sides. Cox's third husband, Jesse Crump, was her music director on tour and also played piano on some of her recordings. For her first release Paramount advertised, "The Uncrowned Queen of the Blues—Discovered at Last," "Ida Cox—the Blues Singer with a Feeling! Paramount Record Star."[5]

"Graveyard Dream Blues" typifies the subject matter frequently used by Cox when she was singing city-style blues and not vaudeville. Her voice was not as powerful as Rainey's or Bessie Smith's but it was as penetrating and convincing. "Chicago Monkey Man Blues," "Mama Doo Shee Blues," "Kentucky Man Blues," "Death Letter Blues" and "Wild Women Don't Have the Blues" were characteristic of the topics and style that made her a favorite in the South and Midwest.

Cox used what in most circles would be considerd a vibratoless voice to convey audacity and intensity equally well. "Death Letter" and "Kentucky Blues" are traditional twelve-bar blues sung in a mournful manner laden with regret. She draws the listener into the situation and rivets attention until the final sobbing note fades. In contrast, "Wild Women" is more of the city-vaudeville ilk, and extends the twelve-bar with an eight-bar verse and one-bar bridge. The brash arrogance of the text is sustained by her swaggering vocals. These clearly demonstrate her ability to orchestrate moods through vocal and textual manipulation. Cox had a peculiar way of placing stress or emphasis on the verb, article, adjective, or conjunction rather than on the subject or object. This gave her phrasing unusual rhythmic pulse, added an expressive flavor to simple melodies, and thus deepened the emotional impact.

Noted boogie-woogie and blues pianist Sammy Price rated Cox as one of his favorites and considered himself honored to have been selected to play with the trio that recorded her final release in 1961.

> I liked her sound. I like that flowing blues sound, . . . good melodic lines, words that make sense, decent diction, or decent diction colloquially, you know. I'm speaking now about colored diction . . . you didn't miss anything that Ida sang. When she said, "'way down yonder in Atlanta, G.A.," she said it soooo plain, and so clear, that you had to be affected by it in some way.[6]

Cox's *Raisin' Cain Revue* proved so popular on the TOBA circuit that it was chosen to be the first TOBA show to open at New York's famed Apollo Theatre in early 1929.[7] She kept busy in the 1930s barnstorming throughout the South, drumming up business in Newbern, Hickory, and Charlotte, North Carolina; along the red dusty clay roads of Milledgeville and Macon, Georgia; through hills and mountains of Alabama and Tennessee; along the route of the Mississippi to Memphis, Natchez, and New Orleans. And when she was lucky she would hit Dallas's Ella Moore Theatre where they had clamored for tickets just a few years earlier.[8]

In 1939, Vocalian recorded several sides of Cox with an all-star ensemble that included "Hot Lips" Page, J. C. Higginbotham, James P. Johnson, Charlie Christian, and Lionel Hampton.[9] That same year, Columbia Record scout John Hammond, whose love for blues and jazz carried him all over the eastern seaboard scouting for talent, spotlighted Ida Cox in his 1939 "Spirituals to Swing" concert at Carnegie Hall.[10]

Hammond's persistent admiration for Cox led him to search for and persuade her to return to the recording studio again in 1960.

She had suffered a disabling stroke which forced her into retirement and was reluctant to leave Knoxville where she was actively involved with her church. Repeatedly, she protested that "she was a regular churchgoer and she didn't feel that it would be right for her to sing the blues again." Fortunately, Cox relented and in 1961 recorded what was to be her final album for the Riverside label.[11] An updated version of "Death Letter Blues" proved that Cox still had the artistry to deliver the blues in spite of her poor health. The young pianist that she encouraged forty years earlier in Dallas was now a member of the Coleman Hawkins quintet that backed her, Sammy Price.

> Ida Cox, now when we recorded Ida here in New York . . . she had the same [feeling]. . . . I think this can be due to . . . [my] having learned how to play the piano based on Jesse's [Crump] piano playing, this had a deep influence on me. So naturally, some of this musical style, and blending of her voice, I acquired. And there was a certain quality, texture, that she had not lost. That still inspired me. This is probably why I was able to play for her as well as I was.[12]

Price's sentiments were also expressed by John Wilson in a *New York Times* review of the album. Of the old singer's voice, he wrote: "[the] artfulness of her phrasing is just as entrancing as it ever was. The personal quality that made her singing immediately identifiable in a crowded field in her young days remains."[13] She was a queen of the blues, who, with the regal bearing, dignity, and beauty befitting her position, mesmerized and bewitched her audiences with her compelling rhythms.

It was this sense of self, understanding of her art, and awareness of her audiences' needs and desires that gained Cox such a high level of appreciation by audiences, fellow musicians, and critics. She was confident of her singing ability and was aware of her people's standards of physical beauty. "I know Ida Cox knew how to dress, she was regal, she knew how to wear costumes, she had a tiara, and a wand with rhinestones and a cape and all this."[14] That image of Ida was still vivid in Price's memory thirty years later. Her larger-than-life presence had inspired him as a fledgling blues pianist in Dallas; had awed the young Victoria Spivey as well as countless others. Cox sustained a tradition of singing and a standard of musical integrity long after its popularity had faded. "The Uncrowned Queen of the Blues" died of cancer in mid-October 1967, leaving a legacy of fine showmanship, tireless dedication to her art and her audience, and a body of blues literature that reveals her deeply personal view of life. She had outlived her esteemed colleagues—Bessie Smith, the Empress of the Blues, and Ma Rainey, the Mother of the Blues—but had kept alive their legacy.

Lucille Hegamin, "The Cameo Girl"

Lucille Hegamin, born to John and Minnie Nelson of Macon, Georgia, in 1897, grew up singing in church and theater programs.[15] At fifteen, Hegamin left her family in Macon to tour with the Leonard Harper stock company in neighboring towns. Later, as often happened with entertainers in those days (early 1900s) she was stranded in a town near Chicago. The enterprising, young, "singing entertainer" left the show and went to Chicago, and began the long climb up the show business ladder. By 1917, the beautiful, sloe-eyed young woman with a creamy complexion was billed as "The Georgia Peach" when she performed on the Chicago cabaret scene. With her pianist-composer husband, Bill Hegamin, whom she had married in 1914, she performed at the Deluxe, the Elite #2, and Bill Lewis's Mineral Inn for a while. She also appeared at the Panama Café with a trio of soon-to-be famous women, Florence Mills, Ada "Bricktop" Smith, and Cora Green and performed with Tony Jackson at the Elite and Jelly Roll Morton at the Deluxe.[16]

The Hegamins left Chicago around 1918 to try the West Coast. Her reputation as a cabaret performer led to engagements in Los Angeles, San Francisco, and Seattle. The blues craze had struck the Coast, so patrons demanded them rather than the popular ditties she had been singing in Chicago. "My biggest song hits were 'Corrina,' 'Beale Street Blues,' and 'Tishomingo Blues.'"[17]

Back on the East Coast and in New York City in 1919, the couple joined the burgeoning number of black entertainers, writers, and artists in their struggle for recognition. Cabarets were the main source of employment for Hegamin. Her career was given a boost when she was featured on a Spring Spectacular at the Manhattan Casino sponsored by Happy Rhone, the band leader. Spectaculars, a combination of a dance followed by a midnight cabaret, attracted hundreds of Harlemites who paid "$.75 [which] was sufficient to keep the undesirable element away."[18] Those appearances led to recording sessions with the Arto label. By the time her first record hit the stores, Hegamin was already firmly established in the New York pantheon of popular stars. Her version of "Arkansas Blues" was so popular that it was copied on Banner, Bell, Black Swan, HyTone, Globe, and four other labels.[19] She introduced and used as her theme song "He May Be Your Man," which was identified with Edith Wilson many years later.

Hegamin's theater dates began after her first recordings were released, but she did not tour widely. Although she performed with many distinguished musicians, her longest associations were with Bill Hegamin and, after their divorce, with J. Cyrill Fullerton, another pianist. The Blue Flame Syncopators listed on many of her recordings in 1921 and 1922 included at one time or another: Wesley Johnson, trumpet; Herb Flemming, trombone; Don Redman, alto sax; Sam Wooding, Bill Hegamin, Fullerton, and Fred Tunstall, piano; and Maud Jones, violin. Switching to Cameo in 1922, she cut about thirty-five sides, some of which were issued by Muse and Tremont under her pseudonym, Fanny Baker.[20] Two ballads in 1926 on Columbia, and two risqué numbers on Okeh in 1932 were the last by Hegamin until the 1960s album on the Prestige and Spivey labels.

We can surmise that the blues "craze" caused her to shift her priorities to promote her career. Hegamin appeared in a few revues in New York and Philadelphia. She was featured in a Club Alabam' show as "The Cameo Girl" and the name stuck. Her stage career ended in 1934 with her final performances in Atlantic City clubs. She retired from the stage and became a registered nurse in New York.[21]

Her performances on the Spivey label in the 1960s are those of a mellowed artist with a fine sense of swing, but the voice is still merely pleasant, not especially distinctive and with little emotion. Hegamin, "The Cameo Girl," died at seventy-three in March 1970 after a protracted illness.

Rosa Henderson

Rosa Henderson, Edmonia Henderson, Mary Dixon, and Monette Moore are among the dozens of other women who achieved some notoriety as recorded blues singers during the 1920s. Of that group, some were unfairly dealt with by historians and critics of popular music. One was Rosa Henderson, considered by Hammond as an underrated artist who was a victim of the glutted market.[22] A Kentucky songbird, she was born Rosa Deschamps in Henderson, the source for one of her many professional recording names. Her output was prolific (approximately 100 sides, of which only 8 were rejects) and involved the use of at least twelve pseudonyms, including Flora Dale, Mae Harris, Josephine Thomas, Rosa Green, Sara Johnson, Gladys Waite, and Sally Ritz. Vocalion, Columbia, Perfect, Emerson, Victor, and Paramount were among the labels that captured her voice. Of course, these also account for her lack of a

strong identity, although she appeared at major houses and with revues such as the Quintard Miller Company. Two of her titles are of
historical interest in that they illustrate the political awareness of
blues composers and singers. "Barbadoes Blues" and "The Black
Star Line Blues" were of topical interest because Marcus Garvey had
raised the political consciousness of many blacks.

Chippie Hill

Bertha "Chippie" Hill broke into the recording scene on the Okeh
label in 1925 when she was twenty. She brought with her eight
years of professional experience gained as a singer-dancer with the
Rabbit Foot Minstrels, and in various cabarets and whiskey joints in
New York's rough waterfront neighborhoods.[23]

Hill, born in 1905 in Charleston, South Carolina, to Ida and John
Hill, the parents of sixteen children, received her first exposure to
music in local churches. Like many of the blues women she left
home in her early teens and was working steadily in New York City's
Tenderloin district by the age of fourteen. Because of her youth and
tiny size, she was dubbed Chippie by the owner of Leroy's, a cabaret
where she worked as a dancer with Ethel Waters in 1919.[24]

Chippie Hill's career was minor compared to singers discussed
previously, but her small record output was prestigious. She had a
deep, heavy voice as big as Bessie Smith's but not as refined. The
hard edge was developed from her experiences singing and dancing
in dives and fending for herself in the city. A hard worker, Hill moved
to Chicago in the mid-1920s and performed at the Plantation and
Dreamland with the musicians Armstrong, Oliver, and Austin.

Hill's style does not evoke images of the bereft, helpless female.
Instead, one hears a woman who has seen and heard it all, who can
be down, but refuses to be counted out. She sings more like a blues
man than any of the women of her time, concentrating the melody

in the lower half of her range, using little vibrato in her simple melodic units with few variations. An aggressive, belting, shouting
style that deemphasizes moaning distinguishes Hill from the Smiths,
Wilson, Rainey, and Spivey. Her voice was especially suited for
the subject matter she chose to sing about. "Leavenworth Blues,"
"Streetwalker Blues," and "Pratt City Blues" have the biting gritti-
ness of city streets. Backed by Armstrong and Richard Jones on
piano, her "Trouble in Mind" conjures up a smoke-filled, crowded
room, tables littered with whiskey bottles, ashtrays, and half-filled
glasses, a piano and trumpet player, sweaty and bleary-eyed, and a
huge woman whose voice defies any male aggression. Her small
stature dispelled that stereotype. Armstrong's cornet and Jones's
piano interlace, scoot in and out, ripple up and down and around
Hill's crisp, hard voice, creating marvelous contrasts and helping to
make the recording a classic in blues discography.[25]

None of the photographs or news accounts of Chippie's performance portrayed her in the sparkling, modish attire generally worn
by the blues stage stars. Hill continued performing in Chicago's cabaret network in 1928–29, and toured briefly with Lovie Austin and
the Blues Serenaders.[26] A few sides were issued on Vocalion from
late 1927 to 1929 but as the blues era was already on its way out,
they did not make any impact on the race market.

Chippie married John Offet in the early 1930s and settled down in
Chicago to raise seven children. She worked in clubs sporadically in
the 1930s but was inactive during World War II. Somehow she was
convinced to give the club circuit another whirl in 1946 and, with
the Lovie Austin Blues Serenaders and Montana Taylor, she cut what
was to be her last album on the Circle Label in Chicago. On that
issue, she swings "Trouble in Mind," this time with a few minor
changes in the text. The voice is still vibrant, authoritative, and
straight Chicago-style shout. This album fills one with regret that
such a magnetic, dynamic, forceful singer and fine swinging musician had had such limited exposure.

From 1946 to 1950, Hill worked in clubs in Chicago and New York and appeared in concerts at the Ziegfeld Theatre, Carnegie Hall in New York, and in Paris. She was booked for a run at a Greenwich Village club in 1950 when a hit-and-run accident took her life.[27]

Sara Martin, "The Colored Sophie Tucker"

Born in Louisville around 1884, Martin was approaching forty when she began recording in 1922.[28] Martin, the daughter of William and Katie Dunn, must have worked locally before she started out as a singer on an Illinois vaudeville circuit on the outskirts of Chicago around 1915. She was singing in the cabarets and clubs of New York City when Clarence Williams hired her for the Okeh label.[29] She and Williams collaborated on several blues during her tenure with Okeh, the earliest being "Uncle Sam Blues," which was immortalized by Ida Cox, and "A Green Gal Can't Catch On."[30] General Phonograph ads promoted Martin as a "famous moanin' mama" because the veteran stage personality was renowned for her dramatic presentation on stage for years before she recorded.[31]

Martin's voice had a pleasant richness and falls somewhere between Bessie Smith's and Ma Rainey's in texture. Her ability as a moaner was not evident on the early Okeh issues, which used Sylvester Weaver on guitar or Clarence Williams on piano, but the beauty of her voice contrasts well with the delicate and simple instrumentation. "I Got to Go and Leave My Daddy," and "Got to Leave My Home Blues" sound like citified country blues, innocent and wordly in the same instant. The voice is not heavy with pleading and moaning, as the lyrics might suggest, but pure and clear like that of ballad singers, reflecting her cabaret and vaudeville background. Both of these blues depart from the usual twelve-bar and sixteen-bar structure, which lends them the country ballad flavor. "I Got to Go and Leave My Daddy" is in extended couplet form with a lilting melody, contradicting the gravity of the situation, which juxtaposes distress with arrogant bravado.

On fox-trots Martin demonstrated why she was called "The Colored Sophie Tucke," displaying a lively, brassy style reminiscent of Tucker's as well as Rainey's. She began to use that billing in the early 1920s to capitalize on Tucker's popularity.[32] Her repertoire ranged from the traditional twelve- and sixteen-bar blues such as "Tired of Waiting Blues," "Sweet Man Blues" and "Goodbye Blues," to such vaudeville comedy songs as "Squabbling Blues" and "Take Your Black Bottom out of Here."

Martin tended to use more swinging, danceable rhythms than some of her peers. The rolling boogie-woogie beat of the piano in her version of "Uncle Sam Blues" creates a lighthearted atmosphere, in contrast to the rendition of Clara Smith. Nevertheless, when she sang a traditional blues her voice and styling had richer, deeper qualities that matched the content in sensitivity and mood: "Mean Tight Mama" and "Death Sting Me" approach an apex of blues singing.[33]

Martin's popularity on the TOBA show circuits from 1922 to 1924 certainly indicates a performer who lived up to the audience's expectations. She wore lavish gowns to compliment her buxom figure, and made two or three costume changes per show. One photo in a review of an Indianapolis engagement showed her in a lace gown, her head crowned with a tiara; the stage was draped with shimmering gold curtains lined with pink satin. A gold-and-black valance down one side proclaimed "Sara Martin Sings Only for OKEH Records."[34] Evidently such costuming was her trademark in an already crowded field, because her reviews usually devoted more space to how she looked rather than to how she sounded.

Martin's acting flair and personality were the source of her continued popularity on stage throughout the 1920s. She used special gimmicks to highlight her singing, including a family act with her three-year-old son and her banjo-playing husband, William Myers.

Leigh Whipper's *Golden Brown Reasons of 1926* provided a loose plot as a foil for her dramatic singing. She appeared in many revues and musicals from 1927 to 1929 in New York, Detroit, and Pittsburgh, as well as Cuba, Jamaica, and Puerto Rico.[35] Mamie Smith and Eva Taylor were also featured in the New York shows. One film appearance is credited to her, *Hello, Bill.*[36]

Although Martin remained with Okeh until 1928, she also recorded under two pseudonyms, Margaret Johnson and Sally Roberts, on other labels. Her religious recordings with Sylvester Weaver on guitar displayed her full, rich voice. After a few recording sessions in early 1928 on QRS with Clarence Williams, Martin retired from the show scene for almost a year. Her featured role in *Dark-Town Scandals Review* in 1930 was her last major appearance in show business. She retired from the stage and turned to the church. Her attempt at gospel singing was not as successful as it might have been if she had started earlier, according to Thomas Dorsey, with whom she worked in Chicago churches in 1932.[37] Her final years were spent in her hometown, Louisville, where she operated a nursing home. She died there in 1955 after a very full life.[38]

Lizzie Miles, "The Creole Songbird"

Born Elizabeth Landreaux, 31 March 1895, on New Orleans's famed Bourbon Street, Lizzie Miles was the daughter of a musical mother who occasionally sang traditional folk and creole songs on public programs. The only New Orleans native in the array of artists to achieve acclaim nationally, Miles was a fair-skinned creole raised as a Catholic. She stated that she began singing with other little children after catechism school, and on Sundays was taught along with other youngsters by a Mrs. Atkins, who gave concerts in her backyard. (This was a common practice in black neighborhoods.) As she became better known, she earned fifty cents with more singing at picnics, house parties, and Saturday night fish fries.

Her first job as a band singer in a cabaret was in Bucktown, the black section of New Orleans, where she said she made good money because Storyville was "going full blast" and people would leave there after work to come to Bucktown.[39] Later, Miles sang in various New Orleans halls with such noted musicians as King Oliver, Kid Ory, Bunk Johnson, and Alphonse Picou. She earned her stage name because she was always smiling: "Miles of Smiles from Lizzie Miles." She left for Chicago, made her way to the Dreamland where Oliver's band was playing, and was hired after singing "I Wish I Could Shimmy Like My Sister Kate." Louis Armstrong, Lil Hardin, and Baby Dodds were members of Oliver's band at that time, which places it late in the decade before 1920. She also sang at the famed Elite #2, and at the Entertainers, where trumpeter Freddy Keppard was playing.[40]

After working briefly with a circus, Miles was stricken with the flu and had to retire from singing for a year. She went home for a period sometime around 1918, then returned to the cabaret scene in Chicago, before going on to New York with Oliver to try the recording field. A few test recordings netted zero so she sought work in the New York cabarets. Thanks to Lucille Hegamin, with whom she lived, Miles got on at Dash's Inn. Next, she worked at the Capital Club on Lenox Avenue for two or three years.

In 1924, pianist Danny Wilson, saxophonist Ollie Lee Gaire, and Lizzie decided to give Paris a try after Ada "Bricktop" Smith wrote about her financial success there. Miles was soon known as "La Rose Noir," "The Black Rose."[41] She sang in English and French and fit the French ideal of black beauty, just as did Edith Wilson, Alberta Hunter, Florence Mills, Josephine Baker, and "Bricktop"—either light (Mediterranean) or swarthy (African) complexion, dark wavy hair, and a sensual, cosmopolitan performance style. All of them were fluent in more than one language, were versatile in their choice of material and styling, and were able to sing risqué lyrics without bawdy lewdness. Although it was reported that she experienced difficulty with labor permits while in France, Miles disclaimed the problem in a letter to the black newspapers.[42]

Around 1926, she returned to New York's cabaret scene, which included a brief stint at the Cotton Club. Her mother's illness was the cause of her return to New Orleans in 1938, according to Miles's statement. That was the same period, however, in which most singers like Miles, Hunter, and Wilson were experiencing displacement by younger jazz singers, such as Ella Fitzgerald, Billie Holliday, and Maxine Sullivan. For the first time, she was not working as a singer but as a barmaid who occasionally sang with the jukebox. Like Wilson, Miles had bit parts in a few movies either as a maid or a performer during the 1930s.[43] She returned to the stage in a New Orleans lounge around September 1950, wearing the exotic dresses she had purchased for her mother three decades earlier.

Miles did not record prolifically but all of her sides are topnotch. She admired Sophie Tucker and went to hear her often as a young singer. Tucker's influence is evident in Miles's belting vaudeville style, as is that of her own sister, Edna Benbow Hicks; this is obvious in Miles's rendition of "Some of These Days," "All of Me," and "Someday, Sweetheart."[44] Miles managed her big flexible voice very well whether she was singing "Some of These Days" or "I Hate a Man Like You." Hers was not a light torch-song type of voice, such as Hegamin's or that of the early Edith Wilson and Mamie Smith, but full-bodied with a rich gravelly edge that gives it bounce and energy. Her recording output was small, comparatively speaking, but of consistently good quality, most likely because of her long years of experience with first-rate musicians before her first release in 1922. "State Street Blues" by Spencer Williams, who got Miles her contract with Okeh, was coupled with George Thomas's popular "Muscle Shoals Blues."[45] She also had the distinction of being the first blues woman to have a record released in England, "You're Always Messin' Round with My Man" (HMVCE) in 1923.[46] She eventually recorded for Okeh, Columbia, and RCA Victor. A throaty growl is charcteristic in all of her singing whether it is bawdy vaudeville songs, fox trot ballads, or blues.

Although not a dyed-in-the-wool blues singer, Miles did justice to blues when she chose to perform them. She might have found a place in the renewed interest in blues, just like Wallace and Hunter, had she lived longer. Her delivery and style in her last recording demonstrated that age mellowed rather than diminished her performing ability. She officially retired in 1959 with the following comment to jazz buffs at the New Orleans Jazz Museum: "I have chosen to live a life of a nun, not a modern one, but an old-fashioned Godly one and have given up the outside world. I take part in nothing. I only attend church and spend the rest of my time in prayers for these troubled times all over the world, making penance for my past sins and trying to serve God as I should. It is my way of thanking Him for all His wonderful blessings."[47] "The Creole Songbird" died on 17 March 1963, after attending mass at the Lafon Old Folks Home in New Orleans.[48]

Clara Smith, "World's Greatest Moaner"

Critics such as Carl Van Vechten and John Hammond consider Clara Smith as nearly as good as Bessie Smith though somewhat less consistent in quality. She was highly regarded by her audiences and is one of the most underrated of all the artists classified as "classic" blues singers.[49] This is mainly because some of her earliest recorded titles were not of the best quality, as were Bessie's, but she gained a following that supported her career steadily until her death in 1935.

Clara Smith was a handsome woman with a broad face and a big

smile. Her large, wide-set eyes and broad nose gave her a resem-
blance to Bessie. She was less noted for the kind of flair that Bessie
showed in her performances and there were no press indications of
Clara's being a flashy dresser like Mamie Smith. However, her
record-buying public was significant enough to cause Columbia to
keep her under contract and recording until 1932.

Information about Smith's personal life is sparse. She was born in
Spartanburg, South Carolina, in 1894 or 1895 and, like many of her
peers, she began working on the southern vaudeville circuit while
still in her teens. By 1918, she was a headliner on the TOBA and
appeared with various tent shows and at major theaters. In 1923 she
moved to Harlem where she was put under contract by Columbia.[50]

Smith brought to the Columbia label a vocal style that rivaled
Bessie's in appeal and power. Joining the soon-to-be celebrated
Bessie Smith and Edith Wilson, Clara remained with the company
for more than a decade except for one release on Okeh in October
1930 under the pseudonym Violet Green. Her output of more than
120 sides used the talents of the finest jazz artists of the era—
among them Fletcher Henderson, Don Redman, James P. Johnson,
Coleman Hawkins, and Louis Armstrong. Although featured in comedy duets with Bessie Smith or Lonnie Johnson, her forte was the
brassy, "down on the no-good cheating man" type of blues, which
she delivered in a wailing style filled with tears and anguish.

Smith's voice conveys a down-in-the-mouth mood, alternating
between a hard, dry sound and a tremulous, tragic whine. Van
Vechten aptly described her voice as one that "flutters agonizingly
between tones."

> Music critics would say that she sings off-key. What she really does
> . . . is to sing quarter tones. Thus she is justifiably billed as the
> 'World's greatest moaner.' . . . [Her] tones uncannily take on the col-
> our of the saxophone; again of the clarinet. Her voice is powerful and
> melancholy, by turn. It tears the blood from one's heart.[51]

Several months earlier he had written, "To hear Clara Smith sing this song [Nobody Knows the Way I Feel This Mornin'], is an experience that no one, who has had the privilege, will soon forget. Her voice, choking with moaning quarter tones, clutches the heart. Her expressive and economic gestures are full of meaning. What an artist!"[52]

Conscious of the theatrical quality of her music, Smith took advantage of each opportunity for dramatizing her lyrics by shedding tears, emitting mournful wails, and clutching her stole or the stage curtains around her body in obvious anguish.[53] She blended a country style with the flair of vaudeville in an interesting, dynamic manner—the moans combined with the tremulous quavers of a tragic theatrical heroine.

> Texas people are your friend,
> Texas people are your friend,
> When one don't want you,
> Other people take you in.[54]

In "Texas Moaner Blues," a traditional twelve-bar blues, she emotes in a country style similar to Ma Rainey's; a sharp contrast to her version of "Nobody Knows," which is a city blues filled with despair and invective.

Columbia Records had a finely matched pair with Bessie and Clara on their artists' roll. Clara's wavering tonality lends a poignancy to her renditions, which sometimes belies her power and strength. "My Man Blues," a lighthearted vaudeville-type quarrel over a man, showcases the two—Bessie's deep chocolatey voice against Clara's brighter, somewhat lighter voice. Stylistically, their phrasing and sliding melodic lines are quite similar. Clara Smith sang straight country blues as well as Ma Rainey did, or the city blues like Sippie Wallace. Her moaning, slow, down-to-earth handling of "Uncle Sam Blues"—no melodic frills, no catchy special effects—gives it a sardonic flavor quite different from the swinging upbeat rendition recorded by Sara Martin. Smith's version, therefore, takes on a more serious dimension. Her well-managed rhythmic sense coupled with a resonant vibrato produced a rich sound. Syncopated, well-placed breaks and melismatic phrase endings in "Mean Papa Turn in Your Key" make this blues performance one of her best. In most of her work, Smith was in command of her material, musicianship, and mood.

Her voice slides up to the tone, stretching some words out and emphasizing unlikely words, giving a loping syncopated swing to an ordinary melody. Her earliest recordings with Fletcher Henderson are small gems with subtle interplay of voice and piano, relaxed and unhurried. The distinctive quavering is utilized just enough to add a convincing flavor of angst; for example, "All Night Blues" is sung to a typical fox-trot beat, but Smith uses soulful tremors on certain words. The tearful voice contrasts with the smooth, languid piano and thus rivets attention.[55] "Court House Blues" and "Ship Wreck Blues" are other engrossing examples of her gripping, emotion-laden delivery.

"Awful Moaning Blues" demonstrates why she was billed as the "Queen of the Moaners." The introductory moans prime the listener for a pitiful tale of a woman alone in a friendless world, the stark lyrics rendered with a feeling tone that clearly reveals an artistry of the highest level. Many of Clara's followers felt that she equaled Bessie in many ways. Clara Smith cannot be labeled a vaudeville or ballad singer who sometimes performed the blues; her voice and style are categorically city blues with a touch of country soul.

By mid-1924, ads appeared in the major black newspapers featuring full-length photographs of Smith stylishly posed and draped in flowing attire, and news articles announcing her engagements in cities such as Pittsburgh, Baltimore, and Chicago became more common. Over the next ten years, Smith toured the TOBA circuit, covering every major theater from Florida and Alabama to Chicago, Cleveland, and Kansas City. Her casts and revues changed as flashy dancing, fancy costumes, and scenery became the drawing cards at mid-decade. Being a savvy showperson, she shifted with the public by acting in more comedy routines, as did Mamie Smith and Edith Wilson.

Smith's penchant for melodrama was balanced by her fine comedic talents, as demonstrated in recordings such as "West Indies Blues," heavy in dialect, and her duet with Bessie Smith, "I'm Going Back to My Used to Be."[56] *Chicago Defender* critic Coy Herndon wrote: "Clara Smith is more than a mere blues singer, her voice is a typical blues singing type, combined with a wonderful personality, but she is a comedienne . . . of the highest order. Her blues gained numerous encores and her facial expressions, combined with a distinct personality, caused the audience to ache from laughter."[57] Witty ad libs interspersed between her blues renditions became the high point of her shows, such as the lavishly mounted *Club Alabam' Revue,* which featured comedian Doc Straine, one-time partner of Edith Wilson. The revue opened in New York in early 1927 and traveled for over a year, receiving wide acclaim for the high quality of its costumes and scenery, and for Smith's wit.[58]

Smith's voice improved with the years and her best recordings were made between 1925 and 1928. Her blues had shifted from the beleaguered, mournful type to more aggressive and explicit expression. The comedy that was wowing them at live performances was also being channeled into suggestive lyrics on recordings. She also recorded six traditional black spirituals including "Get on Board" and "Livin' Humble" during the same period, but judging by their promotion, a gross picture of grinning blacks on a ship watching a man overboard being snagged by an anchor, Columbia did not consider these songs to be religious.[59]

After twenty years on the road, including ten as a headliner, and 125 recorded selections, Clara Smith's career was ended abruptly by a fatal heart attack on February 1935. Her assertion that she was just a singer, not a blues singer, showed that she perceived herself as an artist whose talent and repertoire were flexible and versatile; but blues singing was her forte. Clara Smith is notable for singing blues with an authority derived from a thorough understanding of the idiom. She did not sacrifice pathos, anger, elation, or other moods in her performance, which reflected a fine sense of her vocal abilities, as well as a recognition of the balance needed when shifting from the serious to the comic. She was indeed a "queen of the blues"—a sampling of her recordings confirm that; but she was also a professional who was attuned to the tribulations of the black city woman and her country sisters. And though she may not have remained in the public's mind as long as the much revered Bessie, that is our loss, not hers.

Trixie Smith

Trixie Smith, a southerner who migrated North while still young, was born in 1895 in Atlanta. She supposedly attended Selma University in Alabama before her trek to New York City at age twenty.[60] Initially she performed under cork as a single on the "colored time. . . . a pleasing singer of humorous Negro songs, to which she imparted a trick of delivery that kept her in demand by the managers. . . . [She] admitted that she had no ambitions other than to keep the 'pot' boiling and merely drifted from one theatre to another to earn a living."[61] The 1922 Manhattan Blues contest changed all that for her, making fame and better fortune a reality for a few years. She had already received recognition as a blues singer with vaudeville shows when her first recordings were issued by Black Swan in late 1921. One of the sides, "Trixie's Blues," was the number that won her the silver cup in a contest sponsored by the 15th Regiment at the Manhattan Casino. The event was staged for such illustrious persons as the then-governor, Nathan Miller; Enrico Caruso's widow; and Irene Tremaine Castle, who along with her husband Vernon, had become wealthy from teaching high-society patrons how to do the Charleston, Eagle Rock, and other dances based on black dance forms.[62] Mrs. Castle presented the trophy to Miss Smith.[63] Trixie, described as the "dark horse" in the contest probably because she was the lone black contender, was discovered by Bob Slater, producer of stage shows.[64] As might be expected, she used that victory for promotional purposes throughout her career.

Smith's voice leaves much to be desired when judged entirely on its timbre, depth, and resonance. She recorded fewer than fifty sides between 1923 and 1939 on several labels under three names: Trixie Smith, Tessie Ames, and Bessie Lee.[65] Among the many musicians on her early recordings on the ill-fated Black Swan label were Fletcher Henderson, James P. Johnson, and Louis Armstrong. Unfortunately, the 1922–23 recordings reveal that since much of the material Trixie sang is rather vacuous, her lightweight voice does not make the songs particularly memorable. "Love Me Like You Used to Do" was a foxtrot torch song, as was "My Daddy Likes It Slow."[66] She evidently sang these songs, and others, as a vaudeville star whose value was enhanced by the contest she had won. When Black Swan was taken over by Paramount she moved to that label; later she went to Decca. The Paramount issues of "Freight Train Blues" and "Railroad Blues" are probably her best and most well-known on that label. Her last sessions with Paramount were in 1925. She faded into obscurity except for a brief return to the club scene in New York in the late 1930s.

The texts of Smith's train blues are interesting because of what they tell us about the itinerant life of young women. The backing by Buster Bailey, clarinet; Howard Chambers, cornet; Charlie Green, trombone; and Fletcher Henderson, piano, on "Choo Choo Blues," a 1924 release, is commendable, but it comes off as a jejune novelty number rather than a hard blues. "Railroad Blues" (1925) is so much better that the listener cannot help wondering if these are by the same person. There is a superb shouting quality to the latter which indicates that Smith probably could have produced a higher caliber of recordings had she had a steady contract with a company such as Columbia. The unevenness in her recordings may not provide an accurate picture of her abilities but they are all we can rely on. She sounds amateurish on "Choo Choo" and professional on "Railroad." Two versions of "Messing Around" recorded with Freddie Keppard also lack distinction in the vocals.[67]

Smith's vocal abilities probably did not develop early enough to enable her to produce better recordings during the 1920s and the shift to recording blues men encroached on her career as it did on other blues women. Her "Freight Train Blues" in 1938 makes it clear that she was just beginning to bloom as an artist. Her best recordings were toward the end of the 1930s when her second version of "Freight Train Blues" came out. Here her voice had matured and mellowed and she was swinging with confidence, belting out in the style of Helen Humes, a newcomer of the 1930s. The fine interplay between Smith's steady, solid vocals and the superb interpolations of Sidney Bechet and Charlie Shavers on clarinet and trumpet makes this recording a gem. Still, she did not bring the same level of real grief to it as Clara Smith did in her 1924 recordings. Price, who played piano on that set, considered Trixie to be a good blues singer but he felt that a drinking problem was instrumental in her uneven performances. He claimed that she often would not start a recording session without a few drinks under her belt.[68] However, I have found no verification for that or the rumor that she was intoxicated when she had her fatal accident in 1943.

Trixie Smith was representative of singers who performed the blues in the context of vaudeville comedy routines, such as Susie of "Butterbeans and Susie" and "Sweet Pease" Spivey. Vaudeville remained her mainstay until the 1930s when she toured for a while with Mae West.[69] Most of her performance reviews emphasize her versatility, whether she was headlining a revue or appearing with others. Perhaps her early blackface routines were the basic training that equipped her for endurance on the TOBA time. Comic talent sustained her performing career in revues and musicals, sometimes in nonsinging roles, throughout the decade of the 1930s. She appeared in one film, *The Black King,* in 1932. She also had minor roles in a few Broadway plays. From 1940 until her death, Smith performed occasionally for benefits.[70]

Others who thrived briefly over the decade included the following:

Ajax: Bessie Brown, Josephine Carter, Helen Gross, Ethel Hayes, Edna Hicks, Leitha Hill, Edith Johnson, Virginia Liston, Nettie Potter, Susie Smith (a.k.a. Monette Moore), Grace White, Lena Wilson.

Black Swan: Fae Barnes (a.k.a. Maggie Jones), Josie Miles.

Brunswick: Mary Johnson, Viola McCoy, Lena Wilson.

Columbia: Eliza Brown, Martha Copeland, Mary Dixon, Dorothy Everett, Lillian Glinn, Hattie Hudson, Ann Johnson, Maggie Jones (a.k.a. Fae Barnes), Jewell Nelson, Ethel Ridley, Louise Ross, Mary Stafford, Leona Williams.

Emerson: Lillyn Brown, Ethel Finney, Hazel Meyers.

Gennett: Josie Miles.

Okeh: Helen Baxter, Gladys Bentley, Lucille Bogan, Lela Bolden, Ada Brown, Kitty Brown, Martha Copeland, Fannie Goosby, Elizabeth Johnson, Margaret Johnson, Daisy Martin, Hattie McDaniel, Sally Roberts, Irene Scruggs, Laura Smith.

RCA Victor: Edna Benbow Hicks.

Paramount: Marie Bradley, Gladys Bryant, Memphis Julia Davis, Sodarisa Miller, Priscilla Stewart, Lena Wilson.

Pathé: Lavinia Turner.

Perfect: Mamie Harris, Caroline Johnson, Mary Stafford, Nettie Potter (a.k.a. Monette Moore).

Vocalion: Mae Harris, Mamie Harris, Rosa (Rose) Henderson, Sara Johnson, Hazel Meyers, Luella Miller, Sally Ritz, Gladys White, Bessie Williams.

Selected Blues Titles by Women

Advice Blues	Sippie Wallace
Arkansas Road Blues	Victoria Spivey
'Bama Bound Blues	Ida Cox and Lovie Austin
Bedroom Blues	Ethel Bynum and George W. Thomas
Bedroom Blues	Sippie Wallace and G. W. Thomas
Black Snake Blues	V. Spivey and J. J. Johnson
Blood Hound Blues	V. Spivey
Blood-Thirsty Blues	V. Spivey
Caldonia Blues	S. Wallace and G. W. Thomas
Can Anybody Take Sweet Mama's Place?	S. Wallace and Clarence Williams
Chicago Bound Blues	L. Austin
Chirping the Blues	Alberta Hunter and L. Austin
Coffin Blues	Rosa Taylor and Aletha Dickerson
Court House Blues	Clara Smith
Death Letter Blues	Jesse Crump and I. Cox
Death Letter Dream Blues	Madlynn Davis
Detroit Moan	V. Spivey
Dirty Woman Blues	V. Spivey
Dope Head Blues	V. Spivey

Dopey Man Blues	Lillian Henderson
Down-Hearted Blues	A. Hunter and L. Austin
Every Woman's Blues	C. Smith and Stanley Miller
Experience Blues	A. Hunter and L. Austin
The Flood Blues	S. Wallace, Matt Wallace, and Cleo Grainger
Graveyard Dream Blues	I. Cox
Graveyard Bound Blues	Arthur Ray and Monette Moore
Hard Times Blues	Chippie Hill
He's the Cause of Me Being Blue	S. Wallace and C. Williams
I'm a Mighty Tight Woman	S. Wallace
Lazy Man Blues	S. Wallace and C. Grainger
Long Road	Bessie Smith
Mistreating Daddy Blues	L. Austin
Murder in the First Degree	V. Spivey
Nobody Knows How I Feel This Mornin'	Tom and Pearl Delaney
Nightmare Blues	V. Spivey
No. 12, Let Me Roam	V. Spivey
Poor Man Blues	B. Smith
Pratt City Blues	C. Hill
Red Lantern Blues	V. Spivey
Shave 'Em Dry	William Jackson and Ma Rainey
Sad 'n' Lonely Blues	A. Hunter
Shorty George Blues	G. W. Thomas and Hociel Thomas
Spider Web Blues	V. Spivey
Sport Model Mama	V. Spivey
TB Blues	V. Spivey
Traveling Blues	L. Austin
Uncle Sam Blues	Sarah Martin and C. Williams
Underworld Blues	S. Wallace
Up the Country Blues	G. W. Thomas and S. Wallace
Wild Women Don't Have the Blues	I. Cox
You Gonna Need My Help	Sippie Thomas (Wallace)

Notes

Introduction

1   That unquestioning acceptance was the pivotal point for the protagonists in several novels: Janie in Zora Neale Hurston's *Their Eyes Were Watching God* (Urbana: University of Illinois Press, 1978); Sula in Toni Morrison's *Sula* (New York: Knopf, 1973); Shug in Alice Walker's *The Color Purple* (New York: Harcourt Brace Jovanovich, 1982); and Avey in Paule Marshall's *Praisesong for the Widow* (New York: G. P. Putnam's Sons, 1983.

2   Albert Murray, *Stomping the Blues* (New York: McGraw-Hill, 1976). Murray states that the function of the blues music is to drive away the blues, to stomp them until they fade into the background.

3   "Mama's Gone Good-bye," Clara Smith, Columbia 14039-D, September 1924.

4   Willie Dixon, lecture at the Smithsonian Institution, Washington, D.C., 6 February 1982.

5   Sippie Thomas Wallace, interview with the author, Detroit, 24 January 1975.

6   Ralph Ellison, *Invisible Man* (New York: Random House, 1952), 63.

7   Ralph Ellison, *Shadow and Act* (New York: Random House, 1964), 78.

8   LeRoi Jones, *Blues People* (New York: William Morrow, 1963), 102.

9   Linda Dahl, *Stormy Weather: The Music and Lives of a Century of Jazzwomen.* (New York: Pantheon Book, 1984), 120.

10   Lawrence W. Levine, *Black Culture and Black Consciousness* (New York: Oxford University Press, 1977), 225.

11   Jeff Todd Titon, *Early Downhome Blues: A Musical and Cultural Analysis* (Urbana: University of Illinois Press, 1977), 49–51.

12   David Evans, *Big Road Blues: Tradition and Creativity in Folk Blues* (Berkeley and Los Angeles: University of California Press, 1982), 10.

13   Paul Oliver, *Screening the Blues: Aspects of the Blues Tradition* (London: Cassell Ltd., 1968); Oliver, *The Story of the Blues* (New York: Chilton Press, 1969); Samuel Charters, *Poetry of the Blues* (New York: Oak Publications, 1963); Giles Oakley, *The Devil's Music: A History of the Blues* (London: British Broadcasting Corp., 1976); Paul Garon, *Blues and the Poetic Spirit* (New York: Da Capo Press, 1978); Sally Placksin, *American Women in Jazz, 1900 to the Present: Their Words, Lives, and Music* (New York: Seaview Books, 1982) for general information on blues women. For early autobiographical samples see Billie Holiday, *Lady Sings the Blues* (Garden City, N.Y.: Doubleday, 1956) and Ethel Waters, *His Eye Is on the Sparrow* (Garden City, N.Y.: Doubleday, 1951).

14   Chris Albertson, *Bessie* (New York: Stein and Day, 1972) and Sandra Lieb, *Mother of the Blues: A Study of Ma Rainey* (Amherst: University of Massachusetts Press, 1981).

15   Nathan Huggins, ed., *Voices from the Harlem Renaissance* (New York: Oxford University Press, 1976); David Levering Lewis, *When Harlem Was in Vogue* (New York: Knopf, 1981); Jervis Anderson, *This Was Harlem* (New York: Farrar, Straus and Giroux, 1981); and James Weldon Johnson, *Black Manhattan* (New York: Knopf, 1930) provide vivid descriptions of the Harlem night scene of that era.

Riding "Toby" to the Big Time

1   See Mary White Ovington, *Half a Man: The Status of the Negro in New York* (1911; reprinted New York: Schocken Books, 1969) for a discus-

sion of the organizations formed for the guidance and protection of young women traveling alone to cities seeking work. Concerned persons in Baltimore, Philadelphia, and New York formed societies expressly for the purpose of meeting young women as they arrived on trains and boats. They were assisted in finding housing and getting redress from unfair employment practices. Ovington was instrumental in raising the concern about their plight.

2   Allan Spear, *Black Chicago* (Chicago: University of Chicago Press, 1967), 11.

3   Seth M. Scheimer, *Negro Mecca: A History of the Negro in New York City, 1865–1920* (New York: New York University Press, 1965), 222–223.

4   Cited in ibid., p. 52.

5   "Northern Employers and Migration," *New York Age,* 6 October 1923, 4.

6   U.S. Department of Commerce, Bureau of the Census, *Negro Population in the United States, 1790–1915* (Washington, D.C.: Government Printing Office, 1918).

7   E. Franklin Frazier, *The Negro Family in the United States* (Chicago: University of Chicago Press, 1966), 210.

8   See Francis B. Kellor, "Southern Colored Girls in the North," *Charities and the Common* 13 (18 March 1905); and Ovington, *Half a Man,* for discussion of these conditions.

9   Kellor, "Southern Colored Girls," 585.

10   Ovington, *Half a Man,* 80 and 87.

11   Frazier, *Negro Family,* 212.

12   Scheimer, *Negro Mecca,* 94–95.

13   An item in the *Chicago Defender,* 22 October 1910, lauds Miss Marie Burton, a Chicago singer who was recently engaged at the Pekin Theatre. It also discusses her good salary, her volunteer church and club work, and her right to "earn an honest living" rather than "working as a washroom maid."

14   "Mothers Taking Innocent Daughters to Houses of Ill Fame," *Chicago Defender,* 26 March 1910.

15   See the *Chicago Defender,* 8 April 1916; *The Afro-American,* 20 May 1916; and *The Negro in Chicago: A Study of Race Relations and a Race Riot,*

The Chicago Commission on Race Relations (University of Chicago Press, 1922), 379.

16   Ronald Foreman, "Jazz and Race Records, 1920–1932: Their Origins and Their Significance for the Record Industry and Society (Ph.d. diss., University of Illinois, 1968), 24.

17   Oliver, *The Story of the Blues,* 70.

18   Langston Hughes and Milton Meltzer, *Black Magic: A Pictorial History of the Negro in American Entertainment* (Englewood Cliffs, N.J.: Prentice-Hall, 1967), 67–69.

19   *The Afro-American,* 8 November 1924.

20   Jane Addams and Ida B. Wells, *Lynching and Rape: An Exchange of Views,* Occasional Paper 25 (New York: American Institute for Marxist Studies, Inc., 1977), 8–9. According to figures compiled in independent studies, John Culbert in his study *Lynch Law* estimated 3,337 persons lynched in the United States between 1882 and 1927, of whom 75 percent were black; and Ida B. Wells (Barnett) estimated 10,000 before the turn of the century based on public records. From the Introduction by Bettina Aptheker.

21   *Chicago Defender,* 22 February 1922, 6.

22   "Big Protest," *Chicago Defender,* 8 October 1921, 6.

23   Oakley, *The Devil's Music,* 106.

24   *Pittsburgh Courier,* 27 November 1926, 8.

25   See J. A. Jackson, "Wants an Overlord for Vaudeville Acts," *The Afro-American,* 9 February 1923; and "Dudley Has This to Say about Independent Acts," *Chicago Defender,* 5 December 1925, 6.

26   J. A. Jackson, "Season's Bookings Promise Many High Standard Shows," *The Afro-American,* 12 September 1924, 6.

27   J. A. Jackson, "South's Migration Affects Colored Show Business," *The Afro-American,* 29 June 1923.

28   See W. R. Arnold, "T.O.B.A. Dope," *The Afro-American,* 5 February 1927, for a sample of TOBA schedule for one week.

29   For discussions of black entertainers abroad in the 1920s, see Nancy Cunard, *Negro: An Anthology Made by Nancy Cunard, 1931–33* (1934, reprint ed. New York: Negro Universities Press, 1969); Bricktop with James

Haskins, *Bricktop* (New York: Atheneum Press, 1983); Lewis, *When Harlem Was in Vogue;* and "Acts on Big Circuits," *The Afro-American,* 19 May 1922.

30   "Mutual Wants No Colored Atractions," *The Afro-American,* 25 November 1922.

31   Carl Van Vechten, "The Black Blues," *Vanity Fair* 24:6 (August 1925), 57; "Prescription for the Negro Theatre," *Vanity Fair* 25:2 (October 1925), 92; R. J. McLaughlin, "Smutty Song Ruins Revue," reprinted in *Chicago Defender,* 27 November 1926; and William Gibson, "Passing in Review," *The Afro-American,* 24 December 1927.

32   Kennard Williams, "South's Amusements Need a Cleaning Up," *The Afro-American,* 22 November 1924, 6.

33   See Kennard Williams, "In the Spotlight," *The Afro-American,* 6 June 1924; 3 April 1926; and 1 May 1926; "Artists of Old Days Used Clean Materials," *Chicago Defender,* 3 November 1923; "Lower and Lower," *Chicago Defender,* 5 April 1924; Gang Tines, "Deportment Counts," *Chicago Defender,* 6 September 1924; "Theatre Folks and Theatre Goers," *Chicago Defender,* 24 October 1925.

34   Salem T. Whitney, cited by Kennard Williams in *The Afro-American,* 31 October 1925.

35   See *The Afro-American,* 4 April 1919; and the *Chicago Defender,* 14 April 1923, for examples of these ads.

36   *Chicago Defender,* 1 December 1923.

37   *The Afro-American,* 11 September 1926.

38   "Letter Box," *The Afro-American,* 7 July 1928. Also see *Chicago Defender,* 11 November 1923.

39   *The Afro-American,* 29 January 1927.

40   Lieb, *Ma Rainey,* 17; and Albertson, *Bessie,* 143.

41   See Charles Edward Smith, "Ma Rainey," in "Notable American Women, 1807–1950," Radcliffe College Archives, Cambridge, Mass.; conversation with Rainey's brother, Thomas Pridgett, Jr. in *Jazz Info,* 6 September 1940; and Vic Schuler, "The Mystery of the Two Ma Raineys," *The Melody Maker and Rhythm,* 13 October 1951, 9.

42   John W. Work, ed., *American Negro Songs and Spirituals* (New York:

Bonanza Books, 1940), 32–33. During Work's interview with Rainey, she claimed that she picked up the blues from a girl who happened by her tent one morning.

43   "Slave to the Blues," Paramount Records, 8 March 1926.

44   Smith, "Ma Rainey," 1.

45   *Chicago Defender,* 2 February 1924.

46   Lieb, *Ma Rainey,* 167–168.

47   Rev. Thomas A. Dorsey, interview with the author, Chicago, 7 February 1977.

48   Bob Hayes, "Ma Rainey's Review," *Chicago Defender,* 13 February 1926, 6.

49   Sterling Brown, *Southern Roads* (New York: Harcourt, Brace, 1932), 62–63.

50   Thomas Fulbright, "Ma Rainey and I," *Jazz Journal* 9 (March 1956), 1.

51   Dorsey interview.

52   Dorsey interview.

53   *Pittsburgh Courier,* 25 October 1924, and 8 November 1924, 8.

54   Dorsey interview.

55   Brian Rust, *Jazz Records, 1897–1942* (Essex, England: Storyville, 1975), 1333–1337.

56   Dorsey interview.

57   Ibid.

58   "Traveling Blues," Ma Rainey, Paramount 12706, June 1928.

59   Eileen Southern, *The Music of Black Americans* (New York: W. W. Norton & Co., 1983), 435–436.

"Crazy Blues" Starts a New Craze

1   Foreman, Jr., "Jazz and Race Records," 15.

2   Ibid., 24.

3   Ibid., 24.

4   Ibid., 40–41.

5   Levine, *Black Culture,* 224–225.

6   See Perry Bradford's *Born with the Blues: His Own Story* (New York: Oak Publications, 1965); Foreman, "Jazz and Race Records," 24.

7   Foreman, "Jazz and Race Records," 56.

8   "Making Records," *Chicago Defender,* 13 March 1920.

9   John Hammond, interview with the author, New York, 11 November 1981.

10   Foreman discusses this fully in his study of the race record market. He asserts that the term coined by Peer was not a brilliant stroke but more a reflection of the longstanding usage of the term, race, that blacks had adopted in attempts to unify people of color on a positive basis. Thus at the turn of the century "the race" became the accepted point of reference in statements, written and spoken, about achievements of people of color.

11   *Chicago Defender,* 14 August 1920.

12   *Chicago Defender,* 23 October 1920, 4.

13   From a *Dallas Journal* review quoted in the *Chicago Defender,* 2 April 1921.

14   Ibid.

15   Quoted in Foreman, "Jazz and Race Records," 59.

16   *Chicago Defender* ad, 9 September, and article, 23 September 1922.

17   Foreman, "Jazz and Race Records," 71.

18   Ibid., 72–73.

19   See Anderson, *This Was Harlem,* 132, and *Chicago Defender,* 4 June 1921, 6, for further discussion of the Pace Phonograph Corporation, which included Fletcher Henderson, William Grant Still, and the previously mentioned Carroll Clark as officers.

20   See *The Afro-American,* 17 February and 28 April 1922 for examples described.

21   Paul Oliver, *Songsters and Saints: Vocal Traditions on Race Records* (Cambridge: Cambridge University Press, 1984), 266.

22   Foreman, "Jazz and Race Records," chap. 5.

23   See Oliver, *The Story of the Blues,* 64; Albertson, *Bessie;* and "Bessie Smith: Empress of the Blues," *The Afro-American,* magazine section, 26 October 1974, for biographical data on Bessie Smith.

24   Paul Oliver, *Bessie Smith* (London: Cassell Ltd., 1959), 17 and 42.

25   Hammond interview.

26   Dahl, *Stormy Weather,* 100.

27   Langston Hughes as quoted by Carl Van Vechten in "The Black Blues," *Vanity Fair* 24:6 (August 1925), 86.

28   "Sing Sing Prison Blues," Bessie Smith, Columbia Records G30818.

29   E. Franklin Frazier's interviews of young black urban women revealed that some had extremely cynical views of life yet displayed an ambivalence and melancholy that belied their tough exteriors. See *The Negro Family,* 224.

30   Lieb, *Ma Rainey,* 17.

31   Eva Taylor, interview with the author, New York, 27 March 1977.

32   Levine, *Black Culture,* 225–227.

33   Titon, *Early Downhome Blues,* 271–276.

34   Levine, *Black Culture,* 225–227.

35   Oakley, *The Devil's Music,* 114.

36   Ibid.

37   Oliver, *Songsters and Saints,* 146 and 268.

38   Foreman, "Jazz and Race Records," 182.

39   Ibid., chap. 6.

"Wild Women Don't Have the Blues": Blues from the Black Woman's Perspective

1   Frazier, *The Negro Family,* 210 and 212.

2   James Baldwin, "The Uses of the Blues," in *The Best from Playboy,* no. 6 (n.p., n.d.), 97.

3   Kimberly Benston, "Tragic Aspects of the Blues," *Phylon* 36:2 (1975), 169.

4   Ellison, *Shadow and Act,* 78.

5   Richard Wright, as quoted in *Woke up This Mornin': Poetry of the Blues,* ed. A. X. Nicholas (New York: Bantam Books, 1973), 6.

6   Brown, "Ma Rainey," in *Southern Roads.*

7   Quoted in Margaret McKee and Fred Chisenhall, *Beale Black and Blue: Life and Music on Black America's Main Street* (Baton Rouge: Louisiana State University Press, 1981), 170.

8   Lillie Mae "Big Mama Blues" Glover, quoted in ibid.

9   "Quality of the Blues," *The Metronome* 39 (September 1923), 140.

10   Frazier, *The Negro Family,* 210 and 224.

11   "Long Road," Bessie Smith quoted in Albertson, *Bessie Smith,* 36–37.

12   Victoria Spivey: "New York Tombs," Spivey EP101 1062; "T.B. Blues," Okeh 8494, 1927; and "Dopehead Blues," Okeh 8531, October 1927.

13   "Poor Man Blues," Bessie Smith, quoted in Albertson, *Bessie Smith,* 116.

14   "Uncle Sam Blues," Ida Cox, Columbia 12D-81253, 2 October 1923; and "Pink Slip Blues," Vocalian 05258, 1939.

15   "Hard Times Blues," Ida Cox, Vocalian 05298, 1939.

16   "Death Letter Blues," Ida Cox, Paramount 12220, July 1924.

17   "Coffin Blues," Ida Cox, Paramount 12318-A, October 1923.

18   "Graveyard Dream Blues," Ida Cox, Paramount 12022-A, October 1923; Martin's version was recorded on Okeh 8099.

19   "Death Sting Me Blues," Sara Martin, Paramount 14025, 1928.

20   "Dying by the Hour," Bessie Smith, *Bessie Smith: The Empress,* Columbia G 30818.

21   "Take Him off My Mind," Ida Cox, Vocalian 05258, October 1939.

22   Ibid.

23   "New Orleans Goofer Dust Blues," Thelma LaVizzo, *I'm Coming from Seclusion,* Collectors Items 005.

24   Albertson, *Bessie Smith,* 47.

25   "Rambling Blues," Ida Cox, Paramount 12318-B, September 1925.

26   "Slave to the Blues," Ma Rainey, Paramount 12332, 1926.

27   "Blood Hound Blues," Victoria Spivey, RCA Victor V-38570, October 1929; reissued by RCA Victor on *Women of the Blues,* LP534, 1966.

28   Ibid.

29   "Court House Blues," Clara Smith, Columbia 14073-D, April 1925.

30   "Send Me to the Electric Chair," Bessie Smith, *Bessie Smith: The Empress,* Columbia G 30818.

31   See Albertson, *Bessie,* for accounts of these and other violent incidents.

32   "Georgia Hound Blues," Ida Cox, Paramount 12263, January 1925.

33   "Got to Leave My Home Blues," Sara Martin, Okeh 8146.

34   "I Hate a Man Like You," Lizzie Miles, RCA Victor LPV 508.

35   "Mistreating Man Blues," Sara Martin, Paramount 14025.

36   Ibid.

37   "Every Dog Has His Day," Sippie Wallace, Okeh 8205, February 1925.

38   "Up the Country Blues," Sippie Wallace, Okeh 8106, October 1923.

39   I vividly recall that the quiet of many Saturday nights, and sometimes a Sunday morning, was rent asunder when neighborhood women would scream epithets at their wayward husbands who came in drunk, too late, broke, or all these at once. There was always a tingle of excitement as my sister and I surreptitiously crept to our bedroom windows to hear every censored word. Although we relished the vicarious adventures, my fear that someone would be phsyically harmed was borne out at times. Miraculously, life resumed with its usual calm in a day or so and the philanderer often behaved better for a while.

40   Roger D. Abrahams, "Negotiating Respect: Patterns of Presentation among Black Women," *Journal of American Folklore* 88 (January 1975), 76.

41   "Freight Train Blues," Clara Smith, Columbia, September 1924.

42   Eric Sackheim, comp. *The Blues Line: A Collection of Blues Lyrics* (New York: Schirmer Books, 1969), 34.

43   "Please Come Back and Love Like You Used to Do," Trixie Smith, Paramount 12330, December 1925.

44   "K. C. Man Blues," Clara Smith, Columbia 12D-81222, October 1923.

45   "Chicago Bound Blues," Bessie Smith, Columbia, reissued on *Railroad Blues,* Rosetta Records RR1301, 1980.

46   "Railroad Blues," Trixie Smith, Paramount 12262, 1925.

47   "Pratt City Blues," Bertha "Chippie" Hill, Okeh 8420-A, 1926.

48   "L & N Blues," Clara Smith, Columbia 14073-D, March 1925. The "L & N" was the Louisville & Nashville Railroad.

49   "Dead Drunk Blues," Margaret Johnson, RCA Victor, 14 February 1927; reissued on *Women of the Blues,* RCA Victor LPV 534, 1966.

50   "Leaving This Morning," Ma Rainey, Paramount, September 1928; reissued on Riverside RLP 1003, Vol. 1.

51   Garon, *Blues and the Poetic Spirit,* 75.

52   See *The Afro-American,* and *Chicago Defender,* newspapers of the 1920s with bylines by "Gang" Tines.

53   Sammy Price, interview with the author, New York, 1977.

54   Oliver, *Aspects of the Blues Tradition,* 206.

55   Nicholas, *Woke Up This Mornin',* 22.

56   "Street Walker Blues," Bertha Hill, HJCA HC 102, June 1926.

57   Frazier, *The Negro Family,* 223.

58   "My Man-of-War," Lizzie Miles, reissued on *Women of the Blues,* RCA Victor LPV 534, 1966.

59   Garon, *Blues and the Poetic Spirit,* 78.

60   Sackheim, *Blues Line,* 45.

61   "Trouble in Mind," Bertha "Chippie" Hill, Circle J1003A, c. 1946.

62   Alfred Pasteur and Ivory Toldson, *Roots of Soul* (New York: Anchor Press/Doubleday, 1983), 128.

63   "I Don't Love Nobody," Clara Smith, Columbia 14016-D, January 1924.

64   Ibid.

65   Frazier, *The Negro Family,* 223.

66   "Charleston Blues," Bertha Hill, Circle J1004B, c. 1946.

67   "I Don't Care Where You Take It," Bertha Idaho, Rosetta Records RR 1300.

68   "Shave 'Em Dry," Ma Rainey, Paramount 1222A, August 1925.

69   Lieb, *Ma Rainey,* 124.

70 Oliver, *Aspects of the Blues Tradition*, 207.

71 Ibid., 206.

72 Sackheim, *Blues Line*, 40.

73 Ibid., 35.

74 "Stavin' Chain," Lil Johnson, *Copulating Blues.*

75 "Put a Little Sugar in My Bowl," Bessie Smith, *Copulating Blues.*

76 Oliver, *Aspects of the Blues Tradition*, 21.

77 Ibid., 214.

78 Ibid., 214 and 215.

79 Edith Wilson, speaking at a blues workshop at the University of Maryland Baltimore County, October 1978.

80 According to Lucie G. Colvin, a historian, and Dr. W. B. Lamousé-Smith, a sociologist, the use of lewd songs in public is a tradition practiced on special occasions in some West African cultures. It allows women the opportunity to express otherwise taboo feelings. On a specified day, women vent against strict sexual norms without fear of reprisal. Thus the blues women continued that tradition.

81 "Mean Tight Mama," Sara Martin, Milestone MLP 2006, 1928; "I'm a Mighty Tight Woman," Sippie Wallace, Columbia 1442, 1926; "He May Be Your Man (But He Comes to See Me Sometimes)," Edith Wilson, Columbia A 3653, 9 June 1922.

82 "Kitchen Mechanic Blues," Clara Smith, Columbia 14097-D, August 1925.

83 "Every Woman's Blues," Clara Smith, Columbia 3943, June 1923.

84 "Wild Women Don't Have the Blues," Ida Cox, Paramount, 1924, re-issued on Riverside RLP 9374.

85 Ibid.

"Up the Country . . ." and Still Singing the Blues: Sippie Wallace

1 See James Cone's *The Spirituals and the Blues: An Interpretation* (New York: Seabury Press, 1972), discussion on the existential nature of the blues.

2   Helen Humes, interview with the author, New York, March 1975.

3   Alwyn Barr, *Black Texans: A History of Negroes in Texas, 1528–1971* (Austin: Jenkins Publishing Co., 1973), 169–170.

4   Sippie Thomas Wallace, interview with the author, Detroit, 24 January 1975.

5   Jones, *Blues People,* 235.

6   Cone, *Spirituals,* 111–112.

7   Wallace interview.

8   Ibid.

9   Performed by Wallace during interview, 1975. The original recording was issued by Okeh, May 1924.

10   Wallace interview.

11   Ibid.

12   Alberta Hunter's first job after she arrived in Chicago was as a potato peeler. Billie Holiday recalled her days as a domestic working alongside her mother. Ethel Waters, Mamie Smith, Sara Martin, and Chippie Hill each returned to jobs as waitresses and maids when times were bad. The "Kitchen Mechanic Blues" was an ironical portrait of black domestics.

13   *Talking Machine World* 21 (15 May 1925), 116.

14   See the *Chicago Defender,* 21 February 1925, pt. 1, 12, for an example of the ads used.

15   Price interview.

16   "Shorty George Blues," Okeh, 1923.

17   "Special Delivery Blues," Okeh 8238, March 1926.

18   Sippie Wallace, interview with the author, Detroit, October 1976.

19   Godrich and Dixon, *Blues and Gospel Records,* 654.

20   "Jack of Diamonds Blues," Okeh 8328, March 1926. The circumstances of Wallace's marriage and her comments regarding the "Gambling Blues" lead me to the conclusion that perhaps her memory was clouded and she confused that blues with "Jack of Diamonds."

21   Demographics obtained from *Polk's Detroit Directory,* 1923–1924 edition, 35.

22   Announcements in the *Chicago Defender,* 12 June 1926 and 12 August 1929, confirm Mrs. Wallace's accounts of these deaths.

23   "Bedroom Blues," Okeh 8439, November 1926.

24   Wallace interview, 1976.

25   Humes interview.

26   Wallace interview, 1975.

27   Dahl, *Stormy Weather,* 22–29.

28   Wallace interview, 1976.

29   Godrich and Dixon, *Blues and Gospel Records.*

30   "Mighty Tight Woman," RCA Victor BVE 48870-2, February 1929, re-issued on RCA Victor LP 534, 1966.

31   Wallace interview, 1975.

32   Ibid.

33   Ibid.

34   Len Kunstadt, "The Comeback of Sippie Wallace," *Record Research* 88 (January 1968), 3.

35   Brian McCarthy, *Jazz on Record, 1897–1942* (Essex, England: Storyville, 1975), 297. Bonnie Raitt, a young white folksinger, was instrumental in the revival of interest in and enthusiasm for artists such as Wallace, Sykes, and Montgomery in the early 1970s. That exposure to audiences all across the United States created a new demand for Wallace's style of blues singing—the shouting wail.

36   Sippie Wallace, interview with the author, Detroit, November 1983.

37   Sippie Wallace, interview with the author, Detroit, January 1977.

38   Wallace interview, 1975.

39   Ibid.

40   Refer to Cone, *Spirituals,* for discussion on this topic.

41   James T. Jones, "Sippie: Two Roads to the Blues," *The Detroit News,* 9 November 1986, 1B and 8B.

Blues Was Her Business: Victoria Spivey

1   Leonard Kunstadt, interview with the author, 10 March 1977. He said Ms. Spivey acknowledged few as being her musical peers but she considered Dinah one of them.

2   Ralph Rush, "In Memoriam: Victoria Spivey," *Sing Out!* (December 1976), 30.

3   Sheldon Harris, *Blues Who's Who: A Biographical Dictionary of Blues Singers* (New Rochelle, N.Y.: Arlington House, 1979), 481.

4   Eva Jessye, "Victoria Spivey, Texas Girl, in Hallelujah," *The Afro-American,* 27 July 1929, 8. In this article Miss Jessye tells Spivey's story of her childhood.

5   Victoria Spivey, "Blues Are My Business" *Record Research,* no. 81 (January 1967), 7.

6   Ibid.

7   Ibid.

8   Spivey, "Blind Lemon and I Had a Ball," *Record Research,* no. 76 (May 1966).

9   Ibid.

10   Leonard Kunstadt, liner notes, *The Blues Is Life: Victoria Spivey,* Folkways Records FS 3541.

11   See *Chicago Defender,* 24 July 1926, 6.

12   Spivey, "Blind Lemon and I," 12.

13   Rush, "In Memoriam," 20.

14   "Arkansas Road Blues," Okeh 8481, April 1927, reissued on *Legacy of the Blues,* Spivey Music Co.

15   David Jasen, liner notes, *The Blues Is Life: Victoria Spivey,* Folkways Records FS 3541.

16   *Basket of Blues,* Spivey Records LP 1001.

17   Spivey, "Blues are My Business," *Record Research,* no. 53 (July 1963), 12.

18   *Pittsburgh Courier,* 26 November 1927, sec. 2, 3.

19   Spivey, "My Porter Grainger," *Record Research,* no. 79 (October 1969), 8.

20   Okeh Records ad in *The Afro-American,* 21 April 1928, 6.

21   See Foreman, "Jazz and Race Records," 197–200 for discussion of erotic blues and the record industry in the late 1920s to 1930s.

22   "Organ Grinder Man," Okeh 8615, September 1928.

23   "King Vidor's Hopes," *Chicago Defender,* 19 January 1929, 7. Of

course this claim was fallacious because black filmmakers had produced films using all-black casts prior to Vidor's *Hallelujah.* See Donald Bogle, *Toms, Coons, Mulattoes, Mammies, and Bucks: An Interpretive History of Blacks in American Films* (New York: Viking Press, 1973).

24   Jessye, "Victoria Spivey, Texas Girl."

25   Rust, *Jazz Records,* 1578 and 1575.

26   Rush, "In Memoriam," 30.

27   Leonard Kunstadt, liner notes, *Victoria Spivey Recorded Legacy of the Blues,* Spivey Records LP 2001.

28   Notices in the *Chicago Defender* for July 8 and July 22, 1933, list home addresses in Dallas and Tulsa for Spivey.

29   Kundstadt interview.

30   *The Chicago Defender,* 14 May 1938, 19.

31   Decca 7222, 7 July 1936, reissued on *Victoria Spivey Recorded Legacy of the Blues,* Spivey Records LP 2001.

32   "Detroit Moan," *Victoria Spivey Recorded Legacy of the Blues,* Spivey Records LP 2001.

33   Rush, "In Memoriam," 31.

34   Ibid., 30.

35   John Hammond and Sammy Price did not consider Spivey as ranking in the top category of classic blues singers with Bessie Smith, Clara Smith, Ida Cox, Ma Rainey, and Sippie Wallace.

36   *Basket of Blues,* Spivey Records LP 1001.

37   Max Jones, "Black Queen Spivey," *Melody Maker* [England], 30 October 1976, 41.

38   Sippie Wallace and Len Kunstadt interviews confirm that relationship and account of events.

39   See Derrick Steward-Baxter's obituary of Spivey in *Jazz Journal* (December 1976), 24, in which he discusses her volatile temperament.

40   Mr. and Mrs. Frank Driggs, interview with the author, New York, July 1983.

41   David Jasen, liner notes, *The Blues is Life,* p. 2.

"He Used to Be Your Man . . ." But Edith Wilson Has Him Now

1   Bradford's success in recognizing talent later earned him a spot as a scout for Okeh. Max Jones and Sinclair Traill, eds., "Collector's Corner: Perry (Mule) Bradford," *Melody Maker* (27 April 1957): 6.

2   According to census records for 1900, Louisville, Jefferson County, Kentucky.

3   Edith Wilson, interview with author, Chicago, 5 February 1977.

4   Ibid.

5   Ibid.

6   Ibid.

7   Ibid.

8   Ibid.

9   Ibid.

10   Ibid.

11   Ibid.

12   Wilson interview with author, Chicago, 30 October 1976.

13   Ibid.

14   "Wicked Blues," Edith Wilson, Columbia A-3558, 21 January 1922.

15   "The Standard," *Chicago Defender*, 12 November 1921.

16   "Edith Wilson," *Chicago Defender*, 8 October 1921.

17   Wilson interview, 30 October 1976.

18   "My Handy Man Ain't Handy No More" Edith Wilson, Delmark Records, 1976.

19   Oliver, *Aspects of the Blues Tradition*, 205.

20   James Haskins, *The Cotton Club* (New York: Random House, 1977), 50.

21   "Colored Show at Broadway Cabaret," *The Afro-American*, 17 February 1922.

22   Wilson interview, 30 October 1976.

23   Wilson interview, 5 February 1977.

24   "Flossie Not Colored," *The Afro-American*, 24 August 1923.

25   J. A. Jackson, "Meeting and Greeting Artists of the Race in New York," *The Afro-American*, 8 November 1924.

26   Harris, *Blues Who's Who,* 58.

27   John Godrich and R. M. W. Dixon, *Blues and Gospel Records, 1902–1942* (London: Storyville Publications, 1969), 738.

28   Billy Pierce, "New York Notes," *Chicago Defender,* 31 October 1925, 7.

29   Wilson interview, 5 February 1977.

30   "Florence Mills Has Party for Her Friends in London," *Chicago Defender,* 12 February 1927, 6.

31   "Here and There," *The Afro-American,* 17 December 1927.

32   Ibid.; also *Chicago Defender,* 12 January 1929.

33   Harris, *Blues Who's Who,* 581.

34   Wilson interview, 30 October 1976.

35   "'Hot Chocolates' Stars Open Broadway Hall," *Chicago Defender,* 5 October 1929, 6; "'Hot Chocolates' Is High-Spirited," *New York Times,* 21 June 1929, sec. 17, 4.

36   Biographical sketch from liner notes, *He May Be Your Man,* Delmark Records, 1976.

37   "'Hot Rhythm' Opens Fall Season But Fails to Click," *Chicago Defender,* 30 August 1930, 5.

38   Quoted in ibid.

39   Harris, *Blues Who's Who,* 581.

40   Walter Barnes, Jr., "Hits and Bits," *Chicago Defender,* 24 October 1931, 5.

41   See *Chicago Defender,* 6 February 1932; 6 July 1935; and 26 October 1935 for examples.

42   *Chicago Defender,* 26 November 1932.

43   Rob Roy, *Chicago Defender,* 6 May 1933, 5.

44   *Chicago Defender,* 22 April 1933, 5.

45   See *Chicago Defender,* 24 November 1934, 9; 6 April 1935, 10; 6 July 1935, 9; and 26 October 1935, 8; and *New York Times,* 4 December 1933.

46   "Big Name Bands Flee N.Y. Broadway, Musicians Wondering If Race Prejudice Is the Issue," *Chicago Defender,* 21 January 1939.

47   Wilson interview, 30 October 1976.

48   *Chicago Defender,* 29 July 1939.

49   Wilson interview, 30 October 1976.

50   Biographical sketch from liner notes, *He May Be Your Man,* Delmark Records, 1976.

51   Ibid.

52   Wilson interview, 30 October 1976.

53   Ibid.

54   Ibid.

55   Wilson interview, 5 February 1977.

56   Wilson and Montgomery at a Blues Workshop, University of Maryland, Baltimore County, September 1978.

57   Broadcast on National Public Radio, 24 June 1980.

She's Got a Mind to Ramble: Alberta Hunter

1   Mark Kernis bestowed that title on Hunter in his article (of the same title) in the *Washington Post,* Weekend section, 5 January 1979, 10.

2   Rust, *Jazz Records,* 837–844.

3   Harris, *Blues Who's Who,* 254.

4   See Robert Palmer, "A Jazz Career Reborn at 82," *New York Times,* 14 October 1977, sec. C, 26; Hubert Soal, "Rebirth of the Blues," *Philadelphia Inquirer,* 5 March 1978; Norma J. Darden, "No Tea for the Fever," *Essence* (October 1978), 82–87; Jeanne Parnell, "Once Is Not Enough," *Down Beat Magazine* (October 1978), 12–13; and Joseph McClellan, "Back to the Blues," *Washington Post,* 9 January 1979, sec. B, 1 and 5.

5   "I Got a Mind to Ramble," Alberta Hunter, Bluesville BVLP 1052, August 1961.

6   Ibid.

7   Ibid.

8   Darden, "No Tea for the Fever."

9   Ibid., 83.

10   Ibid.

11   Bricktop and Haskins, *Bricktop,* 55–56; and Harris, *Who's Who in Blues,* 254.

12 Alberta Hunter, telephone interview with the author, 23 February 1977.

13 "Chirping the Blues," Alberta Hunter, Paramount 12017, February 1923.

14 "Chirping the Blues," Alberta Hunter, Prestige Bluesville BVLP 1052, August 1961.

15 See the *Chicago Defender*, 28 November 1922; 30 December 1922; 17 January 1923; and 20 January 1923.

16 J. A. Jackson, "Alberta Hunter Has Reached Stardom," *The Afro-American*, 11 May 1923.

17 J. A. Jackson, *The Afro-American*, 13 July 1923.

18 *The Afro-American*, 17 August 1923.

19 "*How Come* in New York," *The Afro-American*, 24 August 1923; "*How Come* to Detroit—Schubert Michigan Theater," *Chicago Defender*, 27 October 1923.

20 See the *Chicago Defender*, 16 June 1923; and *The Afro-American*, 13 July 1923, for ads.

21 Murray, *Stomping the Blues*.

22 "Down Hearted Blues," Alberta Hunter, Riverside RLP (59) 38, September 1961.

23 Paramount ad in the *Chicago Defender*, 18 August 1923.

24 *Chicago Defender*, 22 March 1924 and 29 March 1924; *The Afro-American*, 25 July 1924.

25 "Texas Moaner Blues," Alberta Hunter, Milestone MLP 2010 (original on Gennett, November 1924).

26 "Nobody Knows the Way I Feel This Mornin'," Alberta Hunter, Milestone MLP (original on Gennett, December 1924).

27 Parnell, "Once Is Not Enough." The same story is quoted in Darden, "No Tea"; Lewis A. Erenberg points out that Tucker fashioned her singing heavily on black singers, even to using black dialect, movements, and vocal inflections. Erenberg, *Steppin' Out: New York Nightlife and the Transformation of American Culture, 1890–1930* (Chicago: University of Chicago Press, 1984), 194–195.

28   *The Afro-American,* 7 February 1925.

29   *Chicago Defender,* 18 April 1925.

30   *Chicago Defender,* 3 October 1925.

31   *Chicago Defender,* 30 January 1926; Rust, *Jazz Records,* 839–840.

32   Darden, "No Tea," 148. Evidently, Hunter never developed home-maker's arts because she warned me when we were arranging for my visit with her, in Spring 1977, not to expect anything fancy, but she would fix me some waffles or something. She said her mother always scolded her for never learning how to cook.

33   "Sugar" and "Beale Street Blues," RCA Victor 20771, May 1927. See Billy Jones, "New York Notes," *Chicago Defender,* 12 March 1927; and Rust, *Jazz Records,* 840.

34   Harris, *Blues Who's Who,* 256.

35   "Alberta Hunter in Europe," *Chicago Defender,* 10 December 1927, 7.

36   "Robeson Scores," *Chicago Defender,* 4 August 1928.

37   *Chicago Defender,* 7 July 1928, 7.

38   *Chicago Defender,* 5 January 1929, 6.

39   Harris, *Who's Who in Blues,* 256.

40   "Gets Flattering Offer," *Pittsburgh Courier,* 30 March 1929, 8.

41   *Chicago Defender,* 27 April 1929.

42   *The Afro-American,* 4 January 1930.

43   See *Chicago Defender,* 18 October 1930; 17 January 1931; 30 January 1932; and 5 March 1932; also Harris, *Blues Who's Who,* 256.

44   "Alberta Hunter Will Replace Jo Baker in Cabaret," *Chicago Defender,* 16 September 1933, 6.

45   See *Chicago Defender,* 17 November 1934, 9; and 29 February 1936, 8.

46   See *Chicago Defender,* 19 February 1933; 9 September 1933; 16 September 1933; 11 August 1934; 6 October 1934; and 17 November 1934 for examples of reviews.

47   Roy de Coverley, "Denmark Café Patrons Go for Alberta Hunter Hits," *Chicago Defender,* 11 August 1934.

48   See *Chicago Defender,* 17 November 1934, 8; Harris, *Blues Who's*

Who, 256; and Rudolf J. Hopf, "Come On, Be Happy: The Jack Jackson Story," *Memory Lane* 7 (April 1975), 5 and 6.

49   *Chicago Defender,* 14 August 1937, 11.

50   *Chicago Defender,* 29 October 1938 and 5 November 1938.

51   Harris, *Blues Who's Who,* 256.

52   Bob Hayes, "Here and There," *Chicago Defender,* 3 August 1940, 20; *Chicago Defender,* 26 October 1940, 20; 30 November 1940, 21; and 28 December 1940, 20; Harris, *Blues Who's Who,* 256.

53   Letter from Alberta Hunter to George Hoefer, 21 September 1945, postmarked St. Quentin, France; also see Carl Levin, "Negro Sextet Get in Groove for Eisenhower and Zhukov," *New York Herald Tribune,* 11 June 1945; both in vertical files, Chicago Historical Society.

54   Alberta Hunter, interview with author, New York, March 1977.

55   John Hammond, interview with the author, New York, 11 November 1981.

56   Bobby Short, interview with the author, New York, 10 December 1985.

57   Jim Feldman, "Alberta Hunter's Glory Years," *Village Voice,* 20 April 1982, 78.

Conclusion

1   Wilson interview, 5 February 1977.

2   Price interview.

Other Blues Singers

1   Harris, *Blues Who's Who,* 134.

2   Ivorey Cobb, "Ida Cox, Famed Blues Singer, Headed for New Comeback," *Chicago Defender,* 20 January 1940, 20.

3   *Chicago Defender,* 27 May 1922, 6, for example.

4   Godrich and Dixon, *Blues and Gospel Records,* 381–382 and Harris, *Who's Who in Blues,* 134.

5   *Chicago Defender,* 4 August 1923, 6.

6   Price interview.

7   *Chicago Defender,* 5 January 1929, 7.

8   See *Chicago Defender,* 1934–1936, for routing notices.

9   Godrich and Dixon, *Blues and Gospel Records,* 385.

10   Hammond interview.

11   Riverside Record review for *Jazz Report,* May 1961.

12   Price interview.

13   John S. Wilson, "Surviving Stylist: Ida Cox sings Blues in Classic Ways," *New York Times,* 10 September 1961.

14   Price interview.

15   Leonard Kundstadt, "The Lucille Hegamin Story," *Record Research* 39 (November 1961), 3; and René Brunner, "The Cameo Girl," *Melody Maker* 31 (August 1956), 6.

16   Kunstadt, "The Lucille Hegamin Story."

17   Quoted in ibid.

18   Ibid.

19   Godrich and Dixon, *Blues and Gospel Records,* 743.

20   Ibid., 744–745.

21   Brunner, "The Cameo Girl."

22   Hammond interview.

23   John S. Wilson, *New York Post-Herald,* 10 September 1947, 20; and McCarthy, *Jazz on Record,* 134.

24   Harris, *Blues Who's Who,* 229.

25   Godrich and Dixon, *Blues and Gospel Records,* 793–794.

26   Harris, *Blues Who's Who,* 229.

27   Ibid.

28   "Clarence Williams Is Winning Fame," *The Afro-American,* 15 December 1922.

29   Harris, *Blues Who's Who,* 350.

30   "Uncle Sam Blues," Sara Martin, Okeh; "A Green Gal Can't Catch On," Sara Martin, Okeh 8099, 1923.

31   "OKEH by Sara," *Chicago Defender,* 3 November 1923; and *The Afro-American,* 31 August 1923.

32   See ads in *The Afro-American,* April 1922, for the New Lincoln Theatre in Baltimore.

33   "Mean Tight Mama," Sara Martin, Milestone MLP 2006. "Death Sting Me Blues," Paramount 14025, 1928.

34   New York Public Library, Lincoln Center, Music Division, vertical files, c. 1924.

35   "Sara in New York," *Chicago Defender,* 23 April 1927, 6; and Harris, *Blues Who's Who,* 351.

36   Harris, *Blues Who's Who.*

37   Dorsey interview.

38   Harris, *Blues Who's Who,* 351.

39   Lizzie Miles, interview with Richard B. Allen and Robert W. Greenwood, 18 January 1951, typescript, W. Ransom Jazz Archives, Tulane University, New Orleans.

40   Ibid.

41   Ibid., 13.

42   "Singers Obliged to Leave France," *The Afro-American,* 14 February 1925, 6; "Lizzie Prognosticates," *Chicago Defender,* 21 March 1925, 8.

43   Miles interview, 13.

44   "Queen Mother of the Rue Royale," Lizzie Miles, Cook 1181.

45   *Chicago Defender,* 1 April 1922 and 20 May 1922.

46   McCarthy, *Jazz on Record,* 197.

47   Carey James Tate, "Famed Lizzie Miles' Death Ends Era of Blues Singing," *The Louisiana Weekly,* 30 March 1963.

48   Ibid.

49   Hammond interview.

50   Harris, *Blues Who's Who,* 467.

51   Carl Van Vechten, "Negro Blues Singers: An Appreciation of Three

Coloured Artists Who Excel in an Unusual and Native Medium" *Vanity Fair* 26 (March 1926), 106.

52   "Prescription for the Negro Theatre," *Vanity Fair* 25: 2 (October 1925), 92.

53   Van Vechten, "Negro Blues Singers," 107.

54   "Texas Moaner Blues," Clara Smith, Columbia 14034-D, August 1924.

55   "All Night Blues," Clara Smith, Columbia A3966, July 1923.

56   "West Indies Blues," Clara Smith, Columbia 14019-D, April 1924; and Clara and Bessie Smith, "I'm Going Back to My Used to Be," Columbia 13007-D, October 1923.

57   Coy Herndon, "Coy Cogitates," *Chicago Defender,* 27 February 1926, 6.

58   "Clara Smith—Alabam' Revue," *The Afro-American,* 15 May 1926.

59   Examples may be found in the *Chicago Defender* and *The Afro-American,* 1926 and 1927.

60   Ibid., 474.

61   *Chicago Defender,* 9 February 1935.

62   See Erenberg, *Steppin' Out,* 150–155, for a discussion of the impact of black dance on New York society.

63   "Trixie Wins," *Chicago Defender,* 11 February 1922.

64   "Champion Blues Singer Here," *Chicago Defender,* 11 April 1924.

65   Rust, *Jazz Records,* 1553–1555.

66   "Love Me Like You Used to Do," Trixie Smith, Paramount 12330, December 1925; and "My Daddy Likes It Slow," Paramount 1216A, 1925.

67   "Railroad Blues," Trixie Smith, Paramount 12262, March 1925 and Miles MLP2010, "Choo Choo Blues," Rosetta Records RR1301; "Messing Around."

68   Price interview.

69   Billy Jones, "That Sine," *Chicago Defender,* 21 November 1931, 5.

70   Harris, *Blues Who's Who,* 475.

Glossary of Colloquialisms

coon song: derogatory song used originally by white minstrel men to depict blacks as buffoons, lackeys, grostesque in appearance and stupidly imitative of "high society." Black songwriters and performers also used the coon song when they went on stage.

croker sack: burlap bag used to hold potatoes.

nurses: respected women in black churches who assist worshippers who are overcome with grief at funerals or are possessed of the spirit during worship. They provide smelling salts; cradle their prostrate bodies until they quiet down; cool their brows with dampened handkerchiefs and fans; or carry them out to another part of the church. They can be identified by their crisply starched, white uniforms and nurse's caps.

pickaninny: young black child costumed and made up like a plantation slave child who served as a foil for white acts in the early 1900s.

race member: title blacks used to refer to themselves at the turn of the twentieth century, to incite pride in people of color. The record industry later coined the phrase, "race market," to identify the central target for its recordings of black artists and music.

Sapphire: name given to a black woman who was assertive, aggressive, and self-confident, as well as physically attractive. Sometimes meaning bossy, loud-mouthed, and domineering.

signifying and playing the dirty dozens: verbal combat with two or more "players" who use direct and indirect attacks on the other player to berate or belittle him/her in front of their peers. In the former, the speaker may challenge the listener to "do something" about a personal situation, or may choose to make fun of himself in order to make the other player "feel good." The latter, the dozens, is more aggressive in that it relies on derogatory taunts, usually in rhyme, about the other player's mother. Its aim is to humiliate and/or anger the person to the point of tears or some breakdown in front of the group. (Thomas Kochman, ed., *Rapping and Styling Out: Communication in Urban Black America,* Urbana: University of Illinois Press, 1972, 206, 315, and 316.)

slave seculars: plantation songs or poetry with nonreligious content, for example, "Round the Corn, Sally," "Charleston Gals," and "Run, Nigger, Run."

Storyville: a section in uptown New Orleans which was set up in 1897 specifically as a vice district by the city council. Its name derived from the surname of Alderman Sidney Story, the sponsor of the resolution. The district soon attracted the best black and creole musicians because of the good wages and regular work that could be had. Basin Street, later immortalized by a blues of the same name, was the most important street in the district. Black music flourished there until 1917, when the U.S. Navy Department ordered Storyville closed. Black musicians, such as King Oliver, worked their way up the river to Chicago on the show- and riverboats. (Eileen Southern, *Music of Black Americans,* New York: W. W. Norton, 1971, 358 and 376.)

trucking: a highly individual dance in which the shoulders are hunched up one after the other, the hips sway, and the feet execute in a variety of shuffles, as they move in short steps forward, turning the heel in after each step, while wiggling the index finger of one hand shoulder-high. (Marshall Stearns and Jean Stearns, *Jazz Dance: The Story of American Vernacular Dance,* New York: Schirmer Books, 1968, 41.)

under cork: term for when a performer "blacked up" his/her face with soot of a burnt cork. This originated with the white minstrels in the early part of the nineteenth century and was adapted by blacks, ironically, when they played in minstrel shows. The practice was decried by many blacks at the beginning of the twentieth century, but some entertainers of the race continued to "black up" because that was the only way they could get a job, or because some black audiences liked to see them in "coon" roles. The most respected and talented of the comedians who performed under cork was Bert Williams, who starred in the Ziegfield Follies.

wang dang: all-night parties with live music, gambling, dancing, drinking, sex, and food, at a price. They were often held in bawdy houses or a private house or apartment, with the owner getting the major cut of the proceeds.

Bibliography

Albertson, Chris. *Bessie*. New York: Stein and Day, 1972.

———. *Bessie Smith: Empress of the Blues*. New York: Schirmer Books, 1975.

Anderson, Jervis. *This Was Harlem*. New York: Farrar, Straus and Giroux, 1981.

Baldwin, James. *Tell Me How Long the Train's Been Gone*. New York: Dell Publishing Co., 1968.

Barr, Alywn. *Black Texans: A History of Negroes in Texas, 1528–1971*. Austin: Jenkins Publishing Co., 1973.

Bogaert, Karel. *Blues Lexicon*. Antwerp: Standaard Uitgeverij, 1971.

Bradford, Perry. *Born with the Blues: His Own Story*. New York: Oak Publications, 1965.

Broonzy, William, and Bruynoghe, Yannick. *Big Bill Blues*. New York: Oak Publications, 1964.

Brown, Sterling. *Southern Roads*. New York: Harcourt, Brace, 1932.

Buerkle, Jack, and Barker, Danny. *Bourbon Street Black*. New York: Oxford University Press, 1973.

Cayer, David. "Black and Blue and Black Again: Three Stages of Racial Imagery in Jazz Lyrics." *Journal of Jazz Studies* 1 (June 1964): 38–71.

Chapman, Abraham. *Black Voices: An Anthology of Afro-American Literature.* New York: New American Library, 1968.

Charters, Samuel. *The Bluesmen.* New York: Oak Publications, 1967.

———. *Poetry of the Blues.* New York: Oak Publications, 1963.

Cone, James. *The Spirituals and the Blues: An Interpretation.* New York: Seabury Press, 1972.

Cook, Bruce. *Listen to the Blues.* New York: Charles Scribner's Sons, 1973.

Dahl, Linda. *Stormy Weather: The Music and Lives of a Century of Jazzwomen.* New York: Pantheon Books, 1984.

Ellison, Ralph. *Invisible Man.* New York: Random House, 1952.

———. *Shadow and Act.* New York: Random House, 1964.

Erenberg, Lewis A. *Steppin' Out: New York Nightlife and the Transformation of American Culture, 1890–1930.* Chicago: University of Chicago Press, 1984.

Evans, David. *Big Road Blues: Tradition and Creativity in Folk Blues.* Berkeley and Los Angeles: University of California Press, 1982.

Foreman, Ronald. "Jazz and Race Records, 1920–1932: Their Origins and Their Significance for the Record Industry and Society." Ph.D. diss., University of Illinois, 1968.

Frazier, E. Franklin. *The Negro Family in the United States.* Chicago: University of Chicago Press, 1966.

Garon, Paul. "Blues and the Church." *Living Blues* 1 (Spring 1970): 18–23.

———. *Blues and the Poetic Spirit.* New York: Da Capo Press, 1978.

Godrich, John, comp. "The Victor Race Series." *Blues Unlimited* 11, 12, 13, and 15 (April, May, June, July, and September 1964).

Godrich, John, and Dixon, R. M. W., comps. *Blues and Gospel Records, 1902–1942.* London: Storyville Publications, 1969.

Green, Maud. "The Background of the Beale Street Blues." *Tennessee Folklore Society Bulletin* 7 (1941): 1–10.

Gruver, Rod. "The Autobiographical Theory Re-Examined." *JEMF Quarterly* 6 (Fall 1970): 129–131.

———. "The Blues as Dramatic Monologues." *JEMF Quarterly* 6 (Spring 1970): 28–31.

Handy, W. C., ed. *Blues: An Anthology.* Revised by Jerry Silverman. New York: Macmillan Co., 1972.

Harris, Sheldon. *Blues Who's Who: A Biographical Dictionary of Blues Singers.* New Rochelle, N.Y.: Arlington House, 1979.

Hobson, Wilder. *American Jazz Music.* New York: W. W. Norton & Co., 1939.

Huggins, Nathan, ed. *Voices from the Harlem Renaissance.* New York: Oxford University Press, 1976.

Hughes, Langston. *Famous Negro Music Makers.* New York: Dodd, Mead, 1955.

————. "Songs Called the Blues." *Phylon* 2 (1941): 143–145.

Johnson, James Weldon. *Black Manhattan.* New York: Knopf, 1930.

Jones, LeRoi. *Blues People.* New York: William Morrow, 1963.

Jones, M. "Introducing Lovie Austin." *Melody Maker* 26 (11 February 1950): 3.

Kellor, Francis B. "Southern Colored Girls in the North." *Charities and the Common* 13 (18 March 1905).

Kochman, Thomas, ed. *Rapping and Styling Out: Communication in Urban Black America.* Urbana: University of Illinois Press, 1972.

Levine, Lawrence W. *Black Culture and Black Consciousness.* New York: Oxford University Press, 1977.

Lewis, David Levering. *When Harlem Was in Vogue.* New York: Knopf, 1981.

Lieb, Sandra. *Mother of the Blues: A Study of Ma Rainey.* Amherst: University of Massachusetts Press, 1981.

Lockard, Diane. "The Negro on the Stage of the Nineteen Twenties." Master's Thesis, Columbia University, 1960.

Lovell, John, Jr. *Black Song: The Forge and the Flame.* New York: Macmillan Co., 1972.

McCarthy, Brian. *Jazz on Record, 1897–1942.* Essex, England: Storyville, 1975.

McCarthy, B., Morgan, A., Oliver, P., and Harrison, M. *Jazz on Record.* London: Hanover Books, 1968.

McKee, Margaret, and Chisenhall, Fred. *Beale Black and Blue: Life and*

Music on Black America's Main Street. Baton Rouge: Louisiana State University Press, 1981.

Mezzrow, Mezz, and Wolfe, Bernard. *Really the Blues*. New York: Doubleday, 1972.

Mitchell, George. *Blow My Blues Away*. Baton Rouge: Louisiana State University Press, 1971.

Murray, Albert. *Stomping the Blues*. New York: McGraw-Hill, 1976.

Neff, Robert, and Connor, Anthony. *Blues*. Boston: David Godine, 1975.

Nicholas, A. X. *Woke up This Morning': Poetry of the Blues*. New York: Bantam Books, 1973.

Oakley, Giles. *The Devil's Music: A History of the Blues*. London: British Broadcasting Co., 1979.

Oliver, Paul. *Bessie Smith*. London: Cassell Ltd., 1959.

———. *The Meaning of the Blues*. New York: Collier Books, 1963.

———. *Screening the Blues: Aspects of the Blues Tradition*. London: Cassell Ltd., 1968.

———. *Songsters and Saints: Vocal Traditions on Race Records*. Cambridge: Cambridge University Press, 1984.

———. *The Story of the Blues*. New York: Chilton Press, 1969.

Ovington, Mary White. *Half a Man: The Status of the Negro in New York*. 1911; reprinted New York: Schocken Books, 1969.

Palmer, Robert. *Deep Blues*. New York: Penguin Books, 1981.

Randall, Dudley. *The Black Poets*. New York: Bantam Books, 1971.

Rust, Brian. *Jazz Records, 1897–1942*. Essex, England: Storyville, 1975.

Sackheim, Eric, comp. *The Blues Line: A Collection of Blues Lyrics*. New York: Schirmer Books, 1969.

Scheimer, Seth M. *Negro Mecca: A History of the Negro in New York City, 1865–1920*. New York: New York University Press, 1965.

Sidran, Ben. *Black Talk*. New York: Holt, Rinehart and Winston, 1971.

Spear, Allan. *Black Chicago*. Chicago: University of Chicago Press, 1967.

Stearns, Marshall, and Stearns, Jean. *Jazz Dance: The Story of American Vernacular Dance*. New York: Schirmer Books, 1968.

Stevenson, Gordon. "Race Records: Victims of Benign Neglect in Libraries." *Wilson Library Bulletin* 1 (November 1975): 225.

Stewart-Baxter, Derrick. "Blues and Views." *Jazz Journal* 25 (February 1972): 25, 39.

————. *Ma Rainey and the Classic Blues Singers*. New York: Stein and Day, 1970.

————. "Autobiography and Blues Texts: A Reply to 'The Blues as Dramatic Monologues.'" *JEMF Quarterly* 6 (Summer 1970): 79–82.

Titon, Jeff Todd. *Early Downhome Blues: A Musical and Cultural Analysis*. Urbana: University of Illinois Press, 1977.

Wolfe, Bernard. "Ecstatic in Blackface: The Negro as a Song and Dance Man." In *The Scene before You: A New Approach to American Culture,* ed. Chandler Broussard. New York: Rinehart and Co., 1955.

Work, John W., ed. *American Negro Songs and Spirituals*. New York: Bonanza Books, 1940.

Subject Index

Ajax Records, *247*
alcohol: as blues theme, *97–98;* usage by singers, *69, 91, 129*
Armstrong, Louis, *38, 52, 95, 125, 209*

bands, dance, *61, 190, 192*
beauty, standards of, *32–33, 182*
Beiderbecke, Bix, *52*
benefit performances, *188*
Bentley, Gladys, *14, 100*
black press: ads for artists and titles, *46, 49–50, 61;* criticism of morals, *22, 29–31, 106;* and influence on black women, *31–32;* TOBA improvements and, *25–26, 27, 28*
Black Swan (Pace Phonograph Company), *49, 204, 247*
Blackbirds, 186, 187
blues: alterations of nonblues songs, *67;* as artform, *114;* articulateness and toughness of, *65;* definition of, *5–6;* paradox of, *64–66;* power of, *7–8;* spontaneity of, *67*

blues themes: advice to other women, *109–110;* alcohol, *97–98;* betrayal or abandonment, *76–77, 128–129;* broken or failed love affairs, *3, 6;* death, *74–76;* departure, *93, 95;* dilemma of staying with man or returning to family, *3–4;* disease and afflictions, *97;* erotica, *99–100, 132–133; hell, 77;* homosexuality, *103–104;* infidelity, *76–77, 86, 91–93;* injustice, *64;* jail and serving time, *70;* loss of lover, *74–78;* love, *73–74;* men, *9;* mistreatment, *82, 85, 90;* murder, *78;* other woman, *76;* poverty, *70–73;* promiscuity, *85–86;* prostitution, *98–99;* sadness, *53;* sex, *73–74, 100, 104–106, 109;* suicide, *77, 93, 101;* supernatural, *77–79;* trains, *93, 95–96, 153, 245–246;* traveling, *95–96, 153;* unfaithfulness, *82, 85;* vengeance, *81, 88–89;* violence, *82;* weariness, depression, and disillusionment, *86–87;* weight loss, *77*

Index of Song Titles

292